Leading with Spirit,
Presence,
and Authenticity

Leading with Spirit, Presence, and Authenticity

Kathryn Goldman Schuyler

John Eric Baugher, Karin Jironet,
Lena Lid-Falkman, Editors

A Volume in the International Leadership Association Series
Building Leadership Bridges

International Leadership Association

JB JOSSEY-BASS™
A Wiley Brand

Published by Jossey-Bass
A Wiley Brand
One Montgomery Street, Suite 1200, San Francisco, CA 94104-4594—www.josseybass.com

Jossey-Bass books and products are available through most bookstores. To contact Jossey-Bass
directly call our Customer Care Department within the U.S. at 800-956-7739, outside the
U.S. at 317-572-3986, or fax 317-572-4002.

Wiley publishes in a variety of print and electronic formats and by print-on-demand. Some
material included with standard print versions of this book may not be included in e-books or
in print-on-demand. If this book refers to media such as a CD or DVD that is not included in
the version you purchased, you may download this material at http://booksupport.wiley.com.
For more information about Wiley products, visit www.wiley.com.

Library of Congress Cataloging-in-Publication Data

　　Leading with spirit, presence, and authenticity / Kathryn Goldman Schuyler, John Eric
Baugher, Karin Jironet, Lena Lid-Falkman, editors. — First edition.
　　　pages cm. — (International Leadership Association series)
　　Includes bibliographical references and index.
　　　ISBN 978-1-118-82061-2 (pbk.); ISBN 978-1-118-82048-3 (pdf);
　　　ISBN 978-1-118-82069-8 (epub) -
　　　　1. Leadership.　2. Leadership—Religious aspects—Buddhism.　I. Schuyler,
Kathryn Goldman.
　　HM1261.L434　2014
　　303.3'4—dc23
　　　　　　　　　　　　　　　　　　　　　　　　　　　　　　　　　2014007797
Printed in the United States of America

FIRST EDITION
PB Printing　　10 9 8 7 6 5 4 3 2 1

Contents

The Contributors

Marco Aponte-Moreno, PhD, is an actor and academic. He has been performing in theater and film for the past fifteen years. He obtained his PhD from the Graduate Center, City University of New York, specializing in Hugo Chávez's political discourse. His current academic research focuses on the role of language and theater in leadership development. Aponte-Moreno teaches leadership and communication at University College London, where he is also the director of the graduate program in management.

John Eric Baugher, PhD, is associate professor of sociology at the University of Southern Maine. His recent research and teaching activities concern emotional and spiritual dimensions of transformational learning, bereavement, and end-of-life care. Baugher is a member of the Association for Contemplative Mind in Higher Education and the social science editor for the *Journal of Contemplative Inquiry*. He provides training in spiritual care to hospice and other organizations, and for more than two decades he has been following the lead of dying and grieving persons as a certified hospice volunteer.

Sylvia van de Bunt-Kokhuis, PhD, is co-director of SERVUS, the Servant-Leadership Centre for Research and Education at the Vrije Universiteit Amsterdam. She has an international career in business, corporate governance, and academia. She has published extensively in international academic journals on higher education, talent diversity, community building, and servant-leadership. She is the author of *Academic Pilgrims* (1996), editor of *World Wide Work* (2006), and coeditor of *Competing for Talent* (2009).

Brighid Dwyer, PhD, is the assistant director for research and training in the Center for Multicultural Affairs at Villanova University and serves as one of the university's ombudspersons for bias concerns. She is one of the co-directors of Villanova's Program on Intergroup Relations, a faculty member in the program, and an adjunct faculty member in the Center for Peace and Justice Education.

Catherine Etmanski, PhD, is an assistant professor in the School of Leadership Studies at Royal Roads University and first-year program head for a master's program in leadership studies. She is passionate about teaching arts-based and environmental leadership as well as action-oriented, participatory approaches to research. She enjoys integrating the arts into her work, and her doctoral studies employed participatory theater as a research method. She practices yoga and meditation.

Mark Fulton, MA, is a seasoned consultant, facilitator, and trainer with over twenty-five years of experience leading organizational effectiveness work—that is, helping organizations develop the capability to execute their strategy and achieve their business goals. He has worked with thousands of frontline leaders, senior executive teams, project teams, and groups of employees in a broad range of organizations from large multinational high-technology corporations to small start-ups. His MA from Concordia University is in human systems intervention.

Ralph A. Gigliotti is assistant director of Student Development for Leadership Programs at Villanova University. In this role, he coordinates the leadership education initiatives for aspiring and current student leaders. He has taught courses in communication, leadership, and public administration and is pursuing his PhD in organizational communication at Rutgers, the State University of New Jersey.

Kathryn Goldman Schuyler, PhD, has over twenty-five years of experience in leadership development, organizational consulting, and somatic learning. She has helped hundreds of executives to cultivate healthy organizations and is a professor in the graduate faculty of organizational psychology at Alliant International University. Goldman Schuyler has published widely on leadership and change and is the author of *Inner Peace—Global Impact: Tibetan Buddhism, Leadership, and Work* (IAP, 2012). In her private practice, she teaches children and adults with moderate to severe neuromotor challenges to move, learn, and live well.

Olen Gunnlaugson, PhD, is an assistant professor in leadership and organizational development in the Business School at Université Laval in Québec City, Canada. He views business education as a key societal vehicle for developing the next generation of self-aware, sustainably minded leaders. Gunnlaugson brings an increasingly multidisciplinary background to research and consulting in leadership, communication in teams, and executive coaching. His research has been published in several books and numerous peer-reviewed academic journals and presentations at international conferences.

Karin Jironet, PhD, theologian, Sufi murshida (guide), and Jungian psychoanalyst, is dedicated to leadership development in times of transition. Specializing in applying psychospiritual principles to boardroom dynamics for more than a decade, she counts as her clients the major international banks. Jironet is an internationally published author of articles and books on new approaches to organizational development and leadership.

Her latest book, *Female Leadership*, was nominated for best book of the year by the Gradiva Award, New York 2012. She is a board member of the Dutch Association of Analytical Psychology and cofounder of In Claritas.

Linda Kantor, BSoc Sci, MA Psychology, is a counseling psychologist, hypnotherapist, yoga teacher, and mindfulness trainer based in Cape Town, South Africa. She has taught mindfulness in various contexts from community to corporate. She is a part-time lecturer at the University of Cape Town, where she teaches mindful leadership. She is also a facilitator for the University of Stellenbosch certificate in mindfulness. She is undertaking her PhD, exploring applications of mindfulness in the corporate context.

Hanna H. Lee is the assistant director of the Center for Undergraduate Research and Fellowships at Villanova University. In this role, she advises students and develops programming around nationally competitive scholarships and undergraduate research to help students reach their full intellectual, professional, and personal potential. In addition to fellowships advising and academic programming at Villanova University, she teaches in the Intergroup Relations Program, Global Learning Communities, Service Learning Communities, and Honors Program.

Lena Lid-Falkman, PhD, focuses on value-based, authentic leadership and on leadership as communicative and rhetorical. Her PhD thesis was elected the best in business administration in Europe 2010 by the European Doctoral Programme Association in Management and Business Administration network and was in the top three in the Jablin Dissertation Award for Leadership Studies. Her recent research deals with authentic leadership as communicated through technology such as social media. She is a Marie Curie Scholar at ESADE Business School in Barcelona, Spain.

Guy Nasmyth, MA, is a consultant, trainer, and educator working in the areas of leadership and human systems. He is also associate faculty at Royal Roads University and the University of Victoria in British Columbia. His research and PhD studies have focused on collaboration and leadership as a shared or distributed phenomenon. He has worked in a variety of locations, including Cambodia, Thailand, and India.

Hellicy C. Ngambi is the vice chancellor at Mulungushi University in Zambia. She has over thirty years of management and teaching experience in higher education in Africa and overseas, including executive director, CEO, executive dean, principal, and managing director. She holds the following qualifications: DBL, MSc, MBA, BA, ITP, ACE fellowship, and Prosci certified. She has authored, edited, and published several articles and books, including *RARE Total Leadership: Leading with Head, Heart and Hands*.

M. Beth Page, author, educator, speaker, consultant, and Dream Catcher Consulting founder, helps people explore and act on their leadership vision. Her recent works include *Change Happens*, *Done Deal: Your Guide to Merger and Acquisition Integration*, and a chapter in the best-selling *Awakening the Workplace*. She holds degrees from Pepperdine University, Western Illinois University, and Carleton University. A certified Emotional Intelligence Coach (EQ in Action), she is pursuing doctoral studies at the University of Victoria.

Deana M. Raffo, EdD, serves as assistant professor of management at Middle Tennessee State University, where she coordinates the leadership studies minor. She has had rich professional experiences involving student services, student affairs, and leadership education. Her research interests include leadership and personal development, leadership education, and the introverted qualities in leadership.

Jonathan Reams, PhD, practices the cultivation of leadership through awareness based consulting and leadership development program design and delivery in a variety of settings. He has a position at the Norwegian University of Science and Technology, serves as editor in chief of *Integral Review*, and is a cofounder of the Center for Transformative Leadership. He brings awareness based technology to focusing on how the inner workings of human nature can develop leadership capacities for today's complex challenges.

Juliane Reams, MA, began her career in the fashion design industry, turned to tourism and adventure sports, elementary and primary school pedagogy, and earned a master's degree in counseling. She works as a researcher on leadership development for the Center for Transformative Leadership and for Conscious Leadership Development, specializing in the field of cultivating wisdom.

Yuka Saionji is deputy chairperson of Byakko Shinko Kai, a spiritual organization dedicated to world peace and raising the consciousness of humanity. She is a board member of Miratsuku ("emerging future"), a nonprofit organization working on community building through dialogue. Saionji works with youth around the world on projects for peace and is a member of the Evolutionary Leaders and World Spirit Youth Council. She has a degree in law from Gakushuin University in Japan.

Subhanu Saxena is managing director and global CEO of Cipla and was previously a member of the Global Pharma

Executive Committee of Novartis Pharma AG, where he had responsibility for marketing, sales, global medical affairs, and health economics. He is a highly accomplished global executive, with experience over the past twenty-five years in Europe, North America, Africa, and Asia. He holds an MBA from INSEAD–France and a BA (Hons.) in engineering science from Oxford University. Fluent in English, Hindi, and Sanskrit, with a good working knowledge of French, German, and Russian, he is also a lecturer and teacher of Sanskrit and ancient Indian literature.

Otto Scharmer, PhD, is a senior lecturer at MIT and founding chair of the Presencing Institute. He cofounded the Global Wellbeing Lab and is vice chair of the World Economic Forum's Global Agenda Council on Leadership. He introduced the concept of "presencing," learning from the emerging future, in his books *Theory U* and *Presence* (the latter co-authored with Peter Senge, Joseph Jaworski, and Betty Sue Flowers). His new book, *Leading from the Emerging Future: From Ego-system to Eco-system Economies*, focuses on transforming business, society, and self.

Susan Skjei, MS, has been an educator, coach, and consultant for twenty-five years, specializing in leadership and transformative change. She is completing her PhD at Fielding Graduate University. Formerly a chief learning officer for a large technology company, she developed and directs the authentic leadership program at Naropa University and is a cofounder of the Authentic Leadership in Action Institute in Canada. She is an Acharya (senior teacher) in the Shambhala Buddhist tradition and consults internationally through her company, SaneSystems.

Bob Stilger, PhD, is the founder and co-president of New Stories, a nonprofit that uses the power of story to help people create thriving, resilient communities. His work has stretched to many parts of the world, including Japan, Zimbabwe, South Africa, Brazil, and Australia. Co-president of the Berkana Institute from 2005 to 2009, he teaches at St. Mary's College of California and Gonzaga University. His PhD in learning and change in human systems is from the California Institute of Integral Studies.

Introduction: Of Leadership and Light

Kathryn Goldman Schuyler

This introduction juxtaposes questions about leadership with questions and perceptions about life, since for me the two are highly interwoven. Walk with me metaphorically as I tell you about this book and my experiences in developing it. My intention for this book is to nourish the capacity to be present, so it seems fitting to walk, notice my surroundings, and reflect on them in introducing you to the world of this book.

The day moves toward dusk, with vivid light shining through wind-blown eucalyptus trees, tossing them into a swaying dance between me and the paling blue sky, its intensity shifting as the light changes. The birds make little sounds; I imagine they are communicating to one another about food for the evening, but who knows. Perhaps they are noticing the wind and the light as well. An intense fuchsia color on a small flower catches my eye. Each blossom looks fragile and brilliant at the same time, contrasted with the darker colors of the heavier, larger plants and trees nearby. *Perhaps the intensity of a small bright flower makes as much difference as the long-lasting contribution of a bush,* I muse.

Today, between the second and third virtual meetings with the three associate editors of this book, I watched the America's Cup race from my office in San Francisco. I knew it was taking place somewhere in the billowing fog outside my windows, yet I chose to watch on screen, both because of the fog and because television can literally place the watcher on the racing boats, with the racer's view added to the spectator's view. An amazing aspect of our world: a technology that distances people from the things happening right outside our windows can also bring us close to them in ways that we could never otherwise experience. For me, the combination of these qualities of television as a medium and the race itself brings me closer to understanding what I want this book to be for readers. In the race, we see boats labeled "New Zealand" and "USA," yet the teams are not necessarily from those countries. The science that developed these unique new boats, with sails thirteen stories high that can race at speeds of over thirty miles an hour against the wind, also cuts across our humanly created divisions into nation-states. The funding for the boats only sometimes comes from the countries named: the New Zealanders represent Emirates Airlines and the Swiss company Nespresso, for example. The skipper of the USA boat clearly sounds like an Australian. Only one member of the so-called American team is from the United States. So is this really USA versus New Zealand? What is it?

The America's Cup as a Metaphor for Understanding Leadership

The type of leadership required of both captains is to be fully present to the demands of the moment. Past races must not overly influence them during the current one, and they need mastery of both the subtleties of interpersonal communication among the team members and the technological complexities of these new, huge, racing catamarans. There is no either-or choice: success requires mastery of technology, one's physical and emotional self, verbal and nonverbal communication, the crafts of sailing and racing, and much more. It means being able to use analytical intelligence, technical knowledge, strategic thinking, and environmental sensing and to be inspirational to one's team as well. In this instance, being world class and getting to the pinnacle of success means inevitably that one team must lose; that is the nature of this contest. Such winning does not come solely from the captain's leadership on the boat.

In this and many other settings today, leadership also means mastery of new technology, which may be contributed by unseen people behind the scenes. Changes made over the course of the series of races by technological wizards working in the background may have led to the dramatic shift in wins from one boat to the other in the middle of these sixteen races. In addition, decisions were made by other leaders off the water who inspired, managed, and funded the entire project. Leadership and winning were truly distributed and networked.

Much of this is true for leadership today. There is not just one training or way of developing leadership, and it is not just one thing. Excellent leaders may grow up in one country and lead companies or nongovernmental organizations based in another, with people on their teams from many different parts of the world. Just as the weather cannot be controlled and may be warm and sunny one day and windy with fog the next, leaders lead through all weather, all conditions, with all kinds of people. To accomplish this, they need high levels of mastery of their physical and emotional selves, verbal and nonverbal communication, the knowledge base of their endeavors, how to choose a strong team, and how to inspire appropriate, timely action. Leadership may look as if it comes from the person who is visible, but it actually depends on widely networked interactions.

Although the credit generally goes to the one person designated as "leader," the America's Cup race helped me see graphically how the team, the boat, and the leader can be almost indistinguishable in terms of their respective contributions. Is it the designated leader who matters most? The innate speed potential of the boat that comes from its technology? The talent of the team members and how they coordinate together? Or is success the outcome of the composite of all of these and other factors as well, like the "surround," which in this case means the changing winds and currents? My vote is for the complex and intricate interdependence of all of these components. The issue for leaders, leadership developers, and scholars then becomes which of these we can influence and optimally effective ways to do so.

Although there is only one winner in the game of racing, this is not so in life, business, or global society. Creating a sustainable human presence on the planet means transcending old notions of one winner and many losers. We human beings are waking up to recognize the interdependence of our actions, organizations, and societies in time and in space. As one of my students recently commented after reading the Dalai Lama's *Ethics for the New Millennium* (1999), "I saw how lazy my mind is: I think about cause and effect, but he sees long chains of causation linked with every act, every choice. I thought I was a good thinker until I saw this possibility. We are not accustomed to contemplating the interconnectedness of our actions. This interconnectedness provides a complex, comprehensive, frankly mind-blowing perspective on how we all affect one another."

Embodied Being

It may not be chance that this book follows *The Embodiment of Leadership*, last year's volume in the International Leadership Association's (ILA) Building Leadership Bridges series. I submitted this year's topic because I sensed that the ILA wishes to help its members and the larger community reframe traditional notions about the nature of leadership and contribute to increasingly healthy leadership throughout the world. This book and its structure grow out of an approach to the interdependence of embodiment, spirit, and leadership that has been developing in my work for many years.

Originally we four editors sought to include concrete stories from leaders and consultants about their work, illustrating how spirit, presence, and authenticity contribute to effectiveness in action. However, most submissions discussed concepts, reviewed relevant literature, or spoke to experiences outside the realms of corporate or political leadership. The most graphic examples came from educators who described how they incorporate these themes into their teaching. Perhaps as leadership scholars and practitioners, we are still drawing together knowledge and experience from a range of fields that rarely interact with one another, so our models don't yet encompass the whole of what we seek to address, making it difficult to move to the stage of illuminating these models with specific stories.

For leadership scholars, educators, and consultants wishing to address leaders as full beings who are embodied, in touch with spirit, present, and thereby authentic, there are rich philosophical and practical sources to draw on. Conceptually the writings of Mark Johnson (1987, 2007), Antonio Damasio (1999), and others (Varela, Thompson, & Rosch, 1991) portray human beings as embodied in ways that are different from most people's commonsense notion of a physical body as a thing in which one lives for a while. Their work has not yet penetrated common social science ways of thinking and writing about what a person is as an agent of change. Few people draw on deep practices of embodiment to develop managers, leaders, and consultants. I know of none who have both consulted from such a deeply grounded embodied perspective and used this consulting experience for systematic action research. From my experience of drawing on professional somatic training in my work as an organizational change consultant, I believe that the leadership field as a whole will benefit if it is nourished by experiential forms of embodied learning that have rich theoretical and scientific roots. Among possible examples of such methods are the *Feldenkrais Method* (Feldenkrais, 1949, 1972, 1977, 1979) and Bainbridge Cohen's (2012) body-mind centering.

Such perspectives posit that we as human beings can potentially sense ourselves down to the cellular level. We can feel consciousness in our cells, fluids, tissues, bones—in all components of our selves. Embodiment offers a potential for sensing our interconnectivity with one another and with the air, water, and earth with which we are in constant interaction. The mind is not a separate kind of entity that can think with clarity about the body: instead, it is an embodied process. "It is our organic flesh and blood, our structural bones, the ancient rhythms of our internal organs, and the pulsing flow of our emotions that give us whatever meaning we can find and that shape our very thinking" (Johnson, 2007, p. 3). Through the quirks of the way we perceive, this embodied foundation of thinking and understanding becomes invisible during what humans have come to regard as normal functioning (Johnson, 2007). The work of pioneers like Feldenkrais, Bainbridge Cohen, Varela, Johnson, and others suggests that this fundamental ground of being can be sensed, studied, and brought into leadership education and development. Embodied learning is grounded in understanding the way humans learn: through variation, noticing differences, and playful experimentation. Ideally, such learning also incorporates the human capacity for compassion, which comes from acknowledging the fundamental interdependence of all living beings.

Unending Unfoldment

Another perspective on the hidden-in-plain-view aspects of human beings can be seen in Tibetan Vajrayana traditions (Goldman Schuyler, 2012, 2013) and in Western philosophers like Spinoza. Both show how ordinary life and material things are not distinct from spirit, but instead can be seen as spirit manifesting in form. From this standpoint, one does not live, get points for being good, and then receive rewards later. There is no later. It is not a sequential process, as there are no "things" that are not also spirit. Materiality and spirit are enfolded in one another, perhaps as David Bohm (1980) saw them in describing the universe as "a coherent whole, which is never static or complete but which is an unending process of movement and unfoldment" (p. x). This is similar to Chogyam Trungpa's (1973) notion of authenticity in action. In this context, mindfulness or awareness intrinsically means connecting simultaneously with oneself as an embodied being and with the vastness and interconnected quality of life, developing a view of impermanence (as Buddhists call it) and the constructed nature of human societies.

While going through this experiment and working on this book, I often reflected on the difficulty of having leaders train extensively in meditation or mindfulness, given their time constraints and focus on action. In addition, over the centuries, it has been clear that even to develop wise spiritual leaders is a significant challenge, since they, like political leaders, are often caught by the attractions of power, wealth, and self-image. The action research process suggests one type of path forward. It is a path that connects with the work of Otto Scharmer and Peter Senge on presence. Instead of developing lengthy training processes, perhaps executive guides can support leaders in being fully present and paying attention, while reminding them of their already existing deep personal values and intentions.

Exploring Presence in Action: A Research Project

To explore this richness and complexity in a structured way, I co-created a collaborative action research project several years ago. We invited participants to observe themselves three to four times a week for four weeks during moments that they sensed themselves to be more awake than usual. The project coordinators did not tell participants anything about how they should hold the notion of awake, except for contextualizing it historically in relation to the words of several different spiritual traditions.

The basis of this research was my curiosity about whether human beings actually need to be trained to notice, pay attention, and sense themselves and their environment. Instead, in this research project we opted to regard these as basic capacities that come with embodiment as human beings, so that people do not need to be "trained" in them. I am guessing that the vivid connectedness with experience that human babies and very young children share fades for most people as they learn to talk, drive, think, and write. Perhaps people simply need to be reminded to pay attention, rather than needing training in awareness or meditation. This led to the design of our research as an action research experiment.

A core notion in this research project was that as humans, we have not learned how to fully use all of our equipment: we haven't yet mastered the fine art of living with the rich and complex body/ mind/sensing apparatus (or self) that we are. Rather than assuming that what is needed is ever more training, I became interested in questioning whether simply paying attention might trigger a different way of approaching life and action. This is similar to what I perceive in the method of dialogue, where participants sit together patiently, allowing silence and time between people's words rather than jumping in with preplanned notions of what should go next. Both approaches give space for something new to emerge from being present to one another.

In our research project, we invited participants to pay attention and be aware of moments when they felt "awake" or present and to write or record notes about the experiences. As this book goes to press, my colleagues and I are engaged in analyzing the transcripts of the individual reflections and interviews that comprise our qualitative data. We already see that the participants experienced unexpected insight and support for being present in daily action and felt that this affected how they worked during the rest of the day while they were involved in the experiment. Such individual first-person research can provide a foundation for designing larger change projects. (See Figure I.1 for the way I have modeled this, based on my research, consulting, experience with Buddhist practices, and reflection.)

Figure I.1   Embodied Leadership

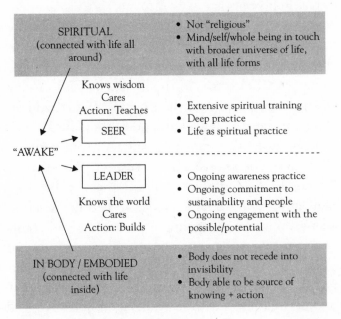

Copyright © 2013 Kathryn Goldman Schuyler.

Rather than doing lengthy training, perhaps leadership development can increasingly incorporate ongoing practices of contemplation (of all types and traditions) to bring leaders in touch regularly with the fullness of life within them (embodiment) and on the planet (spirituality), along with supporting them in actively engaging with the complex systemic problems faced today in our economies and cultures. Such awareness can be enhanced by simple training in easily learned compassion practices (Salzberg, 2011). As Senge (2012) has said, "Until you can stop the habitual flow of your mind, you cannot see what's around you. If you're going to be in a position of authority, you'd better have a high level of awareness of what's going on. Otherwise, all you can do is project your inner dynamics on the outer world. You look at our world today, and we've got a lot of people in positions of authority who don't know anything except how to project their own world-view on the larger world, so we have lots of problems" (pp. 326–327).

When executives sense that they are interconnected with all other sentient beings, they are likely to make different decisions than when they mainly sense pressure for quarterly results, as you will see in several chapters in this book. If CEOs are aware of their breath, their heart, and their feet on the ground and take time to gaze at the vast sky all around as they think about a difficult strategic issue, they may take different things into account in arriving at key decisions. Thus, I suspect that leaders do not need the depth of mindfulness training that has been provided throughout history for those who seek to become wisdom teachers; they need only brief training in awareness and compassion, combined with ongoing practice in being present to themselves, others, and life while working as managers, politicians, or military leaders. This might mean linking experiences in presencing and mindfulness with learning about adaptive leadership (Heifetz & Linsky, 2002).

A Glimpse inside the Creation of This Book

As with leadership, which seems to be an attribute of one person yet is something that occurs only in the midst of an interactive process, the creation of this book has been a team effort. Again, as with the boat, there is a key role for the designated leader, but the selection of the team members and the work of those behind the scenes are all critical components. The editorial team is composed of four people who have never met in person and come from very different backgrounds and experience bases; each graciously gave a great deal of their time to create a book that would make a distinctive contribution to people who care about leadership in today's world.

We made time to talk over coffee virtually, to simply be together so we could speak from our heart-mind, not just from our intellects, even though I was in California, John was on a Greek island and then in Maine, Karin was in the Netherlands, and Lena was in Spain and then in Sweden. We did this so we could express strongly divergent opinions without feeling uncomfortable doing so, as happens much of the time in meetings. We sorted through 120 submissions without having any idea who wrote them, whether they came from widely respected scholars and consultants or from people new to the field, from mature professionals or newly minted PhDs. We read and talked to find those authors who spoke to us from a sense of their own real experiences, who shared data (whether research based or from experience as manager or consultant) and built clear lines of thought that seemed likely to be of interest to the current and potential members of the ILA. They addressed the theme we sought: developing leaders who are present, bring spirit to their part of the world, and lead in ways that enable more authentic action. These are leaders whose spirit, presence, and authenticity help them move their organizations or communities toward improved action on what Ron Heifetz (Parks, 2005) has called "swamp problems"—those problems no one knows how to resolve.

I read all submissions, and each associate editor read a third of them. Then we shared our views in writing, discussed them, and chose twenty that all four of us would read in order to select those that would make up this book.

Living in San Francisco, I often get to watch the fog come floating in and curl around the brightly outlined blocks of buildings as the sun sets. Soft gray fog, shining hard windows reflecting golden light, and sharp edges of buildings standing out against the blur of smaller structures and the gradual enveloping fog, as the sky turns pink and gray—the brilliant blue of the day morphing into a softness and subtlety chilled by strong winds. It is as though the buildings and the city are being packed away in cotton clouds for the night. How do we select pieces that will paint vivid pictures for our readers? Which of the authors will be able to take their submissions to new levels? It is never easy to know.

Our virtual meetings were among the richest I have ever experienced. We have come to know one another and appreciate both the similarities of what we value and the differences among us. I wish such meetings were common in all organizations, in all universities. When she comments, Lena Lid-Falkman brings warmth, experience editing previous BLB volumes, deep knowledge of the way that one exemplary leader (Dag Hammarskjöld) contributed to the global evolution of leadership, plus expertise in rhetoric and the ways that social media are impacting leadership studies. John Eric Baugher brings excellence in scholarly writing that is also personal and reflective, experience in Buddhist practice and research on end-of-life care, as well as extensive understanding of relevant sociological perspectives. Karin Jironet brings years of work experience as a Jungian analyst and executive guide, plus personal experience with Sufism and other wisdom lineages, enriched by having written a book on the feminine in leadership. All are excellent writers and editors who walk their talk of commitment to openness. I seek to bring understanding of interactive processes and a feeling for new possibilities that we are here to birth, honed by over twenty years of practice as an organizational and leadership consultant, decades of grounding in the fluidity and concreteness of the Feldenkrais approach to awareness through movement, and value for both shared silence and well-crafted words. I tried always to create virtual meetings in which we felt truly present with one another, so that our work was itself a manifestation of what we want the book to be in the world.

Finally, we also interacted virtually with Debra DeRuyver, who has managed the creation and evolution of the Building Leadership Bridges for the ILA since 2009. Her ability to be both friendly and highly organized through e-mail and by phone is a blessing in a project manager and contributed always to the quality of the final product. The role of the ILA itself in selecting this theme, placing resources behind it, and sustaining this series is a sign of its intent to make a unique contribution to leadership in today's world.

Overview of the Book

The contributors to this book explored these and similar questions in their own ways. Each part approaches the theme from a different perspective. The associate editors introduce the contents of each part with a thought piece, so I will focus here on the thinking behind the overall structure of this book rather than on the individual chapters.

We don't see spirit, presence, and authenticity as three distinct things; we treat them as related and interdependent lenses through which to appreciate leadership. As an example of the pervading trinity, Buddhist traditions speak of three *kayas*, or different ways of understanding the relationship between spirit and phenomena. Briefly, the first of these could be thought of as the underlying principle of enlightenment—the source of all and everything, which we are here labeling *spirit*; the second is how this enlightenment connects with life through light, which we are here labeling *presence*; and the third is how it manifests in beings who take action, here labeled as *authenticity*. The parts don't follow one another in a linear way, but in a book, one thing must follow another.

My familiarity with these distinctions led me to sense spirit as a lens for something that is not concrete but influences everything else. Therefore, the book opens with part 1, "Spirit," with chapters that offer a frame of reference for renewal of notions of leadership, grounded in theory as well as in daily practice. Another way of describing this part would be to say it provides an expansive view of the nature and role of leadership today, which Karin Jironet explores in her contribution.

Part 2, "Presence," addresses the process of bringing this view into the world of human action. As Senge, Scharmer, Jaworkski, and Flowers (2004) have described presence, it involves experiencing the way the whole is alive in every part of a system, experiencing the "wholeness of nature" (p. 7). They have given the world *presencing* as a path for shifting from reactive learning to deeper levels of learning that lead to "action that increasingly serves the whole" (p. 11). This part contains programs for bringing mindfulness into educational systems. John Eric Baugher's introductory chapter explores the role of individual mindfulness as a foundation, but only a partial one, for societal mindfulness, the direction we would hope such leadership will take in the world.

The book closes with part 3, "Authenticity." To me, trained as a sociologist by Amitai Etzioni when he was focused on bringing about *The Active Society* (1968), authenticity refers to moving beyond trying to be present but really just pretending, to being able to genuinely live values that serve all participants in a given system. Our intent for this part is that it will raise questions for you as to what it is to be authentic as a leader rather than necessarily resolving your questions. Lena Lid-Falkman shares her view of authenticity in introducing the chapters in this part.

The sun has set now, and the sailing racers are long gone. The lights of the city and other cities across the bay sparkle, suggesting to me the many people invisible in the darkness who cause there to be light in this community and in the rest of the world. Even this light can be seen as a symbol of the way that human beings have changed the world we live in, as it makes it possible to live and interact 24/7 and at the same time creates light pollution so that the real points of light, the stars, become invisible.

May this book serve you, all other readers, and the ILA as a tool for asking new questions of yourself about leadership, its function in the world, and how to develop ever healthier leadership for the planet, and may it help you see the light of the stars during those times that we perceive as being dark.

References

Bainbridge Cohen, B. (2012). *Sensing, feeling, and action.* Northampton, MA: Contact Editions.

Bohm, D. (1980). *Wholeness and the implicate order.* London: Routledge

Dalai Lama. (1999). *Ethics for the new millennium.* New York: Riverhead Books.

Damasio, A. (1999). *The feeling of what happens: Body and emotion in the making of consciousness.* New York: Harcourt Brace.

Etzioni, A. (1968). *The active society.* New York: Free Press.

Feldenkrais, M. (1949). *Body and mature behaviour: A study of anxiety, sex, gravitation, and learning.* New York: Harper.

Feldenkrais, M. (1972). *Awareness through movement.* New York: Harper.

Feldenkrais, M. (1977). *Body awareness as healing therapy: The case of Nora.* Berkeley, CA: Somatic Resources.

Feldenkrais, M. (1979). On health. *Dromenon, 2*(2), 25–26.

Goldman Schuyler, K. (2012) *Inner peace—global impact: Tibetan Buddhism, leadership, and work.* Charlotte, NC: Information Age.

Goldman Schuyler, K. (2013). From the ground up: Revisioning sources and methods of leadership development. In L. Melina (Ed.), *The embodiment of leadership.* San Francisco: Jossey-Bass.

Heifetz, R., & Linsky, M. (2002). *Leadership on the line.* Cambridge, MA: Harvard Business Press.

Johnson, M. (1987). *The body in the mind: The bodily basis of meaning, imagination, and reason.* Chicago: University of Chicago Press.

Johnson, M. (2007). *The meaning of the body.* Chicago: University of Chicago Press.

Parks, S. D. (2005). *Leadership can be taught: A bold approach for a complex world.* Boston: Harvard Business Press.

Salzberg, S. (2011). *Lovingkindness: The revolutionary art of happiness.* Boston: Shambhala.

Scharmer, O. (2007). *Theory U.* San Francisco: Berrett-Koehler

Scharmer, O., & Kaufer, K. (2013). *Leading from the emerging future.* San Francisco: Berrett-Koehler.

Senge, P. (2012). "Leaders should be people who are deeply involved in their own realization of being a human being": An interview with Peter Senge. In K. Goldman Schuyler (Ed.), *Inner peace—global impact: Tibetan Buddhism, leadership, and work.* Charlotte, NC: Information Age.

Senge, P., Scharmer, C. O., Jaworkski, J., & Flowers, B. S. (2004). *Presence: Human purpose and the field of the future.* Cambridge, MA: Society for Organizational Learning.

Trungpa, C. (1973). *Cutting through spiritual materialism.* Boston: Shambhala.

Varela, F. J., Thompson, E., & Rosch, E. (1991). *The embodied mind: Cognitive science and human experience.* Cambridge, MA: MIT Press.

Leading with Spirit, Presence, and Authenticity

Part One

Spirit

Awareness and Beyond

Why Moving On Means Letting Go

Karin Jironet

Most of us who try to learn and keep developing professionally have been to a workshop during which our eyes were opened to another way of looking at our actions, and we felt ready to change. Then, after three days back at work, the new perspective seems to have evaporated. We return to the same old ways as before, and the new outlook becomes a memory. The experience itself is no longer in the foreground. We tend to forget it as we go back to business as usual.

This happens because we are enmeshed in, and hence contribute to, a collective mind-set and culture that limit us. Simply resuming our daily life returns us to our usual mind-set. We need not believe in, or even agree with, the concepts that make up our mental categories. They seem to rule our thinking and actions regardless of our wishes. Our conceptual organization and mental categorization do not change overnight. (Mental categories are not solely mental. As Kathryn Goldman Schuyler noted, these are also embodied and as such intrinsic to the way we move and relate in relationships.) It is inherently difficult and complex to replace one image of ourselves with another, regardless of the impression a new outlook can leave.

George Lakoff, professor of cognitive science and linguistics at Berkeley, illustrated this phenomenon by the way he named his seminal work: *Women, Fire and Dangerous Things* (1990). The title refers to a word that denotes women, fire, and dangerous things in Dyirbal, an aboriginal language of Australia.

They co-occur interdependently in the Dyirbal cosmos, stating the obvious to its cultural carriers—similar to the Christian notion of the Holy Trinity of the Father, the Son, and the Holy Ghost—rendering the task of changing these categories of mind nearly impossible. But what of, let us say, the concepts of leadership, power, and goal orientation?

What Is the Relevance of the Concept of Leadership?

Let us agree that for society at large, the signs of rapid transformations are convincing, and they are pointing toward altering our understanding of notions such as global power distribution, hierarchies, organizational development, growth, and the role of the individual—the very cornerstones of any civilization (see Loy, 2003; Tamdgidi, 2007; Wallerstein, 2001). The changes that can be observed in society—interconnectedness, interdependencies, globalization—might also be termed changes in mind-set, that is, a kind of collective awakening to experiences that we have had but have not manifested in conscious awareness due to cultural conditioning.

Perhaps today's widespread reaching out for spirituality is an expression of the realization that the single-minded focus on individual benefits and exploitation of material values will not lead us forward out of what is often described as a crisis—hence, the conclusion that it is spirituality that can now better inform leadership. But if the concept of leadership in its very fundament clings to its old logic, then what could spirituality (e.g., mindfulness) possibly do for leadership? If we agree that the parameters are changing, then the concept of leadership would surely be one of the first to undergo a major revision. But how?

The image of leadership has always been transformed in particular cultural and historical contexts. What is different this time is that the transformation cannot occur within the known leadership engram—with or without spirituality. Leadership as we have known it is no longer a relevant construct for what is needed to meet with changes in society and human consciousness (see Jironet, 2010; Scharmer & Kaufer, 2013). As Otto Scharmer stated in his interview with Kathryn Goldman Schuyler in chapter 1 in this book, "What is required today [is] . . . leadership that is . . . more connected with the sources of our own consciousness on the one hand; . . . [and] on the other hand, . . . needs to link up to the profound societal disruption that we currently face." John Eric Baugher addressed this challenge in his introduction to part 2. He describes the fundamental task that lies ahead of humanity today as that of accepting and assuming responsibility for the harm and suffering we inevitably cause our neighbor. Such a deep ethical response, however obviously called for, is a humbling experience to which Baugher (in press) has applied the term *sociological mindfulness*.

The Problem with Applying Spirituality to the Western Concept for Leadership

It is commonly held that the purpose of spiritual practice is to guide the individual (leader or not) toward renouncing the false self, letting go of the limitations of the ego, and annihilating attachments. As anyone who has seriously followed a spiritual practice knows, this letting go is a long, open-ended, ongoing process, with ups and downs, back and forths, demanding ever more steadfastness and discipline, a patient teacher, and other conditions conducive to practice.

What would leadership look like if it renounced itself, that is, gave up striving to be in the lead or on top with a clear plan for where to go? It would be something very different. Let us consult the mystics for a glimpse of their findings.

Mysticism is represented in all forms of religion, and often it was at the core of what later developed into an established religion. I think it is safe to say that the various mystical paths have more in common than the religions that have been built around their practices. That is because religions are anchored in the culture of a particular time, whereas mysticism is far less so. Owing to my studies and training in, especially, Sufism, I refer to Sufi teachings as an example, although Zen Buddhist or Advaita Vedanta examples of renunciation would serve here just as well.

Sufism is often recognized for its focus on the heart as a center for deep knowing (see Corbin, 1998; Khan, 1988). Notions such as *Wahdat al-wujud* (unity of being), *tawakkul* (reliance on God), and *zikr* (the remembrance of God) are central to all forms of Sufism and to most other mystical paths that I know of. They convey the essence of mysticism—the presence that is experienced as unity with all that is, the realization that the subjective ego is subordinate to the higher force of creation, and that in order not to lose the connection with that creative flow, one needs to remind oneself of it on a regular basis. Engaging in spiritual practices that deepen the individual's experience and realization of these states of knowing is essential for renunciation and, thus, self-realization. Self-realization is the gradual release from the grip and claims of the ego that strives to be at the center and hinders the experience of unity with all that is.

Do renunciation of the ego and self-realization correspond to leadership as we know it? Not really. Leader and leadership are concepts that pursue a logic that yields leaders and followers, teachers and students, goals and actions, perks and disadvantages. It is a logic built on polarization rather than unity, grasping rather than renunciation.

How can we then, without fundamentally uprooting the entire concept of leadership, justify the introduction of spiritual practices, in whatever form, to leadership development? How can we endorse the instrumental use of these when they were developed to reduce the power of the ego? What happens when these practices are used for egocentric purposes and thus strengthen the ego? Without a fundamental shift in our collective outlook when it comes to leader and leadership, notions such as spirituality in business, servant-leadership, mindfulness at work, and so on begin to seem ridiculous. They defy their own intent. If we sincerely wish to play an active role in bringing spirit, presence, and authenticity to the field of leadership development, we must also honestly create awareness around the real challenges humanity faces at this point in time when it comes to leadership, power, and goal orientation.

I believe that these notions can be transformed only by individuals who have the strength to hold on to a new way of looking at the world as a united whole, with awareness of forces that move our lives beyond the ego, and with openness to inspiration for unpremeditated creativity. The challenge is that when immersed in a leader and leadership paradigm, we succumb to the ego's fear of losing power. What is the mystic's approach to this fundamental trial?

The Notion of Power: An Example of the Problem

To a Sufi, power means something very different from what we became accustomed to believing it to be in the twentieth century, an era when power manifestations were tightly linked to accomplishment and scope of influence in the external environment, if not sheer physical power and the power to win over others in competitions. "Power" (as an aspect of *Ishq*, meaning love) to a Sufi means the energy given to a person by his or her ability to be open to the light of the spirit of guidance. To be open in this way, without veils or reservations, but really purely open, is one of the results of the daily practices I referred to earlier.

Let's look a little closer at these practices and the process of letting go. "Letting go of what?" you may ask. "Of the ego," mystics would respond. "The false ego!" they would add, implying that there is a true self, the self or soul, which is veiled by the false self, the ego. "But what is the false self? What ego should I let go of?" you might persist. The crux is that one cannot know this until the letting-go process has taken place. One doesn't know upfront what constitutes the false ego. This is where spiritual and material views first clash: false ego, shadow, unconscious stuff—how to let go of something that you don't really know of? Practice.

The practice itself gradually unveils reality. Through shedding illusions—it is not this; it is not that—the truth (which resides behind form somewhere and is stable and permanent) gradually reveals itself to the open, increasingly purified mind. Attending to a practice is a way of knowing through the heart and mind, combined. This is not simply a distinction between inner and outer power or between how much you can let go of versus how much you can get hold of. It is a difference in the nature of power itself, and this is the second reason for a severe clash of the spiritual and the material mind-sets.

The power developed while following a spiritual path is characterized by surrender, aimlessness, inclusion, acceptance, contentment, open-endedness, and the like. This is contrary to what Western leadership theory identifies as the power of leadership, and from that perspective, spiritual power might well be considered sheer madness. Whatever spiritual practice you introduce in a business context, even in the most benevolently oriented ones, you will come up against this power polarization sooner or later. So then the next question is: If you know this, how do you respond? As far as I understand, there is no conclusive response in the West today, because our culture is at the brink of shifting from one logic of awareness to another that is not yet known.

Many today are dedicated to discovering and understanding the *how* in which ways of personal and public conduct, participation, and creativity can play a defining role in transforming the way we govern organizations. In the next section, I describe In Claritas, a foundation exploring the frontiers of what may come after leadership.

An Experimental Phase of Finding
New Ways: In Claritas

The power of love came into me, and I became fierce like a lion, then tender like the evening star. (Rumi, 2004)

In 2011, Harry Starren, then CEO of the largest leadership institute in the Netherlands, and I created a foundation called In Claritas. Having worked with leadership development professionally for decades, we both felt drawn to delve deeper into exploring how leading could take place in the coming era. We did not have a plan, but allowed a long felt reaction against the fatigue of exhausted pathways to take form. It was all in the spirit of "let's see."

We invited a diverse group of scholars, artists, authors, and business leaders to join a two-day gathering at the Dutch seashore. I recall Harry introducing the theme as an adventure around what the new image of ". . ." could be. He also said it would involve a lot of fantasizing to discover ". . .". And I remember a lot of laughing and how lightly different images flew forth in the group and how associations to these were exchanged freely, without much interpretation or pinning down. Harry and I facilitated the imagination exercise through different modes of experimenting, including musical, poetical, philosophical, and physical ways of engagement. Given our respective spiritual training and practice—Harry has followed the Jesuit path—it seemed natural to alternate activity with repose. We did this in the form of silence and meditations guided toward attunement with the individual higher Self, as well as the soul qualities of the group. Toward the end of the second day, we discovered that we had gradually generated images that were truly embodied and anchored in deeper layers of consciousness. These could translate into concepts that we named *transformation*, *awareness*, and *hope*—three interrelated aspects of how "governance," the guidance of energy and imagination in large groups of people, manifests by ways of continuous renewal, concentration, and uniting intent.

Since that first retreat, the group of affiliates has grown, and we have conducted several retreats in the United States and Europe while developing these concepts further. Although we are building a practice in a very diverse group and each retreat evolves naturally from previous ones, the elements of what now constitutes the In Claritas practice remain very much the same. Rooted in mysticism, this practice is initiatic in the sense that it opens up to new dimensions in the present moment, be it through guided meditations, jokes, creative expression, inner choices, healing of old wounds—in whatever form a first step in an unknown direction is brought about. This approach, oscillating in a creative dimension of subtle and intangible constituents, has regenerating impacts as well as frustrating effects.

In the course of the past three years, we have experienced how affiliates may feel very elevated through being present to an experience of unity with a fundamental reality and then, waking up as it were from that, ask themselves and us, "But what can I do with this? What is the purpose?" In more generic terms, such splitting of experience and action results from insecurity around goal, structure, ownership, and so on rooted in questioning "What is my role in In Claritas?" Their experience simply does not fit into the well-known narrative about leadership and how we do things together. The function of In Claritas, as Harry and I see it, is to sit with and contain this inevitable tension while purposefully listening to the subtle melody that resonates with a flavor of the experience, and in this way strengthen a new engram within the individual and in us all. As a collective, we look for ways of transcending our well-known concepts and ways of knowing the world and our place in it. In such a liminal landscape, where peril and possibility walk hand in hand, we are all dependent on individuals who can hold on lightly to the depth of experience, knowing that will yield the new mind-set.

Leading with Spirit

Chapter 1 contains Subhanu Saxena's story, in which you encounter a man who brings his spiritual practice into business, thereby creating wealth and health for vast numbers of men and women. He speaks of how important it was for him as a child to follow the example of a great leader while dedicating himself to a higher purpose. For me, he represents an example of an individual whose words change the way we understand the world. This is followed in the same chapter by an interview that Kathryn Goldman Schuyler recently conducted with Otto Scharmer in which he speaks about how leaders draw on their spiritual practices and can use presencing to listen deeply to one another and create holding spaces for dialogue across institutional boundaries so as to meet the challenges that companies and nation states urgently need to face.

Jonathan Reams, Olen Gunnlaugson, and Juliane Reams build on this in chapter 2, a case study that describes how deep listening has been developed and implemented within a large Norwegian company. In chapter 3, the last in part 1, Bob Stilger and Yuka Saionji present ways that the Japanese have been bringing communal dimensions of leadership to the challenges of rebuilding the earthquake-devastated portions of Japan, writing from a consulting perspective about enspirited leadership.

References

Baugher, J. E. (in press). Contemplating uncomfortable emotions: Creating transformative spaces for learning in higher education. In O. Gunnlaugson, H. Bai, E. Sarath, & C. Scott (Eds.), *Contemplative approaches to learning and inquiry across disciplines*. Albany, NY: SUNY Press.

Corbin, H. (1998). *Alone with the alone: Creative imagination in the Sufism of Ibn Arabi*. Princeton, NJ: Princeton University Press.

Goldman Schuyler, K. (2012). *Inner peace—global impact: Tibetan Buddhism, leadership, and work*. Charlotte, NC: Information Age.

Jironet, K. (2010). *Female leadership: Management, Jungian psychology, spirituality and the global journey through Purgatory*. London: Routledge.

Khan, H. I. (1988). *The way of illumination*. Bangalore: South Asia Books.

Lakoff, G. (1990). *Women, fire, and dangerous things: What categories reveal about the mind*. Chicago: University of Chicago Press.

Loy, D. (2003). *The great awakening: A Buddhist social theory*. Boston: Wisdom Publications.

Rumi, J. (2004). Sublime generosity. In C. Barks (Ed.), *The essential Rumi*. New York: Harper One.

Scharmer, O., & Kaufer, K. (2013). *Leading from the emerging future: From ego-system to eco-system economics*. San Francisco: Berrett-Koehler.

Tamdgidi, M. (2007). Abu Ghraib as a microcosm: The strange face of empire as a lived prison. *Sociological Spectrum, 27*(1), 29–55.

Wallerstein, I. (2001). *Unthinking social science: The limits of nineteenth-century paradigms* (2nd ed.). Philadelphia: Temple University Press.

Chapter One

Connecting Inner Transformation as a Leader to Corporate and Societal Change

Subhanu Saxena, Otto Scharmer,
Kathryn Goldman Schuyler

I (Kathryn) wanted to bring an executive's perspective and Otto Scharmer's work on leading from the emerging future to this book. This chapter uniquely combines the life story of a CEO who brings deep values about purpose and awareness to his daily work with an interview of Otto Scharmer (who developed the notion of presencing along with Peter Senge) discussing what is needed from leaders today.

I met Subhanu Saxena about six years ago and stayed in touch with him because of my interest in executives and consciousness. He is now CEO of Cipla, the second largest pharmaceutical company in India, which he joined after years on the top management team of Novartis. I introduced him to Otto Scharmer, who invited him to tell his story at the first *Mind and Life Europe Symposium for Contemplative Studies* focused on "Personal and Societal Change from the Contemplative Perspective," which was held in Berlin in October 2013.

Subhanu spoke at the opening of two large open process labs attended by roughly one hundred people each. His charge was to talk about his life as both a global executive and a Sanskrit and Veda/Vedanta teacher in ways that might encourage participants to look at their own life stories and listen for new possibilities within themselves and their worlds. He opened the session by chanting in Sanskrit a melodious, fluid chant that reverberated and echoed around the large concrete space. As he explained, "I thought it was an appropriate way to start this mind and life session with sounds from the Bronze Age, as such mantra allows the person to connect their inner self with their outer self, the universe, and find the universe within."

We open with Subhanu Saxena's story, as told at this gathering, and close with Otto Scharmer's thoughts about how leaders can enable profound shifts in what is possible for us to do together on our planet.

Bringing Life Purpose into Business

yuñjānaḥ prathamam manas tattvāya savitā dhiyaḥ,
agnim jyotir nichāya prithivyā adhyābharat ||
Yoking first the mind, spreading out thought,
Discerning light, the sun has brought forth fire from
        the earth

    . . .

Yuje vām brahmapūrvyam namobhir viślokāyanti
        patthyeva sūrāḥ,
śṛṇvanti viśve amritasya putrā ā ye dhāmāni divyāni
        tasthuḥ ||
I place before thee this ancient prayer, which spreads
        wide and far, as the sun's shining light on its
        path
All the children of immortality can hear it, and
        touch the sacred realms within and without.

(T.S.4.1.1, first six mantras)

I've been asked to talk about how I was able to understand my life purpose and bring it into the world of business. Given

Note: T.S. = Taittiriya Samhita. T.B. = Taittiriya Brahmana. T.U. = Taittiriya Upanishad.

the context of our time together today, I thought I'd start by chanting a mantra and explain how this makes one present in every waking second of your life. These mantras are one of the earliest descriptions of the Vedic conception of yoga of connecting via the mind to that which is beyond the mind and turning external yoga to inner yoga—quite appropriate for the *Mind and Life Symposium*! Mantras flow through me all the time. They are always there. There is a mantra flowing through me every second.

You may be wondering why a CEO of an over twenty-thousand-person corporation is opening with Vedic mantras. Let me tell you a little bit about my story and the topic I'm going to address, which is how as a leader, I connect and engage a large organization to a higher purpose, and how my practice, the teachings I've received, help me or hinder me in achieving that purpose. I hesitate a little bit when I come to meetings like this, because I have to remind people that the purpose of the ancient teachings is not to make a better bond trader, right? It's to know who you are, to take you on a journey of inner discovery. It so happens we work; we're husbands, we're wives, we're fathers. We're talking about application in a specific sphere of our lives, but these teachings infuse every part of our lives and make us who we are and show us who we are. So with that caveat first, let me tell you my story.

Yesterday, mantras I haven't recited for ten years (the trisuparna mantras from Mahanarayana Upanishad) suddenly started resonating within me, so I began reflecting on them. Introspection in a leader is a quality that is not seen so often. How can you get to know who you are and what's around you? There is an Urdu verse: *Before you go and meet people, go and meet the person inside.* For me, I think that the ability to introspect helped me find my higher purpose.

In one of the ancient stories, there are a number of questions posed to a wise king. The last of them is important here: "What's the path that you will follow?" The response always struck me. The response was:

Śrutir vibhinnāḥ smṛtayaścha bhinnāḥ naiko munir yasya vachaḥ pramāṇam,

Dharmasya tattvam nihitam guha‾ya‾m maha‾jano yena gatah. sa pantha‾h.

Religious texts have many varied words. There is no one wise sage whose words are authoritative above everyone else's. Follow the lives of the Great as your path. (*Mahabharata Yaksha Praśna*)

Whatever people say, how they express it could be different. But if you look at the great leaders, how did they live their lives? There are common threads: selfless love, endless passion, uncompromising dedication to the truth.

We follow their stories to be inspired by them. So role models became my way of understanding what I wanted to do. Where I go to find role models for those in the modern world is the ancient texts. The role models who inspired me dedicated themselves to a higher purpose in life, of service, and lived a life of intense external activity coupled with inner calm. Being active, Krishna has been my role model for uncompromising dedication to truth and a clear higher purpose. Everyone looked up to Krishna. He was never a king, but he was above all kings. Why? Because he was the embodiment of truth, dedicating everything he did to a higher calling. And that's my link to what I'm able to do in my life: make a difference and lift those around you to find and achieve their higher purpose. When I look deeper into these role models and how they interacted, they uplifted those around them because they saw the sacred in everyone around them.

I was born in India, grew up in the United Kingdom, and became an Oxford-trained engineer. I'm from a family of Indian classically trained musicians and dancers, and I call my maternal grandfather my first guru. He taught me Urdu poetry, and he would say, "Son, you'll find God in this poetry." So at a young age, I always had a philosophical interest. At university, my friends would ask me, "Tell me about your tradition." I would say, "One God—don't hurt anybody," and I thought they would leave me alone. But they would come back and say, "No, I heard this from this swami, and that from this other guy." I felt inadequate that they'd made me the token expert and I knew nothing about my tradition.

So I asked my parents to get me some books just to keep my friends off my back. I read them intently. I love languages, by the way, so through the years, I've lived in Russia, Switzerland, and France and different places. As I read, I began to feel that the only way I'd really understand was if I studied Sanskrit. So for my graduation present, my parents got me one year of Sanskrit classes at the Institute of Indian Culture. The very first lesson opened this universe of expression that I'd never seen before. I then got lucky: every student dropped out, so I was the only person left. I had an accelerated study program for a year, and then I was asked, "Please help with the teaching."

I found out that my teachers came from Mattur in India, a village where scholars actually speak Sanskrit. It's a village of Vedic scholars, and my teachers were the priests in such a village. So I clearly remember sitting one Sunday evening thinking, "Wouldn't it be lovely to study the Vedas? But I'm here in London. No chance." That Tuesday I went to the Bhavan Institute of Indian Culture and Dr. Nandakumara, my teacher, my dearest friend, said, "My elder brother's visiting, and by the way, he's a Vedic scholar." I couldn't believe my luck.

They say that when the student is ready, the teachers appear. I introduced myself to him, and I was lost to him in the first fifteen seconds of meeting him. I just felt this immediate surrender. I said, "Please teach me the Vedas." He accepted me and taught me. The traditional way of learning the Vedas is to commit them to memory, so that scholars in the village can recite forty-eight hours nonstop. I can only do twelve hours. When he went back to India, he left me tapes. I studied them and then decided to go and study with him in India, so went to the village and studied Veda and also Advaita Vedanta with the Sanskrit commentaries of Shankaracharya, Gaudapada, and my favorite, Suresvara.

That was my life, and then I got into the corporate world. I would say that the first ten to fifteen years of my life was lived as: there's corporate self and there was Subhanu. And which is the real Subhanu? The more I deepened my practice, the more I understood what those teachings were telling me. It liberated me to show up as who I was and hang the consequences. You live one life, so you'd better live it how you want to be. And over the years, I became more and more interested in just being who I really am, and then I began finding corporations that resonated with that, and that's why I want to tell you the story of Cipla, because it's relevant.

Cipla is one of India's largest companies, with over twenty thousand people. We have a market capitalization of $5 billion. The founder of the company, Dr. K. A. Hamied, was a staunch supporter of Mahatma Gandhi, who later on went to live in Gandhiji's Ashram. One day Gandhiji approached Dr. Hamied and asked, "What are you doing here? We need a national university." So he requested him to leave the ashram to set up a national university. After the Aligarh Muslim University was set up, he went on to pursue a PhD in Germany in the 1920s, studying under a Nobel laureate. It was also in Germany where he met his wife, a Lithuanian Jewish woman. They later fled Nazi Germany to set up a pharmaceutical company back home in India.

Once he was back in India, Gandhiji gave him a call and said, "I'm going to come and visit you." On July 4, 1939, Gandhiji visited Cipla and said to him, "The British said they'll give us independence if we support the war effort." To which he responded, "Gandhiji, why are you telling me this? I'm a businessperson." And Gandhiji said, "Medicines are not coming to India. I want you to put the health of the nation before profit and make India self-reliant in medicine." Cipla then endeavored to make Gandhi's vision a possibility by putting the health of patients above profit.

Every single decision the company has ever taken since then is around this central principle: no one should be denied medicines at a price they can afford. That's the higher purpose of Cipla.

The most notable example came during the terrible HIV crisis in Africa. Many of you remember what it was like a decade ago. That was a time when HIV combination antiretroviral therapies cost over twelve thousand dollars a year. Only a few thousand patients in Africa were getting treatment. So the founder's elder son, Dr. Y. K. Hamied, the chairman at this point, went on record saying, "If people are dying, and lifesaving medicines are available and they're not getting them, that to me is genocide."

With the help of Greg Perry, then head of the European Generic Pharma Association, Hamied was invited to address a conference on AIDS at the European Union on September 28, 2000. In front of a world audience, Hamied offered the triple cocktail drug—Triomune for AIDS—to the international community at US$800 per patient per year. Later, with the commitment and support from people, he took yet another bold step of offering the cocktail drug at US$350 per patient per year—less than a dollar a day.

Cipla took that stand, and we changed the course of the disease in Africa. Today HIV therapy in Africa costs below a dollar a day. Nearly 10 million patients are on the therapy. Collectively, we stopped countries becoming extinct, and we're still only scratching the surface. So to join such a company and to be told by the chairman, "I want you to take the message of Gandhi to the world in the field of health care," well, it petrified me, but this is what I wanted to do with my life. I feel privileged having joined such a company and to be continuing this legacy that was given to me and to the organization.

Galvanize an Organization for Its Higher Purpose

Then the question becomes, "How do you really galvanize an organization to do this?" It comes, I think, from a fundamental belief that businesses can be transformative and positive for society if they have the right purpose and the right leadership and the right direction. Our mission is to ensure no one is denied medicines at a price they can afford.

How does an organization come to understand clarity of purpose? It's less what you say and more what you do: when you make decisions that are congruent with that purpose, your organization believes it's real and the stakeholders believe it's real. I'll give you one example. We do a lot of work in India to promote and educate doctors in the field of tuberculosis. It's a time bomb in India: one in three Indians has latent TB. This activity is purely educational and not linked to sales, as this is what needs to be done. When our organization, our people, and doctors see that this is happening, then the purpose becomes real, and it stops being just a mission statement.

Dr. Hamied is still involved in being the living embodiment of the purpose. And that's very much the role I see for myself as the leader. The heart of leadership is very simple, but impossible for most, which is this: whatever you want your organization to be, you have to be that person. This comes from a presence, a mindfulness, and an awareness as to the mission, your energy, and the energy you bring to every discussion.

So clarity of purpose is the first priority. And we are an example, and there are many other companies where you can set a higher purpose for a company. This is not rocket science. And guess what? We're not too unprofitable, we make decent money, we're growing 15 to 16 percent, but we orient everything we do to that higher purpose.

The People

The second ingredient as a leader is the people you bring around you to enable that purpose and the discussion with the leadership team: "How does this team enable the higher purpose?"

To do this, you need to have people whose personal purpose is congruent with the company's purpose. When I interviewed, I saw people who have been with the company for twenty years living this purpose in everything they do. So when you hire people, you spend ten minutes figuring out they can read and write and add, and you really try and understand their inner motivations. What's their life goal, and is there a good fit? I've interviewed many who are incredibly smart, bright, agile individuals, who will be very successful in many scenarios, but if their purpose is not aligned with the company's purpose, they'll be unhappy, and they won't perform, and they'll get frustrated by what the company's about.

One of the things we observed is that those who joined the company in the last couple of years integrated very well into the culture, because they were really Cipla people and didn't know it. I felt that. My first day in the company felt like coming home. A month later, I realize I've been a Cipla man for twenty-five years and didn't know it. As I want employees whose inner purpose is aligned with the higher purpose of the company, I want shareholders who also get the higher purpose of the company.

Presence

The third ingredient is what I call presence. When I interact with the organization, if they think I'm phoning it in, they're not going to go that extra mile. They're not going to really step up and do extraordinary things.

I got an e-mail this morning, "There's a cyclone hitting India; we're all very concerned about it." The team members have already said, "If there are problems, here's what we'd lined up that we'll just send." That comes only if you've got engaged and connected people, and when you are with them, you're with them in the room. I think a leader has to show up. In life, you have to show up as who you are and create an environment where people can show up as who they are. That's the role of presence and the role of being ever aware, mindful of every interaction, and the energy you're giving or receiving from people around you. And that's hard work.

I say that the practice of leadership means that you practice like an Olympian athlete: every day in the office is your gym to become a better leader. There's no simple answer; you've got to keep practicing and working on your craft of leadership.

Live Your Life as a Sacred Offering

How does my practice in that other life (and I'll stop calling it the "other life"; it's my life) from the Vedic tradition inform me as a leader? If you look at the ancient teachings, they come to one central truth, which is to live your life as a sacred offering to a higher purpose—a yagya. Find out what that purpose is and dedicate everything you do to that.

So when you look back on your life, don't ask, "What did I take from the world" but ask, "What did I give to the world?" If you take the teachings and boil it down, this is what you have to inculcate and live in everything you do. And all the practices, in the Indian tradition, the various rituals and forms of worship, are practice for giving: either you give flowers or you offer into a sacred fire. The giving must simply be there so it becomes second nature.

There's a mantra in the Upanishads (T.U.1.11.8):

> śraddhayā deyam, aśraddhayā adeyam
> Give with humility. If it's not there, don't give.
> śriyā deyam
> Give with plenty.
> hriyā deyam
> Give with humility. Not like this hands facing down,
>   but like this, hands facing up.

bhiyā deyam
Give with fear. You may not have a chance tomorrow.

Bring giving into everything you do, and if that comes from an inner deep sense of love and compassion, it becomes easier.

It may be counterintuitive to talk about compassionate leaders. I know no other way but to ask about the welfare of those around me, because that's what my teachings give me. The other piece that my tradition has given me is a discipline. To memorize the Vedas, you can't do it in an afternoon over coffee. So there's something to be said for the discipline that comes from relentless practice. In the Gita 6–35, Krishna says, *asamshayam mahābāho mano durnigraham chalam* ("Without doubt, oh mighty armed one, the mind is hard to grasp, and it wanders"), and *Abhyāsena tu Kaunteya, vairāgyeṇa cha gṛhyate* ("But through practice and dispassion, it can be grasped"). That practice has to be present every second of every day, of every moment.

Shankaracharya talks about this practice with mindful presence as *tailadhāravat*, like an unbroken stream of oil. I'll often take one of these mantras and let it just flow through me all day, just to reflect on what it means—for example, *vayam agner mānuṣāḥ* (T.B. 3–5–1–50): "We are beings born of fire." I just let that flow through me during the day. Even if I want to turn off the Vedic tap, I can't now: somehow it just comes out in everything I do. That's from years of practice. There's no substitute.

Finally there is the notion of seeking out the unique gift in everybody. This is the principle that we are not sheep, we are lions; we already have all the power of the universe in us. You're not going from step 1 to step 2 to step 3; it's already there, and it's always been there. Swami Vivekananda would say, "You cover your eyes and say you're blind." The teachings say, "Look well—your true nature is already there!"

There's a Sanskrit verse that talks to this, which I think is very important for leadership:

> *amantram aksharam nāsti*
> There is no syllable that cannot become a sacred mantra. The inherent potential is already there.
> *nāsti mūlam anauṣadham*
> There is no plant that cannot become a lifesaving medicine.
> *ayogyaḥ puruṣo nāsti*
> There is no such thing as an unworthy person, everyone has their unique gift.
> *yojakaḥ*
> The person who draws out these qualities (*tatra durlabhaḥ*), such a person is rare. You must become that person.

Gandhiji gave us a very simple guide as to how the journey of leadership can be the inner journey of self-discovery. Gandhiji said, "If you want to find yourself, lose yourself in the service of others." The job of leadership is the job of service. And anyone who thinks differently is missing the beautiful gift they've been given to make a profound difference to themselves, to people around them, and to society at large.

An Interview with Otto Scharmer

Otto Scharmer designed two highly interactive labs for Mind and Life's first European Symposium exploring the implications of contemplative perspectives on societal change. The labs focused on health care and on business and were designed to encourage participants to develop their own personal action projects. He asked Subhanu Saxena to tell his story to encourage people to talk openly about themselves as leaders and suggested that I include this story in our book. Several weeks after the symposium, we arranged an interview to talk together about Subhanu, leadership, and societal change.

A New Type of Leadership

Kathryn Goldman Schuyler: What is needed from leaders today, given your perspectives on the change that's taking place in our world, in the economy, in society?

Otto Scharmer: What is needed from leaders today is leadership, and that means a new type of leadership that responds to the collective challenges that we face on all levels: on a local level, on a regional level, and also on a global level.

In most systems today, we face a situation where we collectively create results that nobody wants. We create environmental destruction. We create inequity. We create less and less happiness and well-being in spite of more and more GDP per person. This situation is experienced at a leadership level with a state of collective paralysis.

Most leaders—not only leaders at the top, also grassroots leaders—feel incapable of changing this basic condition of the twenty-first century: that we collectively create results that are completely out of sync with the intentions that we are holding. This mismatch reveals a huge leadership gap. The essence of all leadership is something very simple: the capacity of a system or a community to sense and shape the future. The feeling of collective paralysis that we see so often today signifies the absence or void of leadership on a systems level.

But it's not the old style of leadership that is called for to fill today's leadership gap. We need a leadership that is new in two ways. In the first place, we need leadership that is more connected with the sources of our own consciousness. There is a whole dimension of mindfulness, of presence, of connecting to one's own sources of energy—these open the door for awareness and self to come into the picture. Second, today's leadership needs to link up to the profound societal disruption we currently face.

What do we see in organizations today? We see that people are fatigued by the conventional methods of leadership and change management. They feel this fatigue: they are tired of "same old, same old," precisely because these two dimensions are missing. Unless these new dimensions are brought into the picture and linked with the strategic reorientation and reinvention of the company or enterprise or organization, we are not rising to the occasion. We are not living up to the challenges that we currently face.

Kathryn Goldman Schuyler: How does Subhanu Saxena's story help us see what is needed?

Otto Scharmer: Subhanu's story is a beautiful example of how these two missing dimensions that I just mentioned come into the picture. On the personal transformation or consciousness side of things, he brings his own tradition, the Vedanta tradition, into the organization and into the way he embodies his leadership role. On the societal side, he brings the inspiration that Cipla got through Mahatma Gandhi when Gandhi said, "I want you to put the health of the country first and profit second. I want you to make the health of the country the most important thing as you develop this company and not profit."

This is a reorientation that links the mission of the company with the well-being of the whole, with the well-being of society. This has led to very different business strategies from those that a pharmaceutical company would have chosen otherwise. These two elements and the stories Subhanu shares illustrate how current conventional business leadership needs to be broadened and deepened to incorporate the dimension of consciousness and the dimension of societal evolution at the same time. This is exactly what many young people are looking for when they look for social-mission-driven or hybrid companies that are professional on the one hand and on the other hand are part of a larger story—a larger narrative that they can feel connected to. Having both of these dimensions present means that not only can people feel connected as human beings with their deeper sources of creativity and value, but also professionally, their work and career can be grounded on these values and linked to a larger purpose that they choose to be in service of.

A Renaissance of Spiritual Awareness

Kathryn Goldman Schuyler: I hope you'll return to the question of what young people are looking for, as it is so important. However, I am concerned that people may read Subhanu's story as being so unique, with his grounding in Vedanta and Sanskrit and mantra, that it is not relevant for other executives. I know that you've seen many other leaders who are also doing their version of this, as you have described them in your recent book, *Leading from the Emerging Future* (Scharmer & Kaufer, 2013).

Otto Scharmer: Subhanu's story is unique because it is an Indian international pharmaceutical company. In this case, I think it is appropriate to bring in the cultural tradition that comes from India, particularly since historically it has given rise to all other religions in the East and the West. You can see India being at the crossroads and the source of both the Eastern and the Western traditions.

In general, when I work with leaders of global companies and organizations, people are more reluctant than he is to bring in their own spiritual context from a particular tradition. Yet we are currently in the midst of a huge awakening or renaissance of what I would call spiritual awareness—not religious awareness. The difference between spiritual and religious awareness is that religious awareness usually brings the belief systems and dogmas of a particular religion, while spirituality focuses experientially on the degree that you connect to the sources of your own self, your own humanity, your own energy, your own creativity. Spirituality means a shift in the way you experience the world, yourself, and your relationships. It's shifting the inner place from which you operate. When I did the original research for Theory U, I once interviewed a very experienced CEO who had led many episodes of transformative change in his organization. I asked him what he saw as the most important learning he'd had as a CEO throughout all these years. He responded: "The success of an intervention depends on the interior condition of the intervener." When I heard that sentence I thought: What do I know about this interior condition? Nothing! In management research we know everything about what leaders do and how they do it. But what do we know about the interior condition, the inner place from which leaders operate? Nothing. We know nothing because that inner place lies hidden in the blind spot of our everyday experience.

What I also learned in those interviews is that many accomplished leaders have their own inner cultivation practice. Most of my 150 interviewees had one, and so do I. What people do varies a lot, but most of them practice in the early morning. I have found that when you create an extended moment of mindfulness or contemplation as part of your daily routine, some ten, twenty, or thirty minutes that allow you to connect with what is most essential for you and to let go of everything that isn't, it helps you to stay grounded and calm throughout the rest of the day. The moment I open up my inbox or enter the office I know what is going to happen: chaos and disruption will jump into my face. I can't control that. What I can control is the inner place from which I respond to life. Am I panicked and reactive? Or do I stay grounded in my own intention, in the future that I want to create?

What's interesting is that many of the leaders who use some version of a contemplative practice think, "I am the odd one who is doing stuff like this, and everyone else isn't, so I am not talking to any of my colleagues about this." Each of them thinks he or she is the exception—what they don't see is that many of us are using some type of practice to connect to source. That observation is really what prompted Joseph Jaworski,

Peter Senge, Betty Sue Flowers, and me to co-author the book *Presence* (2004)—to give voice to all these different views. In writing the book *Theory U* (2007), I held the same intention.

Theory U is basically two things: it's a framework and language that brings the deeper levels of awareness and consciousness into view for leaders and change makers. It looks at all levels of systems change through the lens of an evolving consciousness. Second, it provides a method that helps to shift the inner place from which we operate, not only individually but also for teams, organizations, and larger systems. It's basically a how-to method for shifting ego-system awareness to eco-system awareness.

Through the language of Theory U and presencing, I try to bring this profound shift into the picture, because my experience is that a great many leaders worldwide have gone through an experience of change so that they have actually connected with deeper levels of their own experience without fully realizing it. Theory U offers a framework and language that allows leaders to talk about these deeper levels of experience that they already have experienced but usually don't talk about because they seem so different from our usual work life awareness. I find this to be a universal phenomenon across all boardrooms, high-performing teams, and highly innovative teams in most organizations today. I have been surprised by how widespread this experience is. When I put up the Theory U framework and ask people for stories and examples, I have been surprised to see that the stories from across different sectors, systems, cultures, and industries are basically the same. This is really a deeper level of our human condition that we can connect with and tap into. Today it's much more available.

Many young people really have—I don't know what the word is, a yearning. They have a longing to shape their work and life in a way that gives them access to this level of experience and relationship, rather than only experiencing it in a moment of peak performance that happens on very rare occasions. That's what

I see young people and also midcareer people really wanting, but the reality is that the current way of running a business listed on the New York or other stock exchanges makes it very difficult.

Working in such companies brings a set of conditions that make it hard to be a leader like Subhanu. I often ask midcareer executives who join my classes at MIT, "Why do you come to this class?" And they say, "The higher I get in the organization, the less inspired I am by the work I am doing." These are people who are very successful in this world. Yet, as they progress in the system and have more senior leadership responsibilities, they are required to do things that contradict their deeper aspirations for what they would like to do. They are underinspired by their company. This essentially points at a blind spot in terms of institutional evolution where what we need is a new breed of companies that link profits and the business mind-set with social mission, companies that put business in the service of society, as Subhanu's company does when he shares the story from Mahatma Gandhi.

Innovations at the Scale of the Whole

Kathryn Goldman Schuyler: In the United States at least, and perhaps this is global, people have been evolving a new form of corporation called the benefits corporation. Does this go in the direction you have in mind?

Otto Scharmer: It goes in that direction and is a great example. I'm very much in support of this, but it's not enough. This creates a small niche for those socially responsible organizations that meet their criteria. What we really need is to rethink the architecture of the whole system.

The problem with Wall Street is not the top five people who got $2.5 billion over the past few years prior to 2008. The main problem is not greed. That is just personalizing the problem. The primary problem is the system architecture—the way we structure the relationship between the financial economy and the real economy. There are systemic design issues that need to be rethought. It has very little to do with whether personally these bankers are particularly greedy.

When we think about the larger leadership changes today, all three are necessary: the awareness and consciousness, the organizational leadership, and the redesign of the economic system. Society is evolving to the extent that we need to reinvent a new set of institutions that can allow us to move the ego-system economy that we are operating today into an eco-system economy. Basically this means that in addition to the useful market mechanisms that we already have, we need to create pre-market areas of collaboration. Areas of competition need to be in balance with areas of collaboration. Such areas of collaboration need to be supported with institutions and infrastructures. For example, in the second half of the nineteenth century, laissez-faire capitalism gradually moved into stakeholder capitalism or the New Deal kind of the social market economy in Europe, with lengthy struggles to create a whole set of institutional innovations such as social security, the Federal Reserve Bank, standards for labor and environment, and so forth. Similarly, today we also need new institutional forms, but this time to create collaborative innovations where the key players of the major systems that we operate today come together and begin to innovate not only in small pockets but begin to innovate and evolve the system as a whole. We need innovations at the scale of the whole rather than in small niches of the system.

We need to cultivate mindful leadership not only individually but also collectively. Some people say, "If only we would train all Wall Street bankers and really everyone in mindfulness practices, then the world will be a better place, and then the basic issues that we face today in society would be resolved at a root level." What I believe is that this is not at all the case. I think that bringing mindfulness practices to as many people as possible is a necessary condition, but it's not sufficient, because what's really missing most today is to apply the process of mindfulness and compassion to transforming the system as a whole, not only to transforming individual consciousness.

The economy, health, education—all of these systems are collective phenomena, systems phenomena, that are much more than the sum of individual consciousness. We need to apply the process of mindfulness and the process of transforming consciousness to this collective level, which is exactly what I have been trying to describe with the U process. It is fundamentally the same process—the phenomenological process of mindfulness, of meditation. But in leadership, we need to apply it not only to individuals but also to relationships, and not only to relationships but also to the transformation of the larger institutions and systems we operate in. This means creating holding spaces and enabling infrastructures that by and large don't exist today. This is exactly the innovation challenge that we face and why we need to bring together all three aspects of the equation, as I mentioned at the outset.

Kathryn Goldman Schuyler: I know that you're trying to do this in your work, but where do you see examples of such spaces being created, or what is necessary for them to be created? We discussed this during the symposium in Berlin, and I thought it was very important.

"Look At What We Are Doing to Ourselves!"

Otto Scharmer: I think in creating these holding spaces, the most important ingredient is listening to each other. It's also seeing the situation through the eyes of another, seeing yourself through the eyes of another. We need to create spaces where different stakeholders of a system can walk in each other's shoes, can be guests in each other's lives, can go through a process of empathy and compassion that allows you to experience the situation through the eyes of another. All of these are ingredients. If you lead groups and systems through this, and they're walking in each other's shoes, they begin to listen to the situation from different perspectives. It's almost as if you become a collective brain. But we don't just think with the brain. The thinking is stimulated through the senses, through being connected with the world. That is triggering. The same happens on the collective level. What is it that is triggering these "neural connections" on a collective level? It's basically crossing the silos.

After functional differentiation of institutions, of systems, we all operate in silo type of realities. Through what we in the U process call co-sensing or co-presencing, we cut through these silos. You begin to connect and look at reality from different angles, and to do that well, you need a holding place where this can take place. Nature is a very important holding place and one of the greatest allies that we have. Gradually the participants of the system not only see each other, but begin to see themselves. The turning point in almost all of these bigger system stories is when the system begins to see itself.

What does this mean? It means that, for example, a group of engineers or a group of physicians begins to see how they collectively create in patients results that nobody wants and say, "Look at what we are doing to ourselves!" The operative word here is *we.* "Look what *we* are doing to ourselves" is a jump in awareness. Suddenly I no longer see the problem in terms of the others and what they are doing to me. I see the situation and the system in terms of what we are doing to ourselves, which is the starting point for entering a different type of conversation, a more dialogic conversation, a more co-created conversation where new possibilities open up that can be developed, explored, prototyped, and implemented in different ways.

Kathryn Goldman Schuyler: I've seen this kind of process happen in future searches in nonprofits and for-profits and across organizations, but I haven't seen this happen at the level of the global economic system. Are you seeing ways to work with people that enable the creation of new structures that can change the system itself rather than change companies or organizations within it? Even these are hard to change!

Otto Scharmer: Yes. And yet when you look at the challenges that leaders face today, both in government and also in companies, you can see that there is a very significant parallel between nation-states and companies. You can say companies and nation-states share the parallel that they are too big for the small problems and too small for the big problems. In other words, no government in the world can deal with climate change. No government in the world can deal with any of the big challenges that we face as a global community. The same applies to companies. That's why in management, we talk about the extended enterprise. We talk about the business eco-system. We know that the organization itself is the wrong unit of analysis for most problems and leadership challenges that we face. In order to make a real difference, in order to meet and address the challenges at the level they need to be addressed, we need to bring together the entire eco-system. The same applies to the nation-state. Without the business community, without the international community, and also often without the civil society community, the nation-state by itself has very little means to address the key challenges that we face at the level of source.

In all these cases, I think the bottom line is the same. We need to build tri-sector platforms of collaboration that allow diverse groups of stakeholders to meet each other in order to shift the system to move through a process of co-initiating what they really want to do, co-sensing to learn to see the system from all the different angles, co-inspiring where the whole thing could be going, and then co-creating as a process of learning by doing and exploring the future through small-scale experiments. Then, last, co-shaping where the best results from these small-scale experiments and prototypes are scaled and sustained throughout the system.

This is happening naturally at a local level in some places. Why is it happening locally much more easily than globally? I think it is because all of these issues and all of the big global challenges share that they're often related to what has historically been called *the commons*. Markets work well for private goods. They work less well for commons. For public goods, we have governments usually, but the commons is really where we have a lack of institutional intelligence in our societies and in capitalism today. That's the big challenge. And no single sector—not government alone, not business alone, and unfortunately not civil society alone—can solve that issue. We need tri-sector platforms that organize around the commons.

Where do we see this happening naturally? We see it in disaster response, where everyone is pulling together because the need for collective action is so evident that it happens spontaneously to organize around these needs, and we see it on the local level. Because on a local level, the commons and the issues related to the commons are right in your face. It's not abstract; it's very visible. It's common sense in the most literal sense that is being applied when people pull together and collaborate across the three sectors. But the same natural instinct and the same logical response doesn't exist for problems with higher complexity where we either have delayed feedback or we have a global scale where the impact of my action is on the other side of the planet, so I don't see the damage that I create. This dynamic complexity problem leads to a situation where currently we don't have a good answer about how to deal with those commons that are more regional and global. That's the big institutional innovative challenge that we face today.

Awareness-Based Global Action Research

Kathryn Goldman Schuyler: And to conclude?

Otto Scharmer: When I look at what we are doing today, I am really surprised how open people are toward accessing a deeper level of our own humanity and creativity and bringing that into a new type of entrepreneurship that is just beginning now. We see a longing and openness by many players inside the old business community and also in the domain of social entrepreneurship. What we have seen historically is that a lot of great things and energy happen in the sector of social entrepreneurship, but hardly ever does any of that scale up and transform the larger systems. Now, those of us who work with some of the larger institutions like government and big companies realize that inside these institutions there are just as many people who would like to bring this kind of movement into these arenas.

I see potential for a second generation of entrepreneurial change, in which these two emerging movements begin to link and connect with one other—those who operate on a grassroots level outside the established system and those who are inside the established institutions. What's necessary for this to occur is for us to have platforms for collaboration that reach beyond the institutional boundary of organizations, that are tri-sector in nature, and that are like a fourth sector, because they link the other three sectors (business, government, and nongovernmental organizations) in a unique way. This would allow the key change makers across all three sectors to collaborate with each other.

All three of these sectors need to let go of certain old behaviors and tune into new and more collaborative behaviors. To establish such new arenas of collaboration and co-creation is a huge challenge and opportunity ahead of us, and it's given many names. I view this as an awareness-based global action research university that builds capacity for transforming ego-system to eco-system economies.

Going forward, I think two things will make a difference. Such collaborative infrastructures are essential: we need to develop the fourth sector institutions on the one hand and, on the other hand, the collective leadership capacity to create such deeper container and innovation spaces. Without the skill and capacity to develop such transformative spaces, the same old people come together and have the same old conversation, which is of no use.

The bottleneck is the lack of fourth sector infrastructures and the lack of leadership capacity to use them for systems transformation. This is where we, the current generation of change makers on Earth, have a huge responsibility and can make a huge difference. In the generation before us, people were talking about macro changes and doing very little in terms of personal transformation or seeing such personal transformation as relevant to themselves. In the generation after us, today's younger people are often much stronger on the micro, meso, personal, and relational levels, but are not that strong on the macro and political levels. The call for our generation is to bring all these levels together, because if we don't start this, we really mess up big time in this century, and we can't allow that to happen.

Kathryn Goldman Schuyler: I think that there's hope as well. Every time you talk, I feel like I understand more clearly what I've been trying to understand for decades and how to bring this about in the world.

References

Scharmer, O. (2007). *Theory U*. San Francisco: Berrett-Koehler.

Scharmer, O., & Kaufer, K. (2013). *Leading from the emerging future: From ego-system to eco-system economics*. San Francisco: Berrett-Koehler.

Senge, P., Scharmer, C. O., Jaworkski, J., & Flowers, B. S. (2004). *Presence: Human purpose and the field of the future*. Cambridge, MA: Society for Organizational Learning.

Chapter Two

Cultivating Leadership through Deep Presencing and Awareness Based Practices

Jonathan Reams, Olen Gunnlaugson,
Juliane Reams

Throughout the past century, leadership development has focused primarily on leaders' behaviors or skills. While these are important, there is also a growing understanding of the need to cultivate the subtle, internal qualities of the leader's self as fundamental to leadership. Following from this view, it is our proposition that cultivating and enacting key forms of awareness based interventions and encouraging practices of deep presencing are foundational to leadership development.

In this chapter, we examine deep presencing (Gunnlaugson & Walker, 2013) in the domain of self-awareness and through the lens of leadership skill development. In particular, we build on the work of presence (Scharmer, 2007; Senge, Jaworski, Scharmer, & Flowers, 2004) by introducing deep presencing as a key leverage point for engaging the leader's self in the workplace. We then explore this further by linking it to the concept of self as soul (Reams, 2007b, 2012). Cultivating leadership skills is then considered through the lens of cognitive development (Kegan, 1994; Kegan & Lahey, 2009; Torbert & Associates, 2004) by examining how awareness based practices serve in cultivating personal and professional growth in the leader and organization as a whole. Finally, we use Fischer's (1980) skill theory as an approach to illustrate the practical importance of cognitive development in the context of leadership skills, and we offer examples from a corporate leadership development program.

Deep Presencing

Since its inception, Theory U (Scharmer, 2007) has challenged the assumptions of traditional leadership and management thinking and in turn offered a significant change method that has been implemented across a broad assortment of international businesses and communities. Scharmer (2000) emphasizes the leader's self as tool and "the capacity of the 'I' to operate from the emerging larger whole both individually and collectively" (p. 22).

While Scharmer (2007) has directed attention to self as the "blind spot" of leadership, it has been noted that there may be a blind spot in how this is conceived (Reams, 2007b). Scharmer (2007) frames the self in the state of presencing as "a moment when we approach our self from the emerging future" (p. 163). To clarify this process, we introduce deep presencing (Gunnlaugson & Walker, 2013) to extend and shed new light on what is at stake for leaders in the presencing process. In our view, conventional presencing conceptions and practices tend to underestimate the depth and nature of change involved with the leader's self-sense and so risk oversimplifying or outright ignoring the fundamental source from which leaders draw their power, influence, and creativity.

A particular challenge that we perceive as fundamental to this is that a leader's attention and awareness are prone to becoming insular and disconnected in volatile, uncertain, complex, ambiguous (VUCA) and crisis situations within organizational culture. Bohm (1992) and others have explored how our thinking process becomes problematic and incoherent when left unchecked without sufficient awareness and mindfulness in our day-to-day functioning. Without this requisite awareness, we tend to get caught up with and in turn conditioned by this unconscious mental process, giving rise to unconscious social practices of mind and tendencies to identify with and in turn defend these images by filtering or manipulating our experience of reality to conform to them. Thus, learning to let go, moment to moment, of our preconceived notions of who we are and what we know as we engage in day-to-day management activities becomes an essential leadership practice to counter the inherent self-deception of mind and the energy invested in these images of self and the subsequent social world it creates (Arbinger Institute, 2010). Through deep presencing practice, the possibility of a more coherent, or unconditioned perception of the leader's self and the reality that is co-unfolding can be gleaned as it is emerging.

Our basic position is that deep presencing provides an ontological path into the essence of beingness from which leaders can sense, articulate, and bring forth new visions of change within their organizations. Deep presencing offers an ontologically distinct means for accessing stillness, discernment, and generative action amid destabilizing organizational conditions of uncertainty and disorientation (Gunnlaugson & Walker, 2013).

What does this more fundamental shift in a leader's self-sense involve? In part, it is learning how to be in, and more fully orient from, what is arising from our engagement with the present moment. This involves noticing, suspending, and letting go of our preconceived and conditioned notions of who we are (Reams, 1999) to access a more direct perception that arises within the deep presencing phenomenological world-space. Deep presencing, in this sense, becomes a more foundational presencing practice for leaders, that brings forth and illuminates a new internal set of conditions. Deep presencing calls on the need for shifting not only the self-sense but the self-constitution of leaders and is required to more directly access the source of the emerging personal and social reality by engaging directly in the process (Gunnlaugson & Reams, 2013).

Accessing deep presencing requires mastering the paradoxical practice of embodying and abiding in stillness while in action

(Gunnlaugson & Reams, 2013). Sufficiently grounding one's self in stillness is helped by more traditional contemplative practices such as meditation (Cayer, 2005; Gunnlaugson, 2011; Senge & Wheatley, 2001), and perhaps even more by embodied awareness practices (Goldman Schuyler, 2010). To the extent that the generative dimension of deep presencing is driven by this underlying quality of dynamic yet still awareness, leaders discover a place within themselves to activate a seeing through past associations and reactions into sensing more directly into what is emerging through the present (Jironet & Stein, 2012).

During this process, insights, intuitions, and visions can emerge insofar as deep presencing work supports these creative openings or clearings for emergence. With ongoing practice, one becomes more confident and fluent with this process. Accessing deep presencing through stillness requires mastering the practice of embodying or contacting stillness in action and stillness in between action (Gunnlaugson & Reams, 2013). Meditation traditionally gives access to this ground of stillness, but in deep presencing, there is a need to learn how to access a creative perception through stillness in our relating, our knowing, and our conversations. On the whole, embodying stillness offers ontological renewal by giving us access to interior qualities of being (awareness, presence, equanimity, joy, and levity, among others).

Deep Presencing as a Means for Engaging Soul in Action

To extend deep presencing further, we now examine how a conception of self as soul can aid our understanding here. While the conception of self as soul goes back to Plato (1954, 1992), Socrates, and earlier, more recently Teilhard de Chardin (1955) pointed to an important distinction with his well-known quote: "We are not human beings having spiritual experiences, we are spiritual beings having human experiences" (cited in Covey, 2000, p. 47). These views place soul, as a spiritual being, as the ontological ground of our existence (Reams, 1999), with human experience being something we have, not what we are. Here we explore ideas about the nature of soul and how we can see it act in the world, and how this can open new conceptual spaces for understanding presencing in particular, and leadership development in general.

We begin with a definition of "soul as a *creative unit of pure awareness*" (Reams, 2012, p. 104). Pure awareness is awareness independent of content, thus not tied to objects of attention. It is also independent of and prior to intellect, emotions, and physical body (Reams, 2007a). It is creative, in that it is dynamically unfolding into the world. Parker Palmer (2004) says that soul can be viewed as shy and requiring stillness to catch sight of, as well as being "tough and tenacious" (p. 58). He notes that we can name functions of soul even if we cannot reduce it to intellectual analysis: "The soul wants to keep us rooted in the ground of our own being, resisting the tendency of other faculties, like the intellect and ego, to uproot us from who we are" (p. 33). These activities point to the ways soul takes action in the world, as a counter to the tendencies of identification with the body, ego, or intellect. I (Jonathan) have direct experience from longtime practice of how this can bring greater coherence to perception and loosen the hold of conventional identifications.

Pursuing this idea further, David Bohm (1992) described a distinction between a creative sense of being, in contrast to our more traditional identified sense of being. He perceived identification with body, ego, or intellect as a fundamental blockage to achieving coherence in perception and action. An identified sense of being also has a more static nature, while our conception of soul is more dynamic. This dynamic nature is characterized in an ancient view that "*I don't know what I am. What I am is unknown, but constantly revealing itself*" (Bohm, 1992, p. 167). Thus in relation to the creative component of the above definition of soul "the creative process of an unfolding sense of being can be seen as soul continually revealing and coming to know itself in the actions of being in the world" (Reams, 2007b, p. 258).

Linking back to some of the language we quoted from Scharmer, Arthur Deikman's (1996) work in psychiatry and religion around mystical states led him to make a relevant distinction between the "I" as being equal to awareness and the self: "This 'I' should be differentiated from the various aspects of the physical person and its mental contents which form the 'self'" (p. 350). Deikman's distinction between this I and the self (small s) can be contrasted with the previous quote from Scharmer (2000), talking about Self with a capital S, while also using the term I interchangeably. Michael Ray (2004) also describes the conception of self at the bottom of the U by using Self (with a capital S). Using the term *soul* can provide a simple clarification and avoid the confusion that can arise from the use of the terms *self* and *Self* or *I* to point to the essence of who and what we are. Thus for leaders, the presence of soul in action generates spaces that open "the spiritual, mental, emotional and physical area we and others have to work in" (Reams, 2012, p. 108).

There are a number of characteristics concerning the nature of how our presence as soul opens spaces. Here we briefly focus on two aspects of this in terms of integrity and construct aware consciousness. Integrity can be described as acting in alignment with our highest calling, the still, small voice of conscience, or the voice of soul. It is a kind of truthfulness, not as a noun but as a verb, a troth (Palmer, 1993), or a living relationship to and unfolding of learning how to live in integrity with the truth of soul. Thus, having integrity can be conceived as an ongoing dynamic alignment of our human embodiment with soul.

To make this more tangible, we can turn to the psychophysiological links between our inner state and neurocardiology (McCraty, Atkinson, Tomasino, & Bradley, 2009). McCraty et al. use the term *coherence* to indicate tangible markers of this kind of integrity. This coherence functions in two directions. As a psychophysiological state, it orchestrates improved functioning throughout the body, including cognitive performance (McCraty et al., 2009). It also enhances the heart's intuitive capacity (McCraty, Atkinson, & Bradley, 2004a, 2004b), including perceiving future events. This research has shown that the electromagnetic field generated by the heart can be measured up to ten feet outside the body. As such, we create a tangible space that others can perceive or sense through the modes of perception available in the heart.

From our current vantage point, psychophysiological coherence could be the function of the heart, which can be seen as the clearest indicator of soul in action in the world and generating these spaces. In terms of practices, McCraty et al. note that a combination of focusing attention on attitudes of appreciation, gratitude, and love with deep breathing enables us to access this coherence.

In terms of adult development and structures of consciousness (Kegan, 1994; Torbert & Associates, 2004), the dynamic unfolding of soul at the mental level can be seen as constructing meaning-making processes and the resulting structures these generate. In cognitive development literature, the term *construct aware consciousness* (Cook-Greuter, 1999) points to a postformal stage of ego development that is characterized by a transparency of these structures, or aperspectival consciousness (Gebser, 1985). In relation to leading processes in hypercomplex (or VUCA) situations, Reams and Caspari (2012) note, "The construct aware stage of development . . . enables a leader to be aware of constructs while they are happening. By the term constructs we basically mean the assumptions, ideas, lenses, projections and underlying mechanisms, both in detail and as whole systems. It is the ability to see how the participants of a process construct meaning individually and collectively and to respond to these" (p. 42). In this way, the intellect and mental structures are tools for soul taking action in the world. Being able to bring soul's quality of awareness to these mental structures and the construction of perspectives can aid in suspending the images of the intellect and allow soul to come through and lead more authentically.

Applying Awareness Based Technologies

So how does the concept of soul in action, as developed through deep presencing and other methodologies, contribute to a practical, grounded, method for leadership development? Here we explore this question through the application of *awareness based technologies*, where the notion of soul in action functions more in the background as a foundation and grounding for how leadership development is undertaken.

The case presented here is a research project connected to the design and delivery of a leadership development program for a Norwegian multinational engineering and manufacturing company supplying offshore oil and gas equipment, Aker Solutions (Reams & Reams, 2013). We include a brief background on the program, describe the theory behind its design and some of the tools used, outline the research project, and share three key stories to illustrate how we see the awareness based approach contributing to the development of leadership skills in program participants.

In 2010 one of us (Jonathan) was approached by the head of Aker Solutions' learning academy about collaborating with them on the design of a new leadership development program. This arose out of an interest in having a dynamic, action research–oriented program, as well as the recognition that standard off-the-shelf programs would not be able to deliver the depth of leadership skills needed for this organization. An awareness based approach with a grounding in practice was proposed, and after an initial pilot run (Reams & Johannessen, 2011), the revised Develop Your Leadership program was accepted by senior management as the new training for midlevel managers.

The program design covers three modules (three, two, and two days) moving from a focus on leading self, to developing one's team, to developing and implementing strategy in the organization. Along with these three modules, participants receive eight coaching sessions that are based on program tools used for enhancing self-awareness. The theories informing the program all have a basis in cultivating and enabling awareness about participants' problems, both internal and external, so that as Kegan and Lahey (2009) say, they can "solve us" rather than being something to "be solved."

The opening work around defining leadership comes from Heifetz (1994; Heifetz, Grashow, & Linsky, 2009), and the subsequent work focuses on how to develop adaptive leadership capacities. This is approached from two modalities. One modality focuses on skill development of common challenges such as setting clear expectations, having conversations that require courage, developing their team members, and articulating purpose and vision for strategy. The other modality is the development of the being dimension of the participants by increasing their self-awareness. They receive 360-degree feedback in the form of the Leadership Circle Profile (Anderson, 2005), which assesses well-known and normed leadership competencies as well as reactive tendencies that limit leadership behaviors. This generates a kind of crucible or holding environment in which they are more open to self-reflection and inquiry (Reams & Fikse, 2010). From here, they are taken through the immunity-to-change process (Kegan & Lahey, 2009), which enables a deep dive into the systems of thought and assumptions operating to sustain their limiting behaviors.

All of this work is informed by a number of theories on constructivist adult developmental theory. Research by Kegan (1982, 1994), Torbert and Associates (2004), Cook-Greuter (1999), Joiner and Josephs (2007), and others describe stages of meaning making or structures of consciousness that become the implicit lenses through which we shape how much depth and complexity of the world around and inside us we perceive. In this way, the methods, tools, and practices used are "technologies" that put awareness into application. While these applications focus explicitly on cognitive awareness, they also foster practices of deep presence in the form of getting "below the neck," that is, in touch with bodily, emotional, and spiritual intelligences.

Research

Our quest to better understand how these awareness based technologies work in practice has led to ongoing research (Reams & Caspari, 2012; Reams & Fikse, 2010; Reams & Reams, 2013) in this area. The most recent project is a study of two cohorts of managers from Aker Solutions in Oslo and Houston. Detailed observation notes were made, totaling 386 pages and covering areas of the process of facilitation, participant dialogues and reflections, body language, tone of voice, energy in the room, the release of tension, frustrated expectations, as well as participants displaying impacts and the quality of presence and of listening.

Currently the analysis process is ongoing, and we are exploring how Fischer's skill theory (Fischer, 1980; Fischer & Bidell, 2006) can contribute to a finely grained understanding of participants' growth in cognitive development relevant for leadership skills. Fischer's skill theory is a neo-Piagetian approach to cognitive development that also integrates elements of operant conditioning from behaviorism. A skill is defined as "a unit of behaviour composed of one or more sets" (Fischer, 1980, p. 482). Skills, whether physical, emotional, or thinking, develop as environmental conditions are encountered where a situation cannot be solved with existing cognitions, and various transformational processes move skills in micro- and macrosteps through the levels of set relations. These levels go through three tiers— sensory actions, representations, and abstractions—with each tier made up of moves from a single set to mappings between sets, through systems of sets to systems of systems of sets, which become the next tier's single set.

Fischer's (1980) definition of *cognition* gives a broad understanding of the concept: "the process by which the organism exercises operant control . . . over sources of variation in its own behaviour. More specifically, a person can modulate or govern sources of variation in what he or she does or thinks" (p. 481). This dynamic view of skills from Fischer could tentatively be linked to our above-described sense of soul unfolding its being through choices in these sources of variation. This also means that we can move from a level of skill that is automatic, to one that is functional, and then, if conditions are right, to an optimal skill level. Finally, with the support of scaffolding, we can perform at an even higher level of skill. This is important for us in our understanding of how participants in this program are supported and how they demonstrate growth.

Stories

Here we depict sample narratives that illustrate how cultivating deep presence through awareness based technologies can look in real life. These stories come from three out of seven participants we tracked closely for this stage of analysis. The results as a whole showed a wide range of individual participant processes over time of going from total resistance to holistically and insightfully experiencing and tracking the aims and intentions of the program, leading to internalizing new patterns of behaviour. (Pseudonyms have been used.)

Espen from the Oslo Cohort

The first story is about Espen, a participant of the Oslo cohort who spoke up a lot and appeared quite self-confident. His main concern was that he was not delivering on tasks. In the program, he was working with a particular issue about always providing an open door for his employees to come into his office with their problems. They did come to him, with the result that he was not finding the time to deliver on many of his own tasks.

Through the immunity-to-change process, he had created a metaphor where he described his employees as entering the office with monkeys on their back, then taking the monkeys off their back and giving them to Espen. He ended up with a zoo in the office that he had to tend.

He admitted that he somehow felt annoyed but that he still wanted the monkeys because it gave him a feeling of control. "Ja, it comes from me!" he said at one point, realizing that he had invited it in because he wanted that control.

Realization of his competing commitment gave rise to a disorienting dilemma and a fearful resistance to giving up the interdependent dynamic he had created. It took Espen time to let go of that control and an intense process to work himself through that and embody the alternatives. As soon as he saw his role in this dynamic, he started to take responsibility for his actions, make experiences and learn from them, and realize that his competing commitment to control maintained this interdependency.

In the last checkout of module 3, Espen shared parts of his process and one experience of how he had made a step in relation to his challenge: "I practiced with my team. We sat in a circle, and I said, 'I cannot manage everything now.' I made a list. Then I said, 'I can help you with that one or that one.' That was very good. For the first time I have the feeling I am delivering things."

From our awareness based approach, we could imagine that a typical way to address such a problem would be to advise Espen on what to do to stop the interdependent cycle. With the awareness based approach from the immunity-to-change process, we simply allowed him to discover his competing commitments and enabled this awareness to grow over time (with the support of coaching), so that he could self-author a solution from a more complex understanding of his internal dynamic.

Kris from Norway in the Houston Cohort

The next story illustrates a different stage of growth that was more subtle and at first harder to see. Kris is from Norway and was in the Houston cohort. As a Norwegian, Kris's attitudes, behaviors, and interventions were more humanistically shaped than the ones of his colleagues. He had quite a strong presence among his peers and often got people's attention. He displayed a good degree of systemic and complexity awareness. His ability to frame matters, articulate his abstract thought, and contextualize issues seemed to be appreciated in the group. He also used metaphorical language to frame issues he wanted to express. One major shift for Kris was that he talked about great changes during the program in his way of designing relationships at work and especially in his private life.

Deeper insights were often "wrapped." An example is a metaphor Kris used in the first module when the group talked about fixing problems through firefighting: "We are good firemen, but 80 percent of us are pyromaniacs." His systemic awareness allowed him to disentangle and realize patterns in the higher ranks of the organization. The firefighting is a company cultural reflex response to challenges of any kind, and he acknowledged his part in it.

After going through the ITC map, Kris displayed signs of moving to a higher level of cognition in a checkout: "It was a very good day. I am realizing more, and I am seeing from the outside and from the balcony . . . I have crazy assumptions. It is so abstract. I don't recognize myself anymore." When things had started to move for him, he lost his usual clear vision, and then his perception was not as tangible to him anymore, but he had turned to something beyond what he was used to. His attention to his insight illustrated that his development was going deeper into his interior processes, making things appear subtler and, at this early stage, more abstract. This is a commonly observed phenomenon—that performance lowers as a person enters a new level of skill complexity.

In the third module, Kris came back to the metaphor and said: "We are all firefighters, and we are pyromaniacs. But there are two fires: a house and a bush in the garden. We fight the fire in the bush, and the house burns down." Analyzing this statement in relation to his previous use of this metaphor, it appears that Kris had found an optimal level of cognitive operating (with some broad generalized scaffolding from participating in the program) where two systems, his use of metaphors and his systemic awareness, were now connected into a higher level of functioning.

Daniel from the Houston Cohort

Daniel was a younger participant from the Houston cohort. He appeared to be a prime example of a very concrete engineering mind and was outgoing, with strong opinions. His body language was often agile and attentive and also showed some resistance, disbelief, or doubt weighing in on specific situations. According to his body language and verbalized concerns, thinking below the neck seemed to be incompatible with his straightforward engineering mind-set.

To give a reference point for the eventual shift in Daniel's mind-set, one of his initial comments in the first module stood out and caused quite a stir. A conversation came up about the cultural differences between the headquarters in Norway and the business unit in the United States. Somebody had claimed that nobody in Norway would lose his or her job because of a mistake, while those in the United States were not protected in that way. Daniel was obviously triggered by this claim, which he responded to eagerly with a physical presence and strong voice: "How do you get a high-performing team in Norway if you can't fire them?" It is unnecessary to mention that the Norwegians present in the room took a deep breath and had their opinions about that statement. And they did. But that is another story.

One day in module 3, we observed Daniel starting a process of inquiry. He followed up a couple of comments as he shared that he was insecure about the "why" that is related to the purpose in working in the oil and gas industry. He added that "it is not like selling a car or a phone" and showed concerns about what differentiates it. After the participants had been shown an extract of a video of Martin Luther King Jr.'s "I Have a Dream" speech, Daniel emphasized King's passion and that he "was not selling his vision because he believed in it . . . It is much easier to sell something that you believe in! Some people have that. I don't have that!" Through statements like this, he showed signs of being strongly embedded in a limiting belief about his identity and skills.

His claim that he lacked passion was then a subject of collective inquiry where the holding environment, supportive energy in the room, and the facilitation scaffolded him to a place where he noticed an attraction to the notion of transformation of being that had been spoken about. Daniel continued to make statements like these: "Some people have that. I don't have that," or, "I am just not like that. It's just not in me." The context and manner in which he spoke gave us clues that in a way he wanted to disidentify with his own limiting beliefs. Clarifying the "why" about purpose was part of making the next step, activating some subtle awareness that had been at work in him during the program. He appeared to be getting tentatively below the neck, or into some more abstract reflections about his own process.

In the third module, the focus is on strategy, purpose, and vision. One of the exercises in the program is for the participants to create a purpose and vision statement for their business area. First, they go into small groups of three to four and practice. Wandering around between the groups, Jonathan observed Daniel giving a flat, technical, and descriptive vision and purpose statement that did not motivate anybody in his group. Responding to that, Jonathan provided him with some personal coaching for him to rework his purpose and vision statement. In the next activity, all participants went back into the big circle where they could volunteer and share their statement. Mark, another one of the participants, presented his vision statement, which also sounded very rational and technical. Daniel responded instantly: "That sounds like a car sale to me. I am turned off these things by my own rationality." Obviously this was a resistant kind of response, but it also implied an insight that displayed perspective taking on his own rationality when he saw that style in someone else.

Daniel then volunteered to present after Mark. The reworking he did earlier enabled Daniel to present a well-redefined purpose and vision statement. His use of more abstract concepts and below-the-neck motivational energy was noted by the other participants, who stated that he was now inspiring, more authentic, and speaking from the heart.

In Daniel's case, we observed the beginnings of movement from a very concrete, technical focus where "soft" things like inspiration and reflection were latent at best. His at times resistant engagement in the process eventually led to a scaffolded opening into a reformulation of his vision and purpose statement that demonstrated greater cognitive abstraction and much improved below-the-neck motivational energy. Thus he displayed clear signs of operating at a higher level of cognition in two domains: abstract thinking and emotional intelligence. It is our hope that even though he required significant scaffolding to achieve this, it would enable his functional and optimal levels of skill to have a better chance of also moving up a level over time and with practice. Touching on our notion of soul, Daniel's shift to a more authentic, coming-from-the-heart presentation of his purpose and vision for work could be viewed as his having more soul in action.

Concluding Reflections

An earlier critique of Scharmer's Theory U (Reams, 2007b) pointed to how a "social consciousness often wants to 'save the world' from its fundamental flaws" (p. 258). In many leadership development approaches today, there is an emphasis on using good intentions, intellect, and willpower to change what are perceived as flawed behaviors. In contrast, the awareness based approach addresses leaders as embodying an innate perfection, allowing for the growth of awareness and a more coherent perception of what is to enable change to follow course more naturally. In this sense, our chapter clarifies the sense of Bill O'Brian's often quoted point that the interior condition of the intervener is critical for the success of interventions (in Scharmer, 2007). From this point of view, the feeling of needing to fix the world, or even one's self (as in needing to "develop" to a higher stage of cognition), can, without the requisite internal awareness we're advocating for, bring about subtle obstacles to enacting the more fundamental forms of change and development that many long for.

In this chapter, we have examined deep presencing, in the domains of self-awareness as well as through the lens of leadership skill development. We have introduced deep presencing as a way for engaging the leader's self as soul in the workplace. By exploring how soul is both the ground and source of awareness and deep presence, our view is that this work requires an integration of an inner quality of presence with skillful means for understanding how to create environments that facilitate a transformation in being, as well as in cognition and skill in action. In this sense, calls for authenticity in leadership can also be met through cultivating soul's presence.

References

Anderson, B. (2005). *The leadership circle*. Whitehouse, OH: Leadership Circle LLC.

Arbinger Institute. (2010). *Leadership and self-deception* (2nd ed.). San Francisco: Berrett-Koehler.

Bohm, D. (1992). *Thought as a system*. London: Routledge.

Cayer, M. (2005). The five dimensions of Bohm's dialogue. In B. H. Banathy & P. M. Jenlink (Eds.), *Dialogue as a means of collective communication* (pp. 161–191). New York: Kluwer Academic Plenum.

Cook-Greuter, S. (1999). *Postautonomous ego development: A study of its nature and measurement*. Unpublished doctoral dissertation, Harvard University.

Covey, S. R. (2000). *Living the seven habits: The courage to change*. New York: Free Press.

Deikman, A. (1996). I = awareness. *Journal of Consciousness Studies, 3*, 350–356.

Fischer, K. (1980). A theory of cognitive development: The control and construction of hierarchies of skills. *Psychological Review, 87*, 477–531.

Fischer, K., & Bidell, T. (2006). Dynamic development of action, thought, and emotion. In W. Damon & R. Lerner (Eds.), *Handbook of child psychology: Theoretical models of human development* (pp. 313–399). Hoboken, NJ: Wiley.

Gebser, J. (1985). *The ever-present origin*. (N. Barstad, Trans.) Athens: Ohio University Press.

Goldman Schuyler, K. (2010). Increasing leadership integrity through mind training and embodied learning. *Consulting Psychology Journal: Practice and Research, 62*, 21–38.

Gunnlaugson, O. (2011). Advancing a second-person contemplative approach for collective wisdom and leadership development. *Journal of Transformative Education, 9*(1), 134–156.

Gunnlaugson, O., & Reams, J. (2013, October–November). *Authentic leadership through deep presencing*. Presentation at the International Leadership Association Conference: Leadership for Local and Global Resilience: The Challenges of a Shifting Planet, Montreal.

Gunnlaugson, O., & Walker, W. (2013). Deep presencing leadership coaching: Building capacity for sensing, enacting and embodying emerging selves and futures in the face of organizational crisis, In O. Gunnlaugson, C. Baron, & M. Cayer (Eds.), *Perspectives on Theory U: Insights from the field* (pp. 128–137). Hershey, PA: IGI Global Press.

Heifetz, R. (1994). *Leadership without easy answers*. Cambridge, MA: Harvard University Press.

Heifetz, R., Grashow, A., & Linsky, M. (2009). *The practice of adaptive leadership: Tools and tactics for changing your organization and the world*. Boston: Harvard Business School Press.

Jironet, K., & Stein, M. (2012). New approaches for leadership: A psychospiritual model for leadership development. In C. Pearson (Ed.), *The transforming leader: New approaches to leadership for the twenty-first century* (pp. 181–190). San Francisco: Berrett-Koehler.

Joiner, B., & Josephs, S. (2007). *Leadership agility: Mastering core competencies for handling change.* San Francisco: Jossey-Bass.

Kegan, R. (1982). *The evolving self: Problem and process in human development.* Cambridge, MA: Harvard University Press.

Kegan, R. (1994). *In over our heads: The mental demands of modern life.* Cambridge, MA: Harvard University Press.

Kegan, R., & Lahey, L. (2009). *Immunity to change: How to overcome it and unlock the potential in yourself and your organization.* Boston: Harvard Business Press.

McCraty, R., Atkinson, M., & Bradley, R. (2004a). Electrophysiological evidence of intuition: Part 1. *Journal of Alternative and Complementary Medicine, 10*(1), 133–143.

McCraty, R., Atkinson, M., & Bradley, R. (2004b). Electrophysiological evidence of intuition: Part 2. *Journal of Alternative and Complementary Medicine, 10*(2), 325–336.

McCraty, R., Atkinson, M., Tomasino, B., & Bradley, R. (2009). The coherent heart: Heart-brain interactions, psychophysiological coherence, and the emergence of system wide order. *Integral Review, 5*(2), 4–107.

Palmer, P. (1993). *To know as we are known: Education as a spiritual journey.* San Francisco: HarperSanFrancisco.

Palmer, P. (2004). *A hidden wholeness: The journey toward an undivided life.* San Francisco: Jossey-Bass.

Plato. (1954). *The last days of Socrates* (H. Tredennick, Trans.). Baltimore, MD: Penguin Books.

Plato. (1992). *The republic* (C. Reeve, Ed., & G. Grube, Trans.). Indianapolis, IN: Hackett.

Ray, M. (2004). *The highest goal: The secret that sustains you in every moment.* San Francisco: Berrett-Koehler.

Reams, J. (1999). Consciousness and identity: Who do we think we are? *New Ideas in Psychology, 17*(3), 309–320.

Reams, J. (2007a). *Spiritual beings having human experiences: How viewing consciousness as primary reframes science and religion.* Paper presented at the Human Persons and the God of Nature Conference, Oxford.

Reams, J. (2007b). Illuminating the blind spot: An overview and response to Theory U. *Integral Review, 5*, 240–259.

Reams, J. (2012). Integral leadership: Opening space by leading through the heart. In C. Pearson (Ed.), *The transforming leader* (pp. 102–109). San Francisco: Berrett-Koehler.

Reams, J., & Caspari, A. (2012). Integral leadership: Generating space for emergence through quality of presence. *German Journal for Business Psychology, 14*(3), 34–45.

Reams, J., & Fikse, C. (2010). Making leadership development developmental. *Academic Exchange Quarterly, 14*, 197–201.

Reams, J., & Johannessen, B. (2011, October). *Leading with impact: Design and pilot implementation of a global corporate leadership development program.* Presentation at the International Leadership Association Conference: One Planet, Many Worlds: Remapping the Purposes of Leadership, London

Reams, J., & Reams, J. (2013, October–November). *Awareness based leadership development.* Presentation at the International Leadership Association Conference: Leadership for Local and Global Resilience: The Challenges of a Shifting Planet, Montreal.

Scharmer, C. O. (2000). *Presencing: Learning from the future as it emerges.* Presentation at the Conference on Knowledge and Innovation, Helsinki School of Economics, Finland, and MIT Sloan School of Management, Cambridge, MA.

Scharmer, C. O. (2007). *Theory U: Leading from the future as it emerges: The social technology of presencing.* Cambridge, MA: Society for Organizational Learning.

Senge, P., Jaworski, J., Scharmer, C. O., & Flowers, B. S. (2004). *Presence: Exploring profound change in people, organizations and society.* Boston: Society for Organizational Learning.

Senge, P., & Wheatley, M. (2001, January). Changing how we work together. *Shambhala Sun, 51*, 29–33.

Teilhard de Chardin, P. (1955). *The phenomenon of man.* New York: Harper.

Torbert, W., & Associates. (2004). *Action inquiry: The secret of timely and transforming action.* San Francisco: Berrett-Koehler.

Chapter Three

Enspirited Leadership in Japan

Bob Stilger, Yuka Saionji

On a gray winter day in 2011, the biggest earthquake in centuries struck Japan's Tohoku region, just off the northeast coast. Soon a devastating tsunami arrived with waters more than sixty feet high and traveling at nearly sixty miles an hour. The next day, the Fukushima Nuclear Energy Plant exploded. Nearly twenty thousand people perished, and a half million were without jobs or homes or both. In late 2013, 300,000 people are still living in temporary housing, and in many communities the local economy is still paralyzed. Yet beneath this tragedy, something new is being born.

Government has done the best it can, and its immediate efforts led to an early stabilization. Government can provide temporary housing and get the roads fixed and trains running, but government rarely effectively leads change. Change happens when people change the way they think and begin to act in new ways. At first it is messy, even chaotic. Then over time, new order begins to emerge. But how does it emerge? What leadership is required? In particular, what enables ordinary people to step forward, offering themselves and their own leadership?

Scholars, consultants, and managers have written volumes about leadership over the past decade. Frequently their writing has delved into spirit, presence, and authenticity. What is it in the world that is calling forth this inquiry? Was it always important, or has something shifted as humanity entered a new century?

Background: Bob and Yuka

We have been exploring these questions for many years. We've each had the opportunity to work around the world with people from many cultures and to explore the ways in which authenticity seems to be essential in these turbulent times. We began work together in Japan after the triple disasters of March 11, 2011.

Over thirty months, we have engaged with more than a thousand people, hosting community conversations, creating reflection spaces, and listening to people's stories. We have done this to help people in Japan find their way forward and because we know Japan's experience will be of benefit to the rest of the world. Throughout we've wondered: What gives people the clarity and the courage to offer their leadership now?

In the first decade of this century, Bob's research was with individuals and then with organizations to determine the landmarks that help people step forward to lead with spirit. He named these as a framework for enspirited leadership. Described later in this chapter, this particular view of leadership has informed and guided Bob and Yuka's work.

Yuka believes that before 3.11, as the disasters are referred to, there was a "stuckness." People couldn't express who they truly were because of strict social conventions, and they lived in a materialistic world, isolated from their own true selves and from each other. Now, she notices that people are placing value on things they cannot see: love, trust, partnership, and collective wisdom.

We have used many forms of dialogue—circle, world café, open space technology, appreciation inquiry—to help people listen to each other and speak their own truths. These forms themselves help people be present to each other and to call in spirit. Often when reflecting on these past several years, we recall arriving in Minamisoma, a town of seventy thousand on Japan's Fukushima coast fifteen miles from the reactors, in the early evening of December 7, 2012. We had come to conduct a community Future Session. As we greeted twenty or so people at the new Future Center, we were told that a 7.3 magnitude earthquake had struck 150 miles off the coast. At that time, tsunami warnings had been posted, but no one knew whether this quake, the most powerful since March 11, 2011, had damaged the Fukushima reactors further. Was more radiation coming their way? Would a tsunami come? There was no way to know. What should we do? We wanted to stay together. We decided to begin a Future Session. If we received an alert, we could take immediate action. But since we were together, we should talk. Quickly we arranged the chairs into a circle.

The magic of the circle worked for us as well. Our own anxiety had been rising. As we sat and checked in with each other, we settled into our own selves and into the collective. The alert passed. There was no major tsunami. We had a powerful evening talking about how to live with uncertainty.

While there are many pressures to return to an "old normal," the landscape of many people's lives is filled with uncertainty. This has been a time of punctuated equilibrium (Gersick, 1991) in which the ways people make meaning in their lives have been cracked wide open. Many have stepped through those cracks, offering their leadership in a time of great need and new opportunity.

One particularly important aspect of these times we have noticed is that people are standing up while standing together. An often-quoted expression about Japan is *deru kugi ga utareru* (the nail that sticks up is hammered down). In collectivist culture, individual aspirations are often repressed in favor of the felt aspirations of the collective. The events of 3.11 have been a push causing people to stand for what they want and believe, and they are doing so while staying connected with the larger collective. When the Dalai Lama visited Japan in 2011, he spoke to these same themes: "With our intelligence, combined with self-confidence, we can overcome all these problems. So tragedy certainly, naturally, brings sadness and demoralizes us; but now you must transform it into enthusiasm and self-confidence and work hard to rebuild your lives, your country" (Watts, 2012, p. 183). A key issue, of course, is what creates this enthusiasm and self-confidence.

Since 3.11, we have organized and hosted hundreds of dialogues and Future Sessions in Tohoku communities as well as in other parts of Japan. Sometimes we have worked together, other times separately, always returning to meet with each other and share our learning. In this chapter, we share some of the stories we have heard, the meaning we are making from this lived inquiry, Bob's own research into enspirited leadership, as well as some of the questions we see that need to be explored as this work continues.

The ideas presented here are our own, formed through countless hours of listening deeply to the people of Japan. This seemed to be the time to write from our hearts. We have chosen to focus directly on our personal experiences and perceptions in the hope of evoking the same quality of personal reflection in readers. There is time to think more analytically and relate experience to scholarship, but given the enormity of what we and the people in Japan have been living with, this chapter primarily describes what we have experienced, heard, and seen.

Stepping Stones

How does one begin to create the new after disasters? It is not an easy path and certainly is not a linear one. The event of 3.11 was not primarily a natural disaster. It was, in fact, human caused. We heard this point of view first voiced by Masami Saionji, a spiritual leader in Japan (and Yuka's mother), when she said three powerful words to us in April 2011: *We caused this*. This perspective was also offered by both Sivaraksa (2012) and Ariyaratne (2012), who each suggested it is essential that we recognize the culpability that we as human beings had in causing these disasters. This opens a space where we can consider how we might cause something else.

There was a dramatic difference in the energetic response to the catastrophic Kobe earthquake of the mid-1990s and the response to 3.11. In the mid-1990s, most people seemed to think Japan was headed in the right direction. This was not the case in 2011. Sivaraksa (2012) and Ariyaratne (2012) both point to a rising dissatisfaction of materialism and consumption as a gauge for happiness and an ensuing quest for a new future and a new quality of life.

In this quest for a new and uncertain future, we have seen that people in Japan have been finding their way forward, guided by certain stepping-stones that have helped them recreate their lives.

Grieve What's Gone

At times the grief has been overwhelming, not only in Tohoku itself but across all of Japan.

A month after the disasters, Bob was hosting a dialogue in Nagoya, far from the disaster area, and asked a man he knew from other sessions how he was doing. His response was casual: "Oh, you know, just working along." Later, in deep dialogue, he said: "I don't watch the news anymore. I can't. I pretend everything is normal with my family, and then I go to my office and pretend even more." Tapping on his heart, he said: "It is all different in here, and I am sad and confused."

More than a year and a half later, the owner of a fish processing plant in the once prosperous fishing community of Ishinomaki told the story of a friend who had died and asked, "Why did I live while he died? Why was it he who was trapped in the car, unable to open the doors or windows, as the waters rose? Why was he allowed only that last gasp of air before the waters closed around him?" He talked about how his view of life had shifted dramatically: "What about all those families in

Japan that have found success? You know, they have a nice house with new appliances and a shiny car. Their children have gotten into good schools. But are they happy? Is this all there is to life? I'm okay today, but sometimes it is so hard to go on. Each time I would begin to give up, volunteers showed up to help shovel the ten tons of mud out of my factory. Some days I was all alone. Just me, the mud, and my grief."

Sometimes it is a tsunami that heralds sweeping change. Other times, the change is less dramatic, perhaps almost invisible. As we have listened to many stories from people whose lives were dramatically changed by this disaster, we have concluded that it is essential to step into grief and let it transform us if we are to offer our leadership from a place of authenticity.

Stand Up

Disaster has provoked people in Tohoku to stand up for whatever they really care about. It has enabled them to set aside their fears and hesitations. They have found clarity and courage to offer themselves in service to whatever is needed now. A tapestry woven with big and small actions begins to emerge and, within it, a picture of the future being born.

In Otsuchi, after three days of finding and removing bodies from the rubble, a former car mechanic could not close his eyes to sleep. Each time he had tried, for the last two nights, all he saw were the bodies. Instead, he went out and watched the fires burning his beloved town. Town, fields, fishing boats: all gone. He turned his back on the ocean and looked to the hills and saw they were still filled with healthy trees. He knew then he would dedicate his life to the descendants of those who had died, and he would help the community learn how to create an economy from the forest. He's doing that today, developing forest-based businesses employing people from the community.

To the south, another man moved to Minamisoma, the largest city near the Fukushima reactors. Arriving as many were leaving, he had come from his nearby village of Itatemura, destroyed by radiation and uninhabitable for the rest of his life. He came because the people of Minamisoma needed help. Today he leads volunteer efforts to decontaminate buildings, soil, and trees in the community. He's also a leader of the Minami Mirai Center, where people are discovering how to build a new future together.

While other young women who could were trying to find a way out of Fukushima, three decided to stay. They created Peach Heart as a support community for young women whose lives were now filled with questions: Would anyone want to marry a woman from Fukushima? Did they want to have children with the radiation danger? Should they if they could? What kind of a life could they make for themselves now?

We've encountered hundreds of stories like these: people coming together to create a "karma kitchen" in Tokyo; people leading efforts to revitalize their village in Shikoku by recreating a village plan from two hundred years ago; those who started intermediary foundations in Tohoku. All over Japan, people are standing up for what they see as possible. None of them expected to be doing what they are doing today. They were spirit called. They stood up to do what was needed now.

Stay Together

Many times we witnessed people turning to each other and entering into deep dialogue. We have seen people speak their own truths with powerful authenticity. They have found places to stand, knowing they were not alone.

The 188 homes in the small village of Osawa were all destroyed in the tsunami, and 150 people died. And a miracle happened. Across Tohoku, when certificates were being issued for temporary housing, a lottery system was used. Done to ensure fairness, the result was that people who had been separated for months from family and neighbors in emergency shelters were scattered even farther to the winds, landing in small new housing settlements with strangers.

In Osawa, three people saw that they were assigned to the same new location. Quickly they went to a government official and asked if certifications could be traded. The miracle was that the official said: "I guess so." Immediately they arranged a massive trade of certificates. Most of the residents of Osawa moved into the same temporary housing. Over the next months, together they built awnings and porches, started their own security patrols, began growing their own food, and organized a festival to celebrate life. Within eight months of the disaster, they told the nonprofit assisting them to go help someone else; they were doing fine.

To the south, in another case that involved temporary housing, the families from the small village of Jusanhama went together to clear land. When the land was clear and ready, they went to the government and said, "Please build our temporary houses here." The government agreed, and now those fifteen families are rebuilding a village that once supported forty.

Rather than turning away and separating, people in Tohoku turned to each other. They knew that if they were able to stay together, they could begin to create a new future.

Go Alone

Sometimes you must go alone before you can stay together.

One of the most dramatic stories we encountered also comes from Jusanhama. When they heard that the tsunami was coming, ten fishers made their way to the harbor and their boats while others were rushing to high ground. Their fathers and grandfathers had told them: "When the big one comes, get to your boats and go out to sea. Get to a depth of more than fifty meters or you will die." They left families and everything they knew behind and raced out to the sea. Ancestral wisdom guided them, but they had no idea if they or their families would survive. Against all odds, they did. Their families were the ones who later cleared the land, together, for their temporary housing.

One of the great tragedies of 3.11 was the number of children who lost their lives. In the village of Ogatsu, the principal of the junior high told his students to run to the hillside and mountains as quickly as they could. It took him eight days to first search the mountains and then the shelters to discover that every child had lived. To the north in the town of Kamaishi, the schools had developed a unique way to train children for disaster that used three principles: don't try to guess what's going on, go as quickly as you can, and go as far as you can—and one piece of ancient wisdom—don't look for your families—to guide them. The last one was the most difficult, but the ancestors knew that most people died because they went looking for others. Fewer children died in Kamaishi than in any of the other coastal cities.

They found the courage to go alone. They took first steps into an uncertain future and with no idea of what would happen. They opened to new possibilities.

Work with What You Have

In Japan working with what you have is called *jimotogaku*, which translates roughly as "learning from the local area." In the United States, it is called asset-based community development. It means that we don't wait for anyone; we assess what we have and imagine new ways in which it can be used. *Jimotogaku* produces a changed attitude—a new look at what one has—and an orientation to start with what you have and follow it wherever it leads.

In Kesennuma, the family that owned a fish processing plant saw almost every part of their fishing community destroyed. What was left? Canvas. Lots of ship's canvas. How could it be used? First, they dyed it deep blue, stenciled in white the names of the communities torn apart by the tsunami, and made big handbags with bright pink, orange, and green handles. Over the coming months, they added new products: iPad covers, coin purses, baseball caps, and a host of other things. A micro-industry was born.

In the Iwate town of Otsuchi, a series of four dialogues were held to help people reimagine their future. They looked at what they had: clear water once used to grow wasabi that could be grown again. Their pure water might be an attractor in creating a tourist destination. Local knowledge of flowers could lead to a new dried and pressed flower business that could be competitive with flowers from Europe popular in Tokyo.

Jimotogaku is the story of beginning with what you have, right now, without waiting. These are not complicated ideas. They are the first steps that can begin to change the entire way in which you see your life.

Hold Hands across the Generations

We believe that the deepest authenticity arises with diversity. One kind of diversity that is almost always present is that of different generations coming together.

Hundreds and hundreds of young people, called "U turns" and "I turns," have come to the region because they feel called to be there. "U" turns are people who grew up in Tohoku and went away to Tokyo for school and jobs; they came back because either the disasters or their grandmothers called them. "I" turns are people with no previous connection to the region who felt called to be there. We've spent many hours in conversation with them. Frequently they came thinking of themselves as the outside experts and quickly came to appreciate the knowledge and experience of the local people. They realized in the process they had come to learn together, not to teach. The power of these relationships was multifaceted. We recall one fisherwoman speaking of how incredibly challenging the first six months were after the tsunami: "So many times, we wanted to give up. It was just so hard," she said. "But these wonderful young people had come to help us. It was because of them that we couldn't give up."

These intergenerational relationships have given both older and younger people access to wisdom and a presence that was unavailable in their lives. They led each other, making a path forward together.

Start Anywhere; Start Now

Jimotogaku leads to the idea of starting, now, anywhere. Make a new path into the future with your own spirit and presence, step by step. We think that authenticity means being willing to be a little unusual and to try things that will, perhaps, not be successful. In Fukushima and in the coastal areas, there is not a past to return to. What future will be built?

In Rikuzentakada, a former government official talked with us about how government can't create anything new: "People need to do that. Government goes in circles, ending up in the same place. Upward spirals are needed now. We need to really unleash the creativity of people to make a new future that combines old traditions with new technologies. We need to plan and build differently for a future we want, not the past. We need crazy ideas."

A farmer in Fukushima says, "We have to open our minds and hearts and become aware of what we are feeling. We have to open up and accept other people. We must change our ideas. We need to tell our children that college probably isn't all that important for them. We must learn how to live in and open up to nature and we must learn how to relate differently to our natural world. Colleges don't teach these important things."

It takes courage to start right where you are. It requires staying in the present moment, looking at what you have, and beginning.

Grieve what's gone, stand up, stay together, go alone, hold hands across the generations, work with what you have, start any way, start now. These are some of the main stepping-stones people have discovered in Tohoku. Each of these stones is a pathway into self and a new future. They lead us into an uncertain future by also leading us into ourselves.

Enspirited Leadership

Ten years ago Bob's dissertation research was on the practices of younger leaders in different parts of Europe and Africa who were creating new organizations to build community. Using a qualitative methodology called organic inquiry, he engaged with a group of seven people in their late twenties and early thirties in a cooperative inquiry about the landmarks that guided their work and their lives.

Just as Bob was finishing his dissertation, he decided that he ought to look back at what scholars had to say about the nature and leadership of the social movements he was part of in the late 1960s and early 1970s. Various works caught his attention. One in particular led him to the metaframe of enspirited leadership.

Doug McAdam and his colleagues (McAdam, McCarthy, & Zald, 1996) defined the social movements of the twentieth century as protest movements designed to create political change. They saw these movements as ideological, strategic, and tactical. People had ideologies—ways of thinking about the world—that guided them, and they developed strategies and tactics to pursue known goals and objectives. Looking for the words that had the same clarity that could describe the new movements of this century, he saw those he worked with as being enspirited, appreciative, and emergent.

The same can be said of the people we've been working with in Tohoku, Japan. They are guided by a deep presence of spirit, they work with what they have, and they follow the path that emerges before them.

We have used the six key landmarks of enspirited leadership (Stilger, 2004) to guide our work in Tohoku:

o *Work from a sense of true calling.* Each time that we have been in deep dialogue with people in the region, we encouraged them to find the work that was meant for them. We invited them to find clarity and courage in stepping into work that they can do best. This counsel has been particularly important for the many young people who have left their career paths behind in Tokyo that felt lifeless and have begun to discover more of who they truly are through their service in Tohoku.

o *Journey in the company of others.* We have reminded those working in the area that they don't need to do anything alone. They need to keep turning to one another for counsel and support. Sometimes the challenges and the grief are almost overwhelming. We have reminded them not to take on more than they can handle and to rely on each other's honest counsel.

o *Live with a spiritual center.* Spirit is always near in Tohoku. A glance at vacant land where homes stood, a walk through towns completely evacuated, or a stop at a graveyard that has been carefully restored: all call in the presence of spirit. We have invited people to find time to be quiet, to meditate, or to engage in other spiritual practice to keep their balance.

o *Demand diversity.* We have counseled people to keep inviting those with different ideas together. It is easy advice for most. They are not concerned about being right; they want to build a new future. People seem more able to listen to the ideas and perspective of others because there is so much work to do.

o *Use reflective learning as a guide.* This is a time of rapid prototyping in the region. People are trying things. We have reminded them that their early efforts will frequently meet with limited success and that they need to take what they have done, come together, and learn. We have suggested to them that their learning will tell them what comes next. They make a path forward, one step at a time.

o *Befriend ambiguity and uncertainty.* The qualities of stillness, calling, receptivity, and reflection present in these first five landmarks lay the foundation for what may be the most important: the capacity to work without certainty. People know there is little certainty in Tohoku. Some still hope for a return to the old normal; others know they must make a new future. We have encouraged them to learn to be at ease with the uncertainty that surrounds them. It is not going away.

Three Questions

As Japan turns to the long task of rebuilding the Tohoku region, what will sustain those who bring their whole being to their work? We've identified three key questions that we think need to be explored:

1. Where will the leadership come from to create a new Tohoku?
   - What can invite people to step forward?
   - Who are the people who are willing to lead but have no need to be followed?
   - Where will they find and support those who know how to work with their own emotions, have clear purpose, and know what they know and what they don't know?
   - What leadership will help people find the clarity to set a course for the future without much attachment to how it will happen?
   - How will they connect with others in honest relationship?
   - How do they learn to prototype at a systems level, proceeding step by careful step?
2. How will spaces for deep relationship and trust be created?
   - How can people find safe and generative spaces, often referred to simply as good *Ba* (Nonaka & Konno, 1998)?
   - How do they create the spaces in which respect, curiosity, and generosity are present and creativity and possibility prosper?

- What will support people in Tohoku in continually inviting in more and more diversity?

- How will they avoid falling back into ways of thinking and doing that isolate one town from another and that segment different people and endeavors into silos where their impact is minimized?

- How can these many voices be connected so that transformation becomes possible?

3. Will people look to their own wealth of resources and knowledge rather than waiting for someone else?

- What will help people remember they are part of a rich web of possibilities and that they don't need to wait for anyone?

- What will help support them in looking inward toward the resources they already have and in discovering new ways to use those resources?

- What will help them build a strong foundation that invites partnership and collaboration from others in Japan and the rest of the world?

Spirit, Presence, and Authenticity

Stepping into these questions seems to us to require leadership that draws on spirit, presence, and authenticity. Such leadership is deeply aligned with Japanese culture, where deep meaning is conveyed beyond words and requires a stillness to understand. In Japan, the cultural competence for communication is listening. In cultures like the United States, the communications competence is speaking. In Japan, listening is a whole-body sport that relies on the presence of spirit and authenticity. Many years ago, Edward Hall (1976) told a lovely story in a book that laid the groundwork for the field of intercultural communications. He talked about how when the husband arrived home from work, he would know something was not okay in the household when he noticed a tiny branch out of alignment in a flower arrangement or that his tea was just a little cool. While Bob developed the concept of enspirited leadership in the global south, both of us have come to understand it deeply in Japan.

This is a time between myths. The old one is dying, the new yet to be born. It is an unusual time. Many names get tossed around: *new paradigm, postindustrial, cultural creative, Gaia*. People cannot actually see what is coming, but many of us sense that we are in the rapids of change where much of what we've relied on for order in our lives is disintegrating. As the myths that have given coherence to our lives have shattered, people seem to have become spiritually ill (Loy, Goodhew, & Goodhew, 2000). Part of our journey now is one of recovering our human spirit.

It is no surprise that a different kind of leadership is needed, one that is sourced in not knowing and is comfortable with proceeding to a destination not yet knowable. The old expression was, "If you don't know where you're going, you'll never get there." The new expression is, "We make the path by walking it together, one step at a time."

References

Ariyaratne, A. T. (2012). Natural disasters and religion: In search of an alternative way. In J. S. Watt (Ed.), *This precious life: Buddhist tsunami relief and anti-nuclear activism in post 3/11* (pp. 196–203). Tokyo: International Buddhist Exchange Center.

Gersick, C.J.G. (1991). Revolutionary change theories: A multilevel exploration of the punctuated equilibrium paradigm. *Academy of Management Review, 16*(1), 10–36.

Hall, E. T. (1976). *Beyond culture.* New York: Doubleday.

Loy, D. R., Goodhew, L., & Goodhew, L. (2000). *The dharma of dragons and daemons: Buddhist themes in modern fantasy.* Somerville, MA: Wisdom Publications.

McAdam, D., McCarthy, J. D., & Zald, M. N. (Eds.). (1996). *Comparative perspectives on social movements: Political opportunities, mobilizing structures, and cultural framings.* Cambridge: Cambridge University Press.

Nonaka, I., & Konno, N. (1998). The concept of "Ba": Building a foundation for knowledge creation. *California Management Review, 40*(3), 40–54.

Sivaraksa, S. (2012). No more back to business as usual: A socially engaged Buddhist approach to making a post 3/11 society in Japan. In J. S. Watt (Ed.), *This precious life: Buddhist tsunami relief and anti-nuclear activism in post 3/11 Japan* (pp. 188–195). Tokyo: International Buddhist Exchange Center.

Stilger, R. (2004). *Discovering new stories: An organic inquiry into enspirited leadership.* UMI Dissertations Publishing, Ann Arbor.

Watts, J. S. (2012). Engaged Buddhism the Dalai Lama's way: Tibetan leader's exceptional energy for Japan's tsunami victims. In J. S. Watt (Ed.), *This precious life: Buddhist tsunami relief and anti-nuclear activism in post 3/11 Japan* (pp. 180–187). Tokyo: International Buddhist Exchange Center.

Part Two

Presence

Sociological Mindfulness
and Leadership Education

John Eric Baugher

On September 10, 2013, World Bank president Jim Yong
Kim and three hundred members of his staff participated in a
Day of Mindfulness Meditation with Thich Nhat Hanh, the
Vietnamese Zen master, author, and peace activist. The all-day
event at the bank headquarters in Washington, DC, was part of
a larger effort to help staff "manage and balance the stresses
of daily life" brought on in part by Kim's major initiatives for
change within the bank (Kamen, 2013). The World Bank also
offers staff lunchtime mindfulness meditation sessions facilitated by the company Visit Yourself at Work at the rate of
twenty-five dollars for one forty-five-minute session or as low
as eighteen dollars per session for ten or more sessions, allowing
one to "feel good about yourself and your wallet the more you
meditate!"

The Visit Yourself at Work website advertises these corporate wellness programs as "a great return on investment," cit-
ing increased productivity, improved worker morale, and other
organizational benefits. Other clients of the company's mindfulness meditation services are America's Health Insurance Plans,
Fannie Mae, Internal Revenue Service, Kaiser Permanente,
US Department of Justice, and Whole Foods. The bridging of
the spiritual and material world, illustrated by the use of mindfulness meditation in such diverse corporate and governmental
workplaces, would have been unthinkable just a few years ago
(Williams & Kabat-Zinn, 2011). How should we interpret the
current "mindfulness revolution" (Boyce, 2011)?

The focus on mindfulness in recent years is part of a broader cultural shift toward exploring and mastering the self through meditation and other technologies of the self that have become readily available in late modern capitalist societies (Foucault, 1994; Taylor, 1997). Some sociologists and religious studies scholars see the use of meditation, "deep listening, and other forms of journeying inward in the "newly 'spiritual' corporate culture" as an expression of "self-absorption" that inhibits seeing clearly existing power relations and the causes of the financial, economic, and social suffering endemic to the current global capitalist system (Ehrenreich, 2009, pp. 112, 206; see also Carrette & King, 2005; McGee, 2005). While their studies offer a rather one-sided interpretation of the diverse applications of mindfulness in contemporary workplaces, they raise legitimate concerns regarding how spiritual practices are presented within the context of the market values of materialism, individual achievement, competition, productivity, and efficiency. As Mirabai Bush, cofounder of the Center for Contemplative Mind in Society and a key contributor to Google's Search Inside Yourself curriculum, points out, important questions arise when contemplative practices are brought into corporate settings: "Will they be taught in merely a technical way with no larger ethical significance? Will they truly serve the participants' lives or just the company's goals of efficiency and profit?" (Boyce, 2009).

Most of the mindfulness meditation programs currently being implemented in the corporate world are designed to reduce stress, which some believe is "the biggest problem in the workplace in the West" (Titmuss, 2013). Skillfully designed initiatives such as Jon Kabat-Zinn's path-breaking Mindfulness-Based Stress Reduction (MBSR) program can help reduce pain and stress in clinical and nonclinical settings (Chiesa & Serretti, 2009; Grossman, Niemann, Schmidt, & Walach, 2004). Similarly, those who receive skillful training in contemplative end-of-life care may benefit from such training by becoming more creative and compassionate in responding to the holistic needs of sick and dying persons (Baugher, 2012a). But training health care workers in mindfulness practices has not altered inequalities regarding who does and does not have access to adequate medical care in the United States. And although MBSR may assist soldiers in regulating emotions in combat situations (Jha, Stanley, Kiyonaga, Wong, & Gelfand, 2010), we might be better off achieving the goal of world peace (Tan, 2012) by changing the conditions that allow war-making to be so lucrative.

As a Buddhist practitioner, I have experienced the power of mindfulness to calm the mind, transform suffering into wisdom, and open possibilities for loving action in even the most unlikely places (Baugher, 2012b, 2013). Yet let us be clear that in the teachings of Mahayana Buddhism, mindfulness is not celebrated as an effective business intervention or as a useful technique for killing with greater emotional calm, but as skillful means for benefiting all sentient beings. In Thich Naht Hanh's words, "If your business is causing environmental problems, then because you have practiced meditation you may have an idea of how to conduct your business in such a way that you will harm nature less" (Confino, 2013). Critical here is the broader view and intention that shapes the practice of meditation toward developing "more insight and more right view on yourself and on the world" such that "you will want to handle and conduct your business in such a way that will make the world suffer less" (Confino, 2013).

The three chapters in part 2 on presence highlight the central importance of mindfulness in leadership education, and each author or set of authors skillfully outlines how mindfulness practices are intentionally incorporated into their work within the context of a particular ethical foundation or view. In chapter 4, Catherine Etmanski, Mark Fulton, Guy Nasmyth, and M. Beth Page draw on the metaphor of dance to symbolize ways of working, relating, and being with one another that invert and upend hierarchical notions of power and leadership (Jironet, 2010; Scharmer & Kaufer, 2013). Mindfulness has rich connotations in their team teaching model, including the shared intention to stretch and grow, disciplined and playful communal practice, and the capacity to flexibly attune to emergent and unexpected learning opportunities. In chapter 5, Linda Kantor's experience of student resistance to the introduction of MBSR in an executive MBA program in South Africa illustrates quite powerfully Jon Kabat-Zinn's (2011, pp. 281–282) observation that "the quality of MBSR as an intervention is only as good as the MBSR instructor and his or her understanding of what is required to deliver a truly mindfulness-based programme." Kantor embraced the learning opportunity that presented in the painful feedback she received from students, and through her flexibility, self-reflection, and clarity of vision, she was able to discern how to skillfully introduce the wisdom of mindfulness practice in a novel context. Anecdotes from former students highlight how mindfulness practice opened many students to wanting to engage themselves and others as whole persons.

In chapter 6, Brighid Dwyer, Ralph Gigliotti, and Hanna Lee situate their work in the Intergroup Dialogue Program at Villanova within the Catholic mission of their university to develop and sustain true community based on truth, unity, and love. Rather than teaching students about intergroup relations, the intergroup dialogue courses at Villanova engage students in "creating a sacred space for shared meaning and mutual understanding among those of diverse backgrounds." Such transformative work resonates with Etmanski and colleagues' reframing of "fighting" for social justice into a "journey of healing" and "mutual learning." Students in the Intergroup Dialogue Program, most of whom are privileged by race and class, develop through contemplative dialogic practice a deepened capacity for seeing connections between their own experiences of privilege and the suffering of others. Critical here is how mindful questioning and other practices of dialogue turn students inward so that the relation between the inward and the outward, between privilege and oppression, may be revealed. In the words of Canadian philosopher Heesoon Bai (2012, p. 71), such "inner work" supported through contemplative education invites participants to "deconstruct and reconstruct ourselves from the inside out," supporting all in decolonizing our minds of the untenable and unsustainable values and beliefs central to contemporary individualistic, materialistic, and militaristic societies (see also Baugher, in press).

As these contributions illustrate, contemplative education can engage students in practices of inquiry that cannot be reduced to the popular understanding of mindfulness as a value-neutral "type of awareness intrinsically devoid of discrimination, evaluation, and judgment" (Bodhi, 2011, p. 26; see also Boyce, 2011). Buddhist scholars have recently critiqued such an understanding as being inconsistent with canonical texts (Bodhi, 2011; Dreyfus, 2011; Simmer-Brown, 2013). Mindfulness practices that calm the mind are certainly needed in our world today, yet leadership education must go deeper than seeking to alleviate the anxieties of individuals and improve interpersonal relationships and task performance within a given organization or social setting. As Otto Scharmer notes in chapter 1, it is certainly necessary to bring mindfulness practice to as many individuals as possible, although what is needed is linking the process of "transforming individual consciousness" with the work of "transforming the system as a whole." The purpose of Theory U is to provide the framework and language for such spiritual awareness at all levels: individual, team, organization, and larger systems.

Change at the individual and organizational levels is an incomplete "mindfulness revolution" (Boyce, 2011) as long as emotionally intelligent action remains embedded in, and often unintentionally reproduces, destructive social structural arrangements. Organizational technologies such as 360-degree feedback discussed in chapter 2 by Jonathan Reams, Olen Gunnlaugson, and Juliane Reams can help leaders better imagine some of the consequences of their action, yet to see what are often the most painful and destructive reverberations of collective action, we need methodologies for knowing realities that are beyond the situated knowledge and interest of individuals who are embedded in the same organizations to which they belong. Whose voices and experience are invisibly excluded in culturally bound processes of "seeing from within an organization" (Senge, Scharmer, Jaworksi, & Flowers, 2004, p. 48)? Whose suffering is "unmarkable" and "vanishes . . . in the ellipses by which discourse proceeds" (Butler, 2003, p. 23)? What realities are too "unthinkable" to be seen and acted on by those privileged by the current order of social things (Lemert, 2007)?

These kinds of inquiries resonate with Scharmer and Kaufer's (2013) recent work on personal, relational, and institutional inversion. Central in the shift from the current ego system economy to what Scharmer and Kaufer call the nascent ecosystem economy is the process of co-creative conversation with diverse others that "bends the beam of attention back onto ourselves," allowing the possibility for seeing the darker sides of collective action and co-creating systemic changes that will benefit all. Critical here is a shift in mind-set from acting in the interest of our own limited well-being toward a focus on the broader well-being of all who are affected by our work. This shift in mind-set resonates with what I call sociological mindfulness, understood as the capacity to see how the many things we do as individuals and members of collectivities are interconnected with the conditions of our own lives and the lives of multiple others, near and far. Whereas mindfulness meditation may reduce stress, opening ourselves to sociologically mindful seeing is an invitation to discomfort, especially in a society that celebrates individualism, consumerism, and material excess (Baugher, in press). Becoming sociologically mindful involves keeping our hearts and minds open rather than closing down and becoming defensive when we get a glimpse of how our habits of living contradict what we claim to really care about as individuals and members of larger collectives.

It is commonly accepted that leading with mindfulness is socially responsible and makes good business sense (Tan, 2012). Yet leading with sociological mindfulness may not easily align with the corporate bottom line given current political, economic, and social realities. Derek Rasmussen is a social and eco-justice activist and an advisor to Inuit organizations in Canada and is also a Dharma teacher trained in the Burmese and Tibetan Buddhist traditions. His teachings on the pith instruction of the Buddha to first do no harm illustrate the sorrows of living without and with sociological mindfulness.

Charity is a common impulse for those in privileged positions, and Rasmussen considers the good intentions of nonindigenous folks who want to help out indigenous peoples in their struggles for environmental justice. However, the quality of leadership needed today is not that of the rescuer, but of the wise who refuse to continue doing harm. Rasmussen (2013) recounts how he was once asked by the chair of the parliamentary committee studying chemicals in the environment why the chamber of commerce he was representing (Baffin Region) was the only one demanding tighter restrictions. His response in essence was, "Other Chambers have chemical producers as their membership; we have chemical products *in* our membership." Rasmussen explains how toxic dioxin plumes emitted from factories in the United States "grasshopper" their way north, where they settle "absorbed into lichen, eaten by caribou, which in turn are consumed by Inuit." Groundbreaking "source-to-receptor" research shows that in a given year, over half of the dioxin that was poisoning the eight hundred Inuit of Coral Harbour in the middle of the Hudson Bay was emitted from just three factories: Ash Grove's cement kiln in Louisville, Nebraska; Lafarge's cement kiln in Alpena, Michigan; and Chemetco's copper smelter in Hartford, Illinois. A sense of compassion leads nonindigenous folks to want to help, and Rasmussen channels that compassionate impulse with the wisdom of the Buddha: the first step in helping is ceasing to do harm: "Stay home. Go on a field trip to Alpena, Michigan, or Hartford, Illinois. Figure out how to clean it up, slow it down, stop it."

Assume for a moment that the plant managers at the Ash Grove, Lafarge, and Chemetco plants have implemented mindfulness-based initiatives in their workplaces that have created a "more family-life atmosphere" and supported their workers in developing self-awareness, self-regulation, and other domains of "emotional intelligence" that enable "stellar work performance" (Tan, 2012, pp. 11–14). Assume also that the organizations have reaped enormous profits from the sale of cement and copper products in recent years, largely due to the effects of the mindfulness initiatives on worker productivity and plant labor relations. Now assume you and I are managers at these plants. Nonviolent protesters including representatives of the Inuit are attracting media attention outside the plant gates. How will we engage with the unthinkable realization that the apparent success of our corporations, bringing economic riches to so many, also brings poison to these unfortunate others? How will we embrace this bitter fruit of our dawning sociological mindfulness? Which of the "habitual reactions of avoidance"—denial, cynicism, depression—well up, potentially preventing the consequences of our actions from "sinking in deeply" (Scharmer & Kaufer, 2013, pp. 175–176)? Our meditative practice is deep and our commitment to seeing reality with clarity and compassion is strong. And as we come to see more clearly our interconnectedness with others, we develop a deeper sense of gratitude for what has been given to us, a profound sense of sorrow regarding the illusions we collectively live by, and a greater willingness to change our ways of being in the world to remove the causes of suffering for ourselves and for our fellow travelers on this beautiful and fragile planet.

Sociological mindfulness, the capacity and willingness to witness the suffering that frequently results from good intended actions in a global capitalist world system, is indispensable as we seek to realize and institutionalize ways of being that are premised on not doing harm. Such a view of mindfulness requires a contemplative and critical pedagogy that pierces the heart with deep insight into the sorrows of the samsaric wheel of capitalist production and consumption (Bai, 2012). In her introduction to part 1, Karin Jironet brings to light how we are now collectively at a point of liminality between dying and emerging paradigms and suggests that perhaps for now, we may just have to sit with the insecurity and unknowingness that define the experience of standing at this threshold. What might we learn from "tarrying with grief, from remaining exposed to its unbearability . . . the slow process by which we develop a point of identification with suffering itself," not as "narcissistic preoccupation," but as a deeper realization of the vulnerability of others, as an "apprehension of a common human vulnerability" (Butler, 2003, p. 19)? In the words of Dzogchen meditation master Nyoshul Khen Rinpoche, such a realization gives rise to an effortless compassion "so limitless that if tears could express it, you would cry without end" (Rinpoche, 1993, p. 367). May we allow ourselves to live, to mercifully hold this sorrowful, joyful birth of wisdom.

References

Bai, H. (2012). Education for enlightenment. In A. Cohen, M. Porath, A. Clarke, H. Bai, C. Leggo, & K. Meyer (Eds.), *Speaking of teaching: Inclinations, inspirations, and innerworkings* (pp. 63–82). Rotterdam: Sense Publishers.

Baugher, J. E. (2012a). The "quiet revolution" in care of the dying. In K. G. Schuyler (Ed.), *Inner peace—global impact: Tibetan Buddhism, leadership, and work* (pp. 215–242). Charlotte, NC: Information Age.

Baugher, J. E. (2012b). Learning to rest: Transforming habits of mind in higher education. In K. G. Schuyler (Ed.), *Inner peace—global impact: Tibetan Buddhism, leadership, and work* (pp. 113–123). Charlotte, NC: Information Age.

Baugher, J. E. (2013, July). Beyond closure: Transforming trauma into spiritual journey. *View*, 26–27.

Baugher, J. E. (in press). Contemplating uncomfortable emotions: Creating transformative spaces for learning in higher education. In O. Gunnlaugson, H. Bai, E. Sarath, & C. Scott (Eds.), *Contemplative approaches to learning and inquiry across disciplines*. Albany, NY: SUNY Press.

Bodhi, B. (2011). What does mindfulness really mean? A canonical perspective. *Contemporary Buddhism, 12*(1), 19–39.

Boyce, B. (2009). Google searches. *Shambhala Sun*. Retrieved from http://www.shambhalasun.com/index.php?option=content&task=view&id=3417&Itemid=244&limit=1&limitstart=2

Boyce, B. (Ed.). (2011). *The mindfulness revolution: Leading psychologists, scientists, artists, and meditation teachers on the power of mindfulness*. Boston: Shambhala.

Butler, J. (2003). Violence, mourning, politics. *Studies in Gender and Sexuality, 4*(1), 9–37.

Carrette, J., & King, T. (2005). *Selling spirituality: The silent takeover of religion*. New York: Routledge.

Chiesa, A., & Serretti, A. (2009). Mindfulness-based stress reduction for stress management in healthy people: A review and meta-analysis. *Journal of Alternative and Complementary Medicine, 15*(5), 593–600.

Confino, J. (2013, September 5). Google seeks out wisdom of Zen Master Thich Naht Hanh. *Guardian*. Retrieved from http://www.theguardian.com/sustainable-business/global-technology-ceos-wisdom-zen-master-thich-nhat-hanh

Dreyfus, G. (2011). Is mindfulness present-centred and non-judgmental? A discussion of the cognitive dimensions of mindfulness, *Contemporary Buddhism, 12*(1), 41–54.

Ehrenreich, B. (2009). *Bright-sided: How positive thinking is undermining America*. New York: Metropolitan Books.

Foucault, M. (1994). Technologies of the self. In P. Rabinow (Ed.), *Ethics: Subjectivity and truth* (pp. 223–251). New York: New Press.

Grossman, P., Niemann, L., Schmidt, S., & Walach, H. (2004). Mindfulness-based stress reduction and health benefits: A meta-analysis. *Journal of Psychosomatic Research, 57*, 35–43.

Jha, A. P., Stanley, E. A., Kiyonaga, A., Wong, L., & Gelfand, L. (2010). Examining the protective effects of mindfulness training on working memory capacity and affective experience. *Emotion, 10*(1), 54–64.

Jironet, K. (2010). *Female leadership: Management, Jungian psychology, spirituality and the global journey through purgatory*. New York: Routledge.

Kabat-Zinn, J. (2011). Some reflections on the origins of MBSR, skillful means, and the trouble with maps. *Contemporary Buddhism, 12*(1), 281–306.

Kamen, A. (2013, September 23). The World Bank and Thich Naht Hanh say omm. *Washington Post*. Retrieved from http://www.washingtonpost.com/blogs/in-the-loop/wp/2013/09/23/the-world-bank-and-thich-nhat-hanh-say-omm/

Lemert, C. (2007). *Thinking the unthinkable: The riddles of social theory*. Boulder, CO: Paradigm.

McGee, M. (2005). *Self-Help, Inc.: Makeover culture in American life*. New York: Oxford University Press.

Rasmussen, D. (2013, April 4). *Qallunology 101: A lesson plan for the non-indigenous*. Retrieved from http://www.buddhistpeacefellowship.org/qallunology-101-a-lesson-plan-for-the-non-indigenous/.

Rinpoche, S. (1993). *The Tibetan book of living and dying*. New York: HarperCollins.

Scharmer, C. O., & Kaufer, K. (2013). *Leading from the emerging future: From ego-system to eco-system economics*. San Francisco: Berrett-Koehler.

Senge, P., Scharmer, C. O., Jaworksi, J., & Flowers, B. S. (2004). *Presence: Human purpose and the field of the future*. New York: Doubleday.

Simmer-Brown, J. (2013, November). *Mindfulness is not enough: Contemplation in education*. Paper presented at the fifth annual conference of the Association for Contemplative Mind in Higher Education, Amherst, MA.

Tan, C.-M. (2012). *Search inside yourself: The unexpected path to achieving success, happiness (and world peace)*. New York: HarperCollins.

Taylor, C. (1997). What's in a Self? In F. J. Varela (Ed.), *Sleeping, dreaming, and dying: An exploration of consciousness with the Dalai Lama* (pp. 11–21). Boston: Wisdom Publications.

Titmuss, C. (2013, July 19). The Buddha of mindfulness: A stress destruction programme. *Christophers Dharma Blog*. Retrieved from http://christophertitmuss.org/blog/?p=1454

Williams, J.M.G., & Kabat-Zinn, J. (2011). Introduction. Mindfulness: Diverse perspectives on its meaning, origins, and multiple applications at the intersection of science and dharma. *Contemporary Buddhism, 12*(1), 1–18.

Chapter Four

The Dance of Joyful Leadership

*Catherine Etmanski, Mark Fulton,
Guy Nasmyth, M. Beth Page*

The twenty-first century is rife with increasingly complex challenges. Global interdependence coupled with rapidly changing technologies, workforce internationalization, demographic shifts, population growth, economic uncertainty, ongoing conflict, and growing disparity are but a few elements contributing to this complexity. These challenges are compounded by the impacts of climate change and the need to move away from a fossil fuel–based global economy. In the face of such challenges, the call for leadership has never been greater. Yet the very concept of leadership is contested—with different scholars or practitioners placing greater or lesser emphasis on the person, the position, the process, or the outcome (Grint, 2005). This gives rise to the question, What kind of leadership is needed today?

While we cannot presume to know the only possible answer to this question, we have nevertheless come to appreciate the intrinsic value of inviting spirit, presence, mindfulness, and authenticity into our work as leadership educators. Moreover, we have come to see these as important, if not necessary, qualities for both teaching and practicing leadership in our complex world.

Through our conversations, we have come to a mutual understanding of these four key qualities. To us, spirit is the active partnership we experience when we operate in alignment

The author names are in alphabetical order. We thank Phyllis Kennelly for sharing her wisdom and guidance, which helped enhance this chapter.

with our environment, each other, the universe, and our higher power or purpose. The partnership with these external forces is activated when we co-create the conditions and articulate our desire to show up as our best selves in the service of our work as educators.

Presence, as Peter Senge, Otto Scharmer, Joseph Jaworski, and Betty Sue Flowers (2004) have described it, is equally about letting go as it is about "letting come" (p. 14). Scharmer (2009) linked the process of presencing (presence + sensing) to surrender, which allows "the coming into being of a new self, the essential or the authentic self that connects us with who we really are" (p. 187). To us, presence begins as a conscious choice and is directly connected to mindfulness. When we choose to focus our attention in the present moment and become mindfully aware of our thoughts, words, and actions, this allows us to fully use ourselves (not only the content of our minds, but also our way of being) as the instrument of our work as leadership educators. In so doing, we become increasingly sensitive to our environment and more instinctively know how to respond to what is emerging. Mindfulness also means limiting distractions and taking care of ourselves so that we can be truly present to each other and our learners.

Authenticity is to be in alignment with what is going on inside ourselves. Skillful authenticity means gauging the need for professionalism while having the courage to share with others what is needed in the moment to enhance the learning. As we journey on this path of living with authenticity, we realize, as educators and as individuals, the importance of creating the conditions for ourselves and our learners to feel safe and comfortable enough to be authentic. In our experience, trust is a key ingredient for creating the conditions for each of us to show up authentically.

Let us be clear at the outset that we are not claiming to be in a constant state of spirit, presence, mindfulness, and authenticity. Rather, we name these qualities as shared values in our work together, endeavor to live into them, and incorporate reminders to ourselves along the way, as we describe in greater detail in this chapter. This way of working together brings us great joy and feels at times like a dance. In dancing together, we have each experienced moments of inspiration: being fully present, mindfully leading with clear intention, and being authentic with our strengths, vulnerabilities, and weaknesses. Of course, we have also experienced very human moments—a misstep or a fumble—some examples of which we will share. Yet we know that the conditions we have co-created with these qualities enable us to be more powerful, but not in the sense of having power over others. Rather, through working with spirit, presence, mindfulness, and authenticity, we are better able to step into the sacred personal power that, as Marianne Williamson (1992) suggested, exists in each of us. We have experienced that working together enables us to learn and grow and brings each of us closer to our true selves.

Given our belief that spirit, presence, mindfulness, and authenticity are fundamental to leadership today, in this chapter, we articulate how we have invited these qualities into our individual and shared leadership practice. To recount the story of our experiences, we have organized the chapter as follows. Just as T. S. Eliot (1944) suggested that it is the still point that gives rise to the dance of the universe, we begin by examining what the analogy of stillness and dancing has come to mean in the context of our work. Next, we introduce ourselves by providing a brief overview of the life experiences that have led each of us to value the four qualities of leadership we have identified. Finally, we provide details on how we intentionally incorporate these qualities into our work by sharing a few examples.

The Still Point and the Dance

As T. S. Eliot drew from spiritual traditions in the writing of his poetry, the idea of a still point is fitting to our discussion here.

This still point can perhaps be understood as a hub of pure consciousness or the source from which all creation emerges. In the context of our work together, the still point has come to symbolize the intentional ways we invite spirit, presence, mindfulness, and authenticity into our practice. Often this includes shared moments of deep dialogue, stillness, silence, or reflection. But as the still point gives rise to the dance, at times our practice also includes stepping on one another's toes as an inevitable part of learning to dance.

In our writing of this chapter, the dance has come to symbolize our ways of working, relating, and being together. Dancing, particularly ballroom dancing, often involves leading and following. This analogy seems to reflect how many people perceive leadership and can be a beneficial metaphor at times. However, referring to the notion of leader versus follower can also encourage traditional and perhaps limiting patterns of thought. It has become our belief—a belief reflected in our practice—that the actions and mind-set of what we traditionally associate with following can also be considered effective leadership. Ultimately this places equal emphasis and responsibility for leadership on both leaders and followers. The focus on leadership, then, becomes the purview of the whole system. Building on the metaphor of dance, this perspective might encourage us to recognize that ballroom is not the only tradition of dance. A range of different approaches to movement might lend texture to the metaphor of leadership as dance.

For example, in our teaching, as we maximize collaboration among the learners through the structure of learning activities, we incorporate the principles of omnidirectional mentorship (Clapp, 2010), which allows us to leverage the content and experiences that we introduce, along with the wisdom that our adult learners bring to the learning environment. This approach encourages the constant sharing of knowledge back and forth among all members of the learning community. "Omnidirectional mentorship is about teaching and learning—with the roles of teacher and learner switching back and forth depending upon the situation, the particular needs of one party or the other, and the type of information being conveyed" (Clapp, 2010, p. 77). As learners motivate and encourage one another, they demonstrate this omnidirectional approach to leadership as dance.

Regardless of which kind of dance our leadership practice emulates, as we learn to dance better together, we increase our understanding that both our actions and our inactions contribute to our collective leadership. In effect, we have often found that letting go of some of our favorite dance moves (e.g., our favorite activities or scheduling preferences) has given rise to new learning and new approaches to leadership.

The Dancers: Who We Are

We are four Canadian educators who teach in a master of arts in leadership program. The university in which we teach has a well-established approach to learning and teaching adult learners, but what is significant to us is the team teaching model employed by the School of Leadership Studies. (In the graduate program where we teach, we draw from adult learning principles and refer to the students as learners. We recognize, of course, that we are all learners in this work.) This model enables four of us, working in collaboration with the program staff and full-time program directors in the school, to collectively plan and deliver an eleven-week blended learning term, which includes a two-week face-to-face intensive residency experience. The four of us have been working together in various configurations since 2011. The following sections introduce each of us as we describe some of the key influences and turning points in our lives.

Beth's Story

My journey of mindfulness began in 2000, when I was introduced to the work of Jon Kabat-Zinn and Thich Nhat Hanh as part of a four-month course on mindfulness. My participation in this course was transformational. It helped me prioritize the qualitative experience of being over the quantitative history of do, do, do that had consumed me. Each time I teach, I feel invited to dance and also to surrender my ego in service of leadership learning—my own and that of others. My practices of meditation, Reiki, and deep reflection support me as I continue my journey to spend more of my life in the present moment. I invite, but do not require, the leaders with whom I am engaging to consider the same possibility for themselves.

My influences have included mentors such as Roger Harrison, who proposed to participants attending a fireside chat to recognize that "partnerships with spirit are relevant and accessible to individuals, groups, and organizations in service of their health, effectiveness and well being" (personal communication, October 21, 2006). Another mentor, Ron Short (1998), reminded me of the importance of mindfully sharing my stories when he asserted, "When we do not take risks and share our stories, what we truly risk is that fear and mistrust will rule" (p. 11). Sharing my story as a vehicle for co-creating a moment of learning in relationship with others has been difficult, as I do not want to use precious time talking about myself. What I have learned through feedback is that my story helps other people connect to their own stories, their compassion for themselves, and ultimately their humanity as leaders.

In addition, as someone who cries at any sentimental occasion, including when I might be offering a heartfelt thanks to a group of learners, I have learned that in sharing my tears, I have given permission to others to express emotion. I have learned that despite corporate environments that have offered messages to the contrary, not only is it okay, it might be touching and sometimes inspirational to allow tears to be present as an expression of emotion. These mentors and others have modeled the importance of using all of my self as an instrument of experiential learning to facilitate transformative shifts.

Consultant Tony Petrella also helped me identify my desire to create environments that are sacred spaces for learning, being, and transformation when he asked me, "What would be possible if you viewed your work as sacred?" I am at heart a professional student who facilitates learning. The reflective question that helps me dance with grace is a simple one: How might I be of service in this learning situation?

Guy's Story

Throughout my years of studying, teaching, and practicing leadership, I have come to understand that spirit, presence, mindfulness, and authenticity are not simply considerations in leadership but rather leadership itself. During my doctoral studies, I resisted notions of duality. This resistance led me away from Enlightenment era philosophies and toward ancient wisdom traditions. In particular, I was influenced by sophisticated indigenous philosophies developed over millennia. Richard Atleo (2005), a Nuu-chah-nulth scholar, described a worldview "that is inclusive of all reality, both physical and metaphysical" (p. xi). (The Nuu-chah-nulth are First Nations peoples originating on the west coast of what is now called Vancouver Island, Canada.) "*Heshook-ish tsawalk* poses the theoretical proposition that everything is one" (p. xi). This elegant philosophical stance continues to influence my approach to leadership and leadership development.

Systems theory too is central to my understanding of leadership. In this paradigm, we see that it is not possible to understand a system simply through looking at its individual and discrete parts. Rather, we must look more holistically at the interrelationships throughout the system leading us to understand leadership not as the actions of just one individual but as patterns of interrelationships throughout the system.

I have also found that the *Tao Te Ching* holds a great deal of relevant wisdom that guides my practice. I try to resist the impulse toward incessant action, instead choosing the gentle and mindful stance of *wu wei*, which can be translated as "without action" (Needleman, 1989), and my observation has been that the notion of *wei wu wei* (action without action) is often the result. As Iain McGilchrist (2009) noted, "There is a wise passivity that enables things to come about less by what is done than by what is not done, that opens up possibility where activity closes it down" (p. 174). I have found this ancient philosophy, apparently so aligned with recent thinking in complexity science (Wheatley, 2006), directly relevant to mindful leadership.

For example, stillness in the classroom tends to inspire deeper reflections whether in the form of learners making meaning through a practice of journaling or simply through the silence that inspires dialogue. This is not taking a passive stance in my responsibility as educator, but quite the opposite: a mindful choice allowing knowledge and wisdom to emerge.

Yet I have found that today's organizations, the context within which the leadership we teach will unfold, may resist deliberate inaction. We just don't have time. We need to get more done, not less. And yet research suggests otherwise (Senge, 1990, p. 303). Senge explained that most often, the overwhelming busyness of organizational leaders is of their own making and not at all an organizational requirement. He recommended a more mindful pace and attitude toward activity: "Action will still be critical, but incisive action will not be confused with incessant activity" (p. 304).

Mark's Story

A moment of awareness: The feeling started in the pit of my stomach. It could almost be described as a wave of heat rising in my body. I was having an emotion, and I was letting go of the need to control it by allowing it to run wild in my system. I was filled with fear on this, the first time that I decided not to suppress the emotion. What would happen? Would people judge me? Was I being unprofessional? My eyes welled with tears as I released the pain I was feeling in the moment. This was the first time I had been willing to be vulnerable—to cry—in front of a group. More than twenty colleagues shared in the first real, open, and vulnerable experience of my life. I was forty-three years old.

As it turned out, I didn't collapse, and I didn't fail. My colleagues responded with support and compassion, and my relationships deepened and became stronger. The power of the moment was not lost on me. I had begun my journey to mindfulness and had tapped into the heart of authentic leadership.

Currently my work focuses on two main areas: developing strategy and high-performance organizational cultures. My projects bring me into rooms with some of Canada's brightest business minds and thought leaders. Whether we are working to mitigate the effects of climate change or create a high-performance culture at a global high-tech company, one thing is evident: authentic leadership is required. More than ever before as leaders, we must risk being vulnerable to make a real difference.

Otto Scharmer (2009) identified three enemies to developing deep authentic leadership: the voices of judgment, cynicism, and fear. To embrace authentic leadership, one must be able to overcome these enemies. Kahane (2007) encouraged leaders to be in touch with their "own assumptions, reactions, contradictions, anxieties and projections" (p. 129). When we have the courage to connect our hearts to our words and our words to our actions, we become better teachers, leaders, consultants, and friends.

At its core, leadership is about relationships. The team teaching model creates the conditions for us to teach by modeling the way (Kouzes & Posner, 2012). As in any other work environment, conflict is natural and things do go wrong (as we note later in this chapter). We know that as faculty, our work is constantly observed by learners; in essence, we work in a fishbowl. Therefore, how we handle these critical incidents and conflicts is noticed and serves to create the culture of the community. To consciously create healthy, high-performance work cultures, leaders must be fully present, mindful, authentic, and willing to risk being vulnerable. It does make a difference.

Catherine's Story

Born to a family of educators and activists, I was groomed early to engage in multiple struggles for social justice. It took years for me to reframe the idea of fighting for justice into a journey of healing and, at times, mutual learning. Pausing long enough to understand how my personal way of being, doing, and perceiving influences the people and processes around me has deepened my understanding of how self is connected to the system and how parts are connected to the whole.

Baldwin and Linnea (2010) have referred to "an inner core of preparation" (p. 40) that can enable us to become more present and better able to learn from the collective wisdom of a group in which we find ourselves. For me, ongoing practices of yoga (asana and meditation) and arts-based practices have helped to support this inner core of preparation. Taylor (2011) described mindfulness (Kabat-Zinn, 1994) and activities that stimulate right-brain thinking (Taylor, 2011) as practices that support us in tapping into emergent learning for wisdom. These include creative arts-based processes (Clover & Stalker, 2007); learning in, with, and through nature (Clover, de Oliveira-Jayme, Follen, & Hall, 2010); and embodied activities, such as sports, martial arts, and yoga. One of the purposes of these practices is to focus attention away from our mundane challenges and toward our inner experience, on nature or on a creative process, while remaining aware and open to listening with no expectations. To support my preparation as a leader and an educator, when I prepare to teach in residency I intentionally augment my practices of yoga and meditation to ground myself, seek greater clarity, move toward enhanced mindfulness, and open myself up to the learning.

In addition, scholars such as Joanna Macy (2007) have beautifully woven teachings from sacred texts into the scholarship of leadership. One teaching that has influenced me comes from the Isha Upanishad: "In dark night live those for whom the world without alone is real; in night darker still, for whom the world within alone is real. The first leads to a life of action, the second of meditation" (Easwaran, 1987, p. 209).

As a reflective practitioner, I have come to understand that a sole focus on the outside world (the "world without") does not serve to perfectly manifest desired outcomes, be they of equity, justice, harmony, compassion, or joy. Yet a complete focus on the goings on of my inner world is equally insufficient. The wisdom of this ancient text offers a balance of inner and outer work as an effective way forward, a balance I continue to learn every day.

Our Story: Reflections on the Still Point and the Dance

Earlier in this chapter, we described what spirit, presence, mindfulness, and authenticity mean to us. In the following sections, we share examples of how we weave these four qualities into our work together. In the spirit of sharing our learning, we have decided to share both the intentional ways in which we remind ourselves of our stated desire to work with these qualities and also the ways in which we have slipped away from mindful action but were able to bring ourselves back with authenticity.

Naming Our Values

As is affirmed by leadership scholars and practitioners such as Kouzes and Posner (2012), we have learned that explicitly naming our shared values is essential to our team's success. The process of planning for a residency in this faculty team begins with an in-depth conversation about the values we individually bring to the work, the values we share, the ways in which we wish to work together, and the ways in which we want to stretch and grow. It is in these early dialogues that our deep relational connections are established and these relationships serve as a foundation for our work. Our practice has been to identify our vulnerabilities while also seeking to establish high standards for our work together. These discussions of heartfelt values have served to humanize us, which has increased our respect, care, and compassion for one another. And it is this deep sense of respect that we believe allows us to be unashamedly authentic in one another's presence—a foundation in our relationship that gives rise to our frequent experience of joy.

In recent experiences, we have explicitly named skillful authenticity, presence, and mindfulness among other shared values. Naming these as values is not simply an exercise of putting words on the page. Rather, we also explored which concrete behaviors would support us in living into these values more fully. As a result, we began incorporating stillness into the curriculum and, more recently, sitting together as faculty in a morning meditation practice.

Incorporating Stillness into the Curriculum

In 2012, we began experimenting with intentional periods of silence in the classroom. When Catherine introduced this idea in a small-group seminar, we collectively observed that this quiet time created valuable space for reflection and integration. In a two-week content-heavy, process-rich program, we know there is a danger that the learners will not absorb content if they do not have sufficient time to reflect, integrate, and apply it in a meaningful way. Although perhaps this is not a new idea, the first step of creating a silent period in the busy agenda demonstrated to the learners that we valued reflection enough to move other content out of the way.

Building on this first experiment, we subsequently introduced a daily fifteen-minute personal leadership integration period into our residency schedule. During this period, learners were asked to maintain silence and choose a practice that enabled them to reflect or otherwise be with themselves and what they are experiencing in the moment. We encouraged people to walk outside (in the forest, by the ocean, or in the gardens of our campus), create using art supplies we made available, journal, meditate if they knew how to do so or wanted to learn, or undertake any other personal practice that helped them feel more connected with themselves. Learners had varied responses to this short period of silence: some reported that it was a personal stretch, while others reported that it was their favorite time of day. As instructors, we observed that committing to this short daily practice had a tremendous impact. It served as a calming mechanism in the midst of the busy pace of residency and offered opportunities for learners to share their own personal leadership practices with one other.

Morning Meditation

In our most recent team teaching experience, we chose to arrive fifteen minutes early to meditate together as faculty before our daily morning meeting. During this time, we each took turns offering a guided practice to the group. These meditations were different each day: we read excerpts from philosophy texts; walked silently through the forest; engaged in an internal scan of our breath, body, thoughts, and emotions; and chanted the student-teacher peace mantra in Sanskrit. We allowed ourselves to be playful and open and to move in and out of our comfort zones. Choosing to meditate together, even for this short period, allowed us to invite spirit, presence, mindfulness, and authenticity into our practice in a very concrete way at the beginning of each day.

We know that the discipline of spending time quietly like this, shifting the focus from a narrative view of self as the central character to a more experiential view focusing on unfolding thoughts, feelings, and sensations, has been shown to enhance concentration (Jha, 2013). Indeed, "mindfulness training uniquely builds the ability to direct attention at will through the sea of internal and external stimulation while also allowing for greater awareness of what is happening in the moment" (Jha, 2013, p. 28). Following this meditation, we noticed a significant shift in how we entered our conversations with one another; we didn't feel our usual sense of urgency to jump directly into our daily task list. We accomplished everything we needed to accomplish, of course, but with a quieter state of mind and at a more human pace.

Fumbling in the Dance

In exploring our approach to mindfulness and authenticity, it is important to recognize that things can and do go wrong. One such event occurred during a learning seminar Mark and Guy were co-facilitating. Guy had paused in his presentation, and Mark took the opportunity to add relevant points, taking the class on a tangent and away from the agenda. The additional material sparked interest and dialogue, and both Mark and the class became engaged in this new perspective. Time slipped past, and the session eventually closed without the opportunity for Guy to complete the seminar as planned. Although the new material was relevant and the seminar had been a success, Guy was feeling uncomfortable about the unplanned shift. He was willing to take a risk, and with care and compassion, he brought the topic up with Mark. Mark's reaction was immediate and genuinely apologetic. Later Mark found the opportunity, without drawing unnecessary attention to the event or himself, to be authentic, apologize to the class, and explore ways that the community might catch up on material missed.

Beth recalls another instance that exemplified how the learners we have the privilege of teaching also teach us. In this cohort, a learner had invited us all to "listen to the final period." Over the course of the residency experience, this phrase became a helpful reminder. On one occasion, I (Beth) was facilitating a plenary session with approximately fifty learners, and as I was responding to a question from one learner, I heard laughter come from the other side of the room. I responded to the laughter and then invited the class to take a break. Another learner approached me to let me know that the person had not finished with her question and that I had not listened to the final period. I thanked her for sharing her reflection with me. I followed up with the learner whom I had interrupted and apologized for not listening to the final period. When the class returned from break, I began by debriefing what had happened and expressed my appreciation for being alerted to a missed opportunity to listen to the very end of the conversation and for the opportunity to continue to learn. It was important to me to circle back to the community to share my learning, make my humanity and compassion available to myself and others, and highlight that learning is always happening in leadership.

Two final examples come from an activity we normally undertake on the first day of residency, where faculty sit in the center of the room and invite the learners to listen to the conversation that unfolds among us. The purpose of this activity is to give learners a window into our team dynamic: how we communicate with and relate to one another and how we resolve differences if they emerge. While we sometimes have a general sense of what we will discuss (e.g., our values), this fishbowl activity is never scripted. Its power comes from our ability to be authentic in the moment, to be present to whatever emerges among us, and to debrief the experience with the learners immediately afterward. On at least two occasions we have experienced friction during the fishbowl activity. On one of them, Catherine felt tension when she disagreed with the direction the conversation was taking, and on another, Mark felt discomfort with the organic approach we were exploring (we hadn't alerted the learners that we were starting the activity; we simply sat down and began a conversation). On both occasions, Catherine and Mark had the ability to identify their feelings and the willingness to name them in public, on the first day of residency, in front of forty or more virtual strangers. During the debriefing of these conversations, learners commented that at first they thought our discussion was superficial or perhaps scripted. However, when they observed tension between us and also observed how we worked through this friction compassionately with one another, they knew the experience was real and that we were being authentic. Given that we ask learners to work in teams, these experiences have provided examples of how to disagree respectfully and continue to work together joyfully to achieve shared goals.

After the Dance: Closing Thoughts

In this chapter we have offered a continuum between the still point and the dance as an analogy for leading with spirit, presence, mindfulness, and authenticity. We have shared stories and examples of how we individually and collectively invite these qualities into our leadership teaching and practice to tap into the still point. We have also provided examples of times we bumped up against one another in the dance, but were able to bring ourselves back into respectful connection by continuing to honor our stated values.

When we ask ourselves what kind of leadership is needed today, we know from our own experience that these qualities have heightened our self-awareness of the dance, that is, of the relationships and interactions among the four of us; among our learners, colleagues, and ourselves; and between each teaching experience and the whole of our practice. When we give them our attention, the behaviors associated with these qualities also have the power to reduce mindless action and infuse our work with a welcomed sense of joy. We believe that this dance of joyful leadership, as we have described it here and as we continue to learn through our ongoing interactions, offers insight into the leadership we so preciously need today.

References

Atleo, R. (2005). *Tsawalk: A Nuu-chah-nulth worldview*. Vancouver, BC: UBC Press.

Baldwin, C., & Linnea, A. (2010). *The circle way: A leader in every chair*. San Francisco: Berrett-Koehler.

Clapp, E. P. (2010). Omni-directional mentorship: Exploring a new approach to inter-generational knowledge-sharing in arts practice and administration. In D. D. Schott (Ed.), *Leading creatively: A closer look 2010* (pp. 66–79). San Francisco: National Alliance for Media, Arts, and Culture. Retrieved from http://namac.org/sites/default/files/images _upload/NAMAC-Leading_Creatively.pdf

Clover, D. E., de Oliveira-Jayme, B., Follen, S., & Hall, B. (2010). *The nature of transformation: Environmental adult education* (3rd ed.). Victoria, BC: University of Victoria.

Clover, D. E., & Stalker, J. (Eds.). (2007). *The arts and social justice: Re-crafting adult education and community cultural leadership*. Leicester, UK: NIACE.

Easwaran, E. (Trans.). (1987). *The Upanishads*. Tomales, CA: Nilgiri Press.

Eliot, T. S. (1944). *Four quartets*. London: Faber and Faber.

Grint, K. (2005). *Leadership: Limits and possibilities*. Aldershot, UK: Palgrave/ Macmillan.

Jha, A. (2013, March/April). Being in the now. *Scientific American Mind*, 24(1), 26–33.

Kabat-Zinn, J. (1994). *Wherever you go, there you are: Mindfulness meditation in everyday life*. New York: Hyperion.

Kahane, A. (2007). *Solving tough problems: An open way of talking, listening, and creating new realities* (2nd ed.). San Francisco: Berrett-Koehler.

Kouzes, J., & Posner, B. (2012). *The leadership challenge* (5th ed.). San Francisco: Jossey-Bass.

Macy, J. (2007). *World as lover, world as self: Courage for global justice and ecological renewal*. Berkeley, CA: Parallax Press.

McGilchrist, I. (2009). *The master and his emissary: The divided brain and the making of the Western world*. New Haven, CT: Yale University Press.

Needleman, J. (1989). Introduction and notes. In Lao Tsu, *Tao te ching* (Gia-Fu Feng & J. English, Trans.). New York: Vintage Books. (Original work published circa 500 BCE)

Scharmer, C. O. (2009). *Theory U: Leading from the future as it emerges*. San Francisco: Berrett-Koehler.

Senge, P. (1990). *The fifth discipline: The art and practice of the learning organization*. New York: Currency Doubleday.

Senge, P., Scharmer, C. O., Jaworski, J., & Flowers, B. S. (2004). *Presence: Human purpose and the field of the future*. Cambridge, MA: Society for Organizational Learning.

Short, R. (1998). *Learning in relationship*. Bellevue, WA: Learning in Action Technologies.

Taylor, M. M. (2011). *Emergent learning for wisdom*. New York: Palgrave Macmillan.

Wheatley, M. J. (2006). *Leadership and the new science: Discovering order in a chaotic world* (3rd ed.). San Francisco: Berrett-Koehler. (Original work published 1992)

Williamson, M. (1992). *A return to love: Reflections on the principles of "A course in miracles."* New York: HarperCollins.

Chapter Five

Why on Earth Are We Staring at Raisins?

Linda Kantor

When I was invited to teach in the executive MBA (EMBA) program at the University of Cape Town Graduate School of Business (GSB), I was at once elated and nervous. For the previous eleven years, I had been teaching Jon Kabat-Zinn's (2000) eight-week mindfulness-based stress reduction (MBSR) program, and I had observed its impact firsthand: that the simple capacity to pay attention in the present moment with both sensitivity and kindness can shift how we relate to ourselves and others.

While teaching mindfulness-based stress reduction to the general public over those years, I often asked myself what the impact would be if business leaders had a greater capacity for mindfulness. If leaders could embrace these practices, would workplace decisions and attitudes begin to reflect a greater understanding of our shared humanity? Could leaders embrace such practices? Might this greater understanding and its benefits expand out into the society at large?

I had long felt the calling to bring mindfulness-based stress reduction into leadership, having witnessed its impact on patients in my private psychotherapy practice. After leading

I acknowledge the pioneering work of Tom Ryan and my colleagues Dave Bond, Chris Breen, Millie Riviera, and, previously, Rodney and Heila Downey, all of whom have contributed to bringing mindfulness to the executive MBA program at the University of Cape Town Graduate School of Business. Thank you as well to Sherry and Trish. I am inspired by all of you.

numerous MBSR programs and training a variety of health care professionals in mindfulness-based interventions, I had seen for myself how increased mindfulness could lead to new ways of being in the world and relating to others. Moreover, having lost my marriage, partially due to the stress as my ex-husband earned his MBA, I knew well the potential damage this type of demanding program could create.

Mindfulness-based stress reduction has soared in popularity worldwide over the past thirty years due to extensive research into its effects. Completing an eight-week program in MBSR has been linked to greater resistance to the emotional and physical impacts of stress. Current neuroscientific research is compelling: mindfulness practice has been shown to lead to increased activity in regions of the brain involved in learning, memory processes, regulation of emotions, self-referential processing, and perspective taking (Hölzel et al., 2011).

After discovering MBSR, I realized that it could work well in the South African context, where stress and trauma levels are high and so, consequently, is the need for cost-effective interventions. I became convinced that I could offer no better contribution to South Africa's ongoing journey of healing than teaching mindfulness skills to its leaders. South Africa's transformation over the past two decades has been nothing short of extraordinary, and yet the country's legacy of apartheid and the resulting ongoing socioeconomic disparities continue to weigh heavily on it. The impacts of violence, poverty, disease, and corruption are evident. For me, teaching mindfulness to leaders suggested the possibility of a trickle-down effect: mindful leadership could lead to mindful corporations, educational institutions, governmental and political organizations, and health care systems.

In South Africa, the concept of Ubuntu (interconnectivity) is well understood as a social touchstone. As Archbishop Tutu (2009) explained, "A person with Ubuntu is open and available to others, affirming of others, does not feel threatened that others are able and good, based from a proper self-assurance that comes from knowing that he or she belongs in a greater whole and is diminished when others are humiliated or diminished, when others are tortured or oppressed or treated as if they were less than who they are" (p. 35).

Nelson Mandela (1994) echoed Tutu's sentiment: "A traveller through a country would stop at a village and he didn't have to ask for food or for water. Once he stops, the people give him food and attend to him. That is one aspect of Ubuntu, but it will have various aspects. Ubuntu does not mean that people should not enrich themselves. The question therefore is: Are you going to do so in order to enable the community around you to be able to improve?" In the new South Africa, although many individuals and organizations are vibrantly engaged in active citizenship, much more is needed to heal the country's deep emotional scars. Mindfulness can reinforce the Ubuntu principles of interconnectedness and community.

The University of Cape Town GSB is set in one of the most picturesque parts of the city, close to the upscale waterfront district and with backdrops of sea and mountain. The school is housed in a converted prison, a powerful symbol of how education can break the shackles of ignorance. Archbishop Tutu has described South Africa as the "Rainbow Nation," which is echoed by the school's motto: "Full-Color Thinking."

From the waterfront, one can see Robben Island, another important symbol of South African history as the place where Nelson Mandela spent most of his twenty-seven years in prison. Mandela's history is an important legacy; any student who earns the EMBA within the context of this difficult history is helping to heal the pain of the nation's tumultuous past. South Africa is still integrating the impact of its past, and at GSB, students raised in poverty and lacking in human rights study next to students brought up in a world of privilege, a dichotomy based solely on skin color.

As an ancillary note, although I am a PhD student at the GSB, most of my peers—myself included—are interested in the practical applications of our work and look to our research to support those applications. Other PhD models are more purely academic, with less focus on real-world applications. I mention this in the South African context, where there is a strong motivation to bring healing and transformation.

I was passionate about mindfulness and its practical impacts, and I was also interested in its value within the context of South African leadership. I felt ready to teach at the EMBA program— or so I thought.

The Quest and the Test

My first year of teaching was the hardest I have ever encountered. I realized quickly that my expectation that students would welcome the ideas in the midst of a demanding, competitive, complex course that was fraught with personal dynamics was unrealistic. I began teaching mindfulness at the GSB thinking that I could simply adapt Kabat-Zinn's (2000) MBSR program. In retrospect, I might have engaged in more mindful reflection before introducing students to lengthy mindfulness practices and open-ended inquiry about the practices.

Kabat-Zinn developed his program thirty years ago, using mindfulness practices to help people who suffered from chronic and life-threatening medical conditions. I was used to working with individuals who were motivated to explore mindfulness practices. MBSR program participants have often been diagnosed with medical or psychological conditions and have realized the need to live a deeper, slower, more mindful existence. People joining MBSR programs learn a range of mindfulness practices. They understand that they will be encouraged to practice for between forty and sixty minutes daily, leading up to one full day of silent practice during week 6 of the program. In the case of training health care professionals, students already have an interest in the subject and are themselves driven to teach mindfulness.

The EMBA candidates' motivations were different from those of other groups I had taught. The EMBA program is an intense, highly demanding experience, with deadlines for assignments, group work, and presentations. The two-year course is designed to enable senior executives to make decisions from within complex situations using learning techniques that harness their critical thinking abilities and develop their theoretical understanding of management concepts. Most students attend the program while working at demanding jobs and maintaining family lives. Moreover, students come from a broad diversity of racial and cultural backgrounds.

The program was structured into three modules per year. I was assigned lecturing slots at the beginning and end of each module. Tom Ryan, the program director, decided that it would be useful to begin and end modules with mindfulness teaching and practice. During the modules, students would practice guided mindfulness at the end of each day using a CD recording as a guide. The mindfulness component was already unique in two ways. First, all students were invited to attend as an integral part of their experience, and they were encouraged to attend the class even if they struggled with the concept of mindfulness or the practice. This course is a prerequisite part of their two-year EMBA journey. Second, in addition to being taught the theory of mindfulness as it was emerging in some of the organizational literature (Langer & Moldveanu, 2000; Weick, Sutcliff, & Obstfeld, 1999), students would engage in meditative practice on campus. They were also given recordings of the practices to use between modules. Another difference from my regular eight-week MBSR program was that I would see students intermittently over two years instead of regularly over eight weeks.

Although I was concerned initially about students being required to participate, I rationalized that when I was at school,

I had to take subjects that I did not enjoy, and so I assumed that these students would accept mindfulness study just as I had accepted the courses I had to take. I was breathtakingly naive. I encountered some of the strongest resistance I have ever confronted. Students' responses ranged from personal attacks on me as the instructor ("Why can't we get someone else to teach this?"), to resistance to some of the materials I used in the program ("Does Rumi's poem 'The Guest House' imply that Satan is the unexpected visitor?" [Rumi, Moyne, & Barks, 1994]), to opposition to the brain science behind mindfulness theory ("What if I don't believe in evolution and that the brain evolves?"), to complaints that mindfulness practice was simply a poor use of their valuable time.

After the initial shock of their resistance wore off, I realized that I could put the feedback I had received to constructive use by using it as a growth opportunity, reflecting deeply on the messages behind the feedback and asking myself some important questions: What was I there to teach? Why? What did these students need? How could I impart something of practical value while honoring my own sense of what the world needs: slowing down, moving into the heart, and building leaders who are compassionate and wise? How could I find common ground with what had brought these students to the program: a drive to become more effective leaders, build new skills, be more productive, and earn more money?

It took me a while to digest the feedback, which was that much harder due to the anonymous nature of student evaluations; I had no idea where the comments were coming from. I decided to stay close to my vision of leaders who discover their innate wholeness and cultivate and value these practices so that their actions come from the clarity and wisdom of presence. My challenge was to turn what I had been teaching in Kabat-Zinn's MBSR program into something that was relevant to my students while maintaining integrity with the deep wisdom inherent in mindfulness practice.

Fortunately, the program director was not swayed by my students' strongly negative feedback. Rather, he increased my time with them. I was surprised, thinking that perhaps he should have me there less frequently. He believed that the benefits of the process we were beginning might not become apparent for five or ten years; we should not stop simply because of the students' initial resistance.

Interestingly, despite students' reluctance at the beginning, during my second year of teaching, the staff observed that students appeared to be less stressed than in previous classes and the group dynamics were less intense. I continued to teach, at first with uncertainty, then gaining more strength and resolve over time. At first, close friends and colleagues were concerned by my willingness to continue. However, I felt compelled to do so, no matter what the outcome. The shift for me was to reflect deeply and know my insecurities and embrace them. I began to view criticism as an opportunity to stand strong for what I believed in and yet not get lost in my own ego.

I began using Marshall Rosenberg's (2003) nonviolent communication model as part of a lesson. Using Rosenberg's four steps—observe, feeling, needs, requests—underpinned by the attitudes of honesty and empathy, I opened up to the class about how saddened and frustrated I was at reading their feedback. I reflected on my need to contribute to them as leaders and to connect with them more effectively. Although something in the class shifted at this point, I believe I was too far along to have established so little trust from many of them.

Hitting the right note in the mindful leadership module, as I called it, has been a work in progress. Slowly, however, the ingredients of the course have come together.

Opening and Learning

Over time I began to hear more about the ways in which students were using and appreciating mindfulness practices.

To quote one student, "The journey that had started with open-ness to new things, followed by measures of skepticism and curiosity, has culminated in a level of awareness of myself and of others that I am hugely appreciative of, and which makes me feel like more of a whole person than I had previously ever experienced in my life." Another student approached me one day and said, "You know, when you had that first class with us and we spent all that time gazing at a raisin, I thought, 'What the heck does this raisin have to do with an MBA? I paid a lot of money for this course.' But I can see now that if I can't look with clarity at a raisin, what am I missing everywhere else? What am I missing about my kids growing up?"

I noticed one day while teaching students walking medita-tion in the school's central courtyard that somehow their slow walking brought a sense of slowing down to other students watching them. A student who had been struggling with the practice suddenly remarked one day, "You know, when I noticed the seagulls and heard them calling overhead, I felt such grati-tude and joy to be in this school." One of my students, a finan-cial manager, told me that he now begins all of his meetings by asking his employees to put away their cell phones and play with some play dough for a while, just noticing the shapes and tex-tures. "Our meetings are so much more creative now," he said.

The shift has been slow and subtle, made possible only by keeping the program going, being open to feedback, and know-ing that teaching mindful leadership to EMBA students is the ultimate mindfulness practice for me. Can I as a teacher remain embodied? Can I stay in my heart? Can I develop the resilience and energy I need to stay present with a large group of students (this year's group has more than fifty students in some mindful-ness sessions)? With larger groups, how do I impart the practices in a context that is safe for sharing? Can I be open to walking into the classroom with my lesson plan and be willing to do something completely different if that is what unfolds?

As the program director had predicted, years later, students from the first group contacted me, acknowledging the impact of the practices. "I'm glad that the GSB has given us the opportunity to be exposed and know the practice, and I hope your current students do not give you as much grief as we did." One student met with me for tea and told me that at the time, she did not understand what I was teaching, but she is beginning to see how she had been running from her feelings and was unable to slow down.

Shafika Isaacs, an EMBA student during the first year that I taught, wrote her dissertation on what she termed the "voyage of mindfulness" in the program (Isaacs, 2010). She explored how and why some of the students benefited from the mindfulness sessions while others did not. She described her daily sitting sessions as follows: "When asked what they thought of the meditation sessions, four told me that it was a waste of time, that they used the time to sleep, and that they did not see the point of it all. Others said they were suspect of the Buddhist connotations. Some used the time to pray, and others said they were open-minded about it. Four diligent types said they were hooked and have been meditating ever since" (Isaacs, 2010, p. 3). She concluded that "the majority, if not all, responded positively to the teaching of the course." Her diagram, figure 5.1, describes how mindfulness is a core competency in the EMBA process. She wrote: "I realized that if one considers the EMBA10 program in its entirety, the course on Mindfulness and its associated attributes and skills that it intends to impart correspond to a host of other courses with similar learning outcomes in mind."

Isaacs's comments were instructive for me. I realized that despite my struggles in figuring out how to get the information across in this unique context, somehow my students had recognized that the practice was valuable and that mindfulness was central to what they were doing in other aspects of the program.

Figure 5.1 Interlinking Attributes

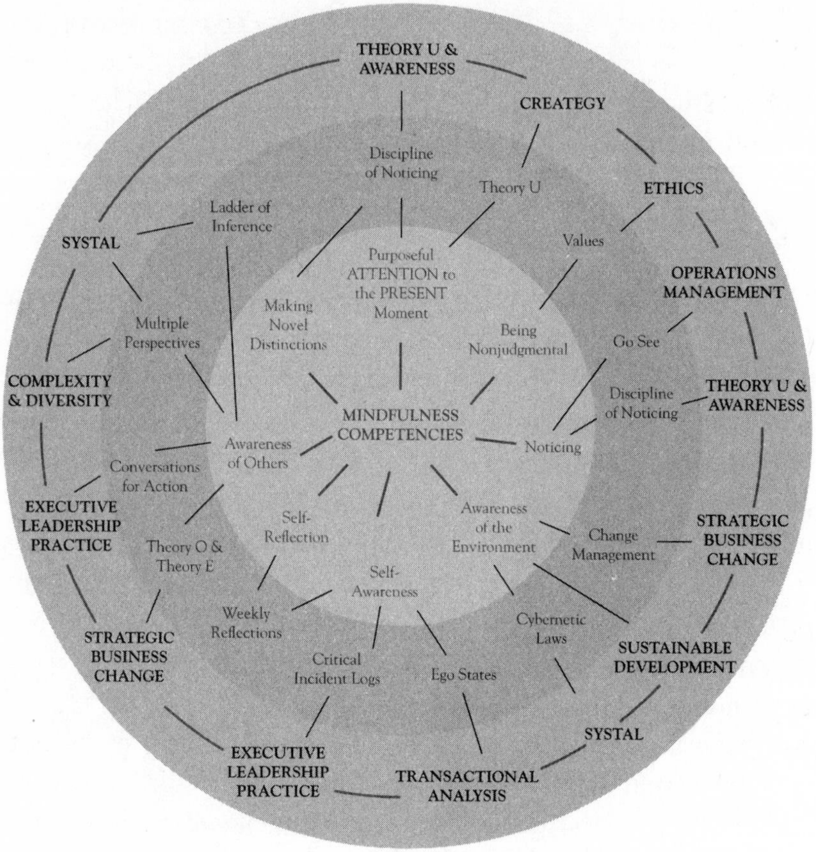

Note: Theory E has a focus on the creation of economic value, formal, structure, and systems. Theory O focuses on the development of human capacity to implement change and to learn from change. Systal is an information technology that provides solutions for various business challenges.

Rainer Maria Rilke (1981) wrote, "How could we forget those ancient myths that stand at the beginning of all races—the myths about dragons that at the last moment are transformed into princesses? Perhaps all the dragons in our lives are only princesses waiting for us to act just once with beauty and courage. Perhaps everything that frightens us is, in its deepest essence, something hopeless that wants our love." My own personal dragons of fear, doubt, and insecurity were being transformed by the commitment to make the work an act of love.

Growing

Mindfulness training as part of a stressful MBA program is a work in progress, and I am constantly learning and adapting. For example, students would often fall asleep during long practice sessions from sheer fatigue (some students called it the "sleep class"). I began focusing on short practice breaks that could be used anytime, especially at times of stress, before a stressful confrontation or on hearing difficult feedback, for example. Formal practice sessions are shorter than in traditional MBSR due to the difficulty of sitting still for extended periods. I found that MBA students' levels of agitation and restlessness were typically higher than those of students in my MBSR groups and concluded that it is easier to start with shorter practices and then lengthen them over time.

The way in which I frame the lesson is also important. For example, MBA students wanted to know that the practice would have some efficacy in their lives; hence, describing the brain science early on was helpful. Reviewing the physiology and neuroscience of stress also helps make the practice relevant regardless of any individual's underlying spiritual beliefs or practices.

My first-year students engage in a range of mindfulness practices and are encouraged to take time daily to practice, including yoga, body scan, walking meditation, and sitting meditation. Practice ranges from ten to twenty minutes, and, at the request of some of my students, I am working on a second CD that they can use in their second year, with longer practices, including a loving-kindness practice. The CD material emphasizes the informal aspect of mindfulness practice: Do they notice when they are on autopilot? Are they aware what gives them energy and what depletes them?

In the first year, the goal is to learn to sit with oneself, which I frame as an act of courage and compassion. We explore what it means to be in the body and to feel embodied. I found that students enjoyed the teachings inherent in the yoga postures. For example, what does it feel like to push into warrior pose? What does it feel like to relax into it? Where does one's sense of power and strength originate? In tree pose, what does it mean to be balanced and aware? What makes us lose our balance? In cat/cow, what happens if we lift up one arm and extend it out to the next person? Does this motivate a desire for more space or a need to be even closer? We explore bringing presence to enjoyable events, and students are encouraged to notice and track pleasant moments. This is the start of learning how to be with what is unpleasant as it arises with a degree of equanimity and wisdom.

Students explore stress and come to understand that their neurobiology can often dictate how they approach stress and conflict in their lives. In sitting practice, they explore opening to the moment more fully, noticing in particular how they react to difficult moments and how to manage the mind with more skill and compassion.

Year 2 is a journey into exploring mindfulness in relationship to others. Students have spent the first year cultivating some sense of inner awareness. What if they bring this awareness outside the body and to their relationships with others? What happens when we have to give or receive difficult feedback? How do we stand steady in those moments? How do we deliver messages nonviolently? The meditation practice is for students to observe themselves in relationships. I use Rosenberg's (2003) nonviolent communication model intensively in the second year as "training wheels" to help students communicate with more awareness, honesty, and empathy.

At first, there was no assignment for the mindful leadership part of the course, and this may have contributed to participants' not taking it seriously. I believe that the invitation for me to grade students' reflection papers has helped in this regard. The reflection paper prompts students to explore and reflect on how they apply all of what they are learning in the program, including mindfulness theory and practice in the context of their lives.

Mindfulness practice develops certain qualities, which we explore at the end of the program. Without realizing it, throughout the practices the students have cultivated the attitudes of mindfulness as delineated by Kabat-Zinn (2000): patience, loving kindness, compassion, letting go, nonstriving, acceptance, trust, and equanimity. These are hardly qualities that one would expect to learn in an MBA program, especially in a country where violence is rife and the destructive legacy of apartheid can still be felt.

Home Is Wherever You Are

I teach students that "home" is always in the here and now. Home is a place inside you that is available moment to moment. Five years later, I remain grateful for the opportunity to teach students who are challenging, open, curious, and on a journey of profound growth. The work of the EMBA is much more than students learning about business; it is about their becoming active citizens. My role is to remind them that they are citizens of their own bodies, hearts, and minds first. If they can inhabit the present moment with more grace, compassion, and self-awareness, it will spill over to other moments.

In the ancient poem "The Guesthouse," the Sufi poet Rumi teaches us how "this being human is a guesthouse, every moment a new arrival." He encourages us to welcome all experiences, "even if it is a crowd of sorrows who empty your house clean, still treat each guest honourably, he may be clearing you out for some new delight" (Rumi et al., 1994, p. 41).

My own capacity to enter the crucible of teaching—coping with students' challenges, probing questions, and sometimes strong resistance—has flourished. It has been a lesson for me in trusting myself and my path even when resistance from those around me is strong. The value of a supportive and visionary leader is clear. The EMBA program director's belief in the mindfulness practices and the permission he gave me to create a mindfulness program for his students modeled for me leadership that was strong and willing to explore something new and different. I am supported by the other lecturers in the program who are involved in the personal growth side, who believe in and embrace mindfulness and use it in their own ways in their teachings as well.

I recall asking Tenzin Palmo, a Buddhist teacher who spent twelve years in a cave in the Himalayas, three of them in silent retreat, when she was speaking in Cape Town, "What do you think is the most important thing I can teach business students?" She looked at me and answered without hesitation, "Teach them to be kind."

Perhaps as we all learn to stand strong and open-hearted in the seasons of our lives, we can embody a model of leadership that is true to Ubuntu, for a kind of leadership that embodies heartfulness. South Africa had no better teacher of this than the beloved Nelson Mandela, whose understanding of interbeing was such that he could state that "the oppressor must be liberated just as surely as the oppressed. . . . For to be free is not merely to cast off one's chains, but to live in a way that respects and enhances freedom of others" (Mandela, 1994, p. 202).

The Dalai Lama refers to the importance of developing a "universal responsibility," that is, a deep concern for all human beings. The understanding that we are all dependent on each other is critical to overcoming the world's problems. The outlook that true individual happiness comes from the capacity to serve not only ourselves but others can develop only when we are able to work with the tendency of the mind to compare, compete, and judge. Practices that cultivate presence and heart connection may give rise to a more humane world, where issues of economy, environment, and energy are considered from a space of deeper understanding of our interconnectedness.

References

Hölzel, B. K., Carmody, J., Vangel, M., Congleton, C., Yerramsetti, S., Gard, T., & Lazar, S. W. (2011). Mindfulness practice leads to increases in regional gray matter density. *Psychiatry Research: Neuroimaging, 191*(1), 36–43.

Isaacs, S. (2010). *Breath by breath: Awakening to mindfulness on voyage EMBA 10*. Doctoral dissertation, University of Cape Town.

Kabat-Zinn, J. (2000). *Full catastrophe living: Using mindfulness in stress, pain and illness*. New York: Dell.

Langer, E. J., & Moldveanu, M. (2000). The construct of mindfulness. *Journal of Social Issues, 56*(1), 1–10.

Mandela, N. (1994). *The illustrated long walk to freedom*. London: Little, Brown.

Rilke, R. M. (1981). *Selected poems of Rainer Maria Rilke*. New York: Harper.

Rosenberg, M. (2003). *Nonviolent communication: A language of life*. Encinitas, CA: PuddleDancer Press.

Rumi, M., Moyne, J., & Barks, C. (1994). *Say I am you: Poetry interspersed with stories of Rumi and Shams*. Athens, GA: Maypop.

Tutu, D. (1999). *No future without forgiveness*. London: Rider.

Weick, K. E., Sutcliff, K. M., & Obstfeld, D. (1999). Organising for high reliability: Processes of collective mindfulness. In R. S. Sutton & B. M. Staw (Eds.), *Research in organizational behaviour, 21* (pp. 81–123). Greenwich, CT: Jai Press.

Chapter Six

Intergroup Dialogue

Mindfulness and Leadership Development for Social Change

Brighid Dwyer, Ralph A. Gigliotti, Hanna H. Lee

Through encouraging active self-reflection, dialogue, and collaboration, higher education institutions can support students in becoming confident and aware global citizens and leaders (Wagner, 2011). This chapter showcases Villanova University's Intergroup Relations (IGR) program, specifically focusing on the dialogue courses as a unique interdisciplinary initiative for integrating mindfulness and authentic leadership development. Thus far, IGR has been contextualized primarily as a social justice initiative, although to truly attend to social justice on university campuses, students must also be engaged in their own work that is centered on personal awareness and reflection. By analyzing Villanova's IGR program, this chapter discusses how intergroup dialogue contributes to student leadership development through the practice of mindfulness. Drawing on the mission of our institution, Veritas, Unitas, and Caritas (Truth, Unity, and Love), Villanova's IGR program helps develop and sustain true community through fostering authentic dialogue. Through an emphasis on dialogue in interpersonal relationships, the IGR initiatives at Villanova equip students with critical skills for effectively navigating their leadership experiences on campus and beyond.

Developing a greater understanding of difference during the collegiate years is essential. Most students come to college from highly segregated communities and high schools (Orfield, 2001; Orfield & Eaton, 2003; Orfield, Frankenberg, & Lee, 2003); as a result, students from all racial backgrounds often have their first interaction with diverse peers upon entering college. It is therefore highly likely that violent assaults in the form of microaggressions and the chilly climate that underrepresented students experience on college campuses are due to students' inexperience with diverse others (Yeung, Spanierman, & Landrum-Brown, 2013). An effective response to these acts of discord centers on dialogue. As Bohm (1996) suggests,

> If each one of us can give full attention to what is actually "blocking" communication while he is also attending properly to the content of what is communicated, then we may be able to create something new between us, something of very great significance for bringing to an end the at present insoluble problems of the individual and of society. (p. 4)

In intergroup dialogue (IGD) classes, facilitators attend to a number of structural blockers that disrupt dialogue, including societal inequity, privilege, and power structures. By participating in IGD, students are challenged to consider their biases as they engage in thoughtful dialogue. As the course progresses, students begin to deeply consider diverse viewpoints and critically reflect on their core beliefs and values. Consistent with Bohm's work, these moments of authentic dialogue have the potential to heal social inequities and make whole the fragments of our everyday experiences.

The Intergroup Relations and Dialogue Program at Villanova

Intergroup dialogue was developed at the University of Michigan as a social justice program to promote interaction and dialogue with diverse others (Zúñiga, Nagda, Chesler, & Cytron-Walker, 2007). IGD engages students in learning that involves understanding social identities and group-based inequalities, encourages building of cross-group relationship, and cultivates social responsibility. Thus, intergroup dialogue fosters engagement that is intellectual and affective, self-reflective and in dialogic relation with others, personal and structural, and that connects dialogue to action. (Zúñiga et al., p. 3)

Villanova's IGR program, modeled after that of the University of Michigan, is based on dialogic communication in which students "actively participate in jointly constructing both the meaning and process of building relationships across and within differences" (Gurin, Nagda, & Zúñiga, 2013, p. 45). Intergroup dialogue courses became part of the curriculum at Villanova in 2011 and have expanded into an intergroup relations program with co-curricular and social components. The Villanova IGR initiative was developed to engage students in authentic communication between peers of different backgrounds.

Villanova is a midsized Catholic institution located in suburban Philadelphia. As a predominantly White institution, it is invested in preparing students to live, work, and serve in a global society that is more racially and culturally diverse than the typical Villanova classroom. As a Catholic University grounded in the teachings and ideals of St. Augustine, Villanova is called to foster a community that lives in harmony with God and one's neighbor. The IGR program has supported the university to more fully realize its mission of service and inclusion.

All elements of the university reflect the centrality of Veritas, Unitas, and Caritas. According to its mission statement, "the University community welcomes and respects members of all faiths who seek to nurture a concern for the common good and who share an enthusiasm for the challenge of responsible and productive citizenship in order to build a just and peaceful world" (Villanova University, 2013, paragraph 2). Our Catholic identity lies at the core of who we are as an institution, and dialogue occupies an important role in the development and sustainability of our community by creating a sacred space for shared meaning and mutual understanding among those of diverse backgrounds.

Villanova's IGD classes are focused on creating understanding relationships among people from different social, economic, racial, and ethnic groups and "building substantive relationships between and within groups" (Gurin et al., 2013, p. 44). Communication skills related to careful listening and meaningful dialogue are cultivated among students. Villanova's IGD courses are one credit and can fulfill a diversity requirement in the College of Liberal Arts and Sciences. Each class is intentionally designed to support diverse perspectives and ideas. This is accomplished by balancing the social identities of students such that there is (as close to) equal representation in the class from a privileged group and an underrepresented group. A class on gender, for example, would ideally have five women and five men to help balance the power differential. Critical mass theory has shown that there is strength in numbers and those from marginalized identities are more likely to be vocal and honest when they are not the lone representative of their social identity group (Kanter, 1977). IGD classes are coordinated by two faculty facilitators who guide students through the four-stage model where they get to know one another and build trust (stage 1), practice careful listening and other communication skills as they begin to share personal experiences (stage 2), discuss contemporary or hot topics on campus or in the media (stage 3), and finally move into being an effective ally as they take action (stage 4) (Zúñiga & Nagda, 2001).

This model allows a deeper conceptualization and operationalization of dialogue for student participants and encourages them to reflect on their involvement in the cultivation of dialogic relationships. For Bohm and Peat (1987), "dialogue can be considered as a free flow of meaning between people in communication, in the sense of a stream that flows between banks" (p. 241). Borrowing from their imagery, the free flow of dialogue requires both intentionality and resilience in flowing between, over, and under the banks of one's interpersonal experiences. This image of a free-flowing stream may also provide a useful illustration of working through obstacles that disrupt the stream of dialogue. In addressing these systemic obstacles, students in the program are expected to complete courses with a sense of engagement in social justice leading toward action. In addition, we expect students will develop a willingness to intervene amid conflict and social injustice and serve as an ally to others. As the myriad obstacles to dialogue attempt to disrupt the flow of meaning, the four-stage model provides students with a useful conceptual framework for cultivating meaningful dialogue.

Villanova's dialogue program also reflects Buber's (1947) work on "the between" and Arnett and Arneson's (1999) emphasis on dialogic civility. Dialogue is a rare occurrence that highlights the interdependent nature of social relationships. It presents an opportunity for two individuals to focus their attention on the "between persons" in a given communicative moment. This conceptualization of the between aligns nicely with this current integration of mindfulness and authentic leadership. Dialogue emerges when two individuals, through an appreciation and deep respect for what the other has to offer, can both be heard despite the distractions of everyday life. This notion of the between speaks to those profound and rare moments when two individuals or groups encounter the space between "me" and "you" where there is common understanding, mutual respect, and genuine inclusion of the other.

As noted earlier, true community hinges on effective dialogue. As Bohm and Peat suggest, when engaging in free dialogue, two or more people with equal status observe the following principles: they listen to each other with detachment, suspend opinion and judgment, allow the free flow of thought and feeling, and accept and appreciate differing beliefs or understanding. The four-stage model of dialogue walks students through this interactive process and orients them toward an authentic understanding of the other. Particularly in the context of our Catholic institution, dialogue equips individuals with the ability to manage difference and fragmentation in a respectful, productive, caring, and mutually beneficial manner. Truth, unity, and love are brought to life in those moments of authentic dialogue. Just as individuals become more whole as they open themselves up to dialogic relationships, communities also thrive when groups of individuals seek mutual understanding. Authentic dialogue breathes life into any community, and as the next section offers, a deliberate approach to cultivating dialogue can extend internal and external peace beyond the walls of Villanova.

Intergroup Dialogue and Nonviolent Communication

Villanovans can serve the campus community more justly by acting as peacemakers and reducing the psychological violence that undergirds many underrepresented students' college experiences. Intergroup dialogue is an effective tool for reducing prejudice on college campuses and encouraging positive intergroup interactions (Gurin & Nagda, 2006). Allport's (1954) and Pettigrew's (1998) research outlines the conditions necessary for optimal intergroup contact: (1) equal group status within the setting, (2) individuals with common goals, (3) opportunities for intergroup cooperation, (4) support from authorities, and (5) the opportunity to become friends. All five of these conditions are met in Villanova's IGD courses. IGD courses provide supportive environments for students from different racial backgrounds to interact cross-racially in a way that promotes intensive dialogue and greater understanding across difference.

Over the past several decades, scholars have investigated the prevalence, effects, and consequences of microaggressions on the body and psyche of people of color (Feagin & McKinney,

2003; Steele, 1997; Sue et al., 2008; Sue & Constantine, 2008; Smith, Allen, & Danley, 2007). Solórzano, Ceja, and Yosso (2000) define microaggressions as "subtle insults (verbal, non-verbal, and/or visual) directed toward people of color, often automatically or unconsciously" (p. 60). The effects of microaggressions include a range of coping strategies, including avoidance, aggravation, resentment, fatigue, emotional withdrawal, hostility, and combative behavior (Smith, Allen, & Danley, 2007). IGD is one way higher education institutions can bring awareness to psychological violence and social injustice and help students become cognizant of microaggressions. In IGD courses, students become aware of how their unconscious everyday actions and speech may have a deleterious effect on others so that they can change their behaviors and serve as allies. By introducing these ideas and practices to students, we can lessen the violence that marginalized students experience on a daily basis and support students in becoming ethically and emotionally intelligent leaders.

Through the process of self-inquiry and self-understanding in IGD, students have the opportunity to develop inner peace and end violence within themselves and their communities. IGD cultivates speaking and listening with compassion, which are essential mindfulness practices of nonviolent communication (Nhat Hanh, 2003). Becoming aware of one's fears, prejudices, and insecurities through ongoing reflection and being awake and attentive to oneself, others, and the environment are foundational to effective leadership (Rogers, 2003; Boyatzis & McKee, 2005). By supporting students in developing self-awareness and social consciousness, IGD prepares them to be effective leaders in a complex, global society.

Mindfulness and Intergroup Dialogue

Mindfulness can be defined as "the awareness that emerges through paying attention on purpose, in the present moment, and nonjudgmentally to the unfolding of experience moment by moment" (Kabat-Zinn, 2003, p. 145). Within modern Western societies that often devalue "the present moment in favor of perpetual distraction, self-absorption, and addiction to the feeling of progress," this simple yet profound concept of moment-to-moment awareness is challenging to embrace (Kabat-Zinn, 2003, p. 147). In particular, college students in the United States face daily stressors and distractions from academic pressures, social interactions, technology, and social media, making the practice of mindfulness even more critical to their learning and development. Today's university students will be entering a global society that requires critical thinking, cultural competence, and leadership skills that are rooted in compassion, mutual understanding, and openness to address numerous challenging social problems. With a focus on openness, acceptance, nonjudgment, and compassion, mindfulness is a practice that supports students in developing a strong sense of self that leads to a deeper insight and understanding of themselves and others.

IGD cultivates mindfulness by encouraging students to engage with one another and be fully present throughout the experience. At the beginning of each course, students and facilitators establish a set of shared ground rules, and facilitators intentionally put forward the agreement that every member be fully present during each session. In addition, part of the student's grade is participation, which is defined as thoughtful reflection on the perspectives of classmates and the respectful sharing of insights and experiences. Students' participation is assessed by their demonstration of active listening, asking questions that create understanding, and respectful communication that honors their peers' experiences. Meaningful participation enhances the quality of the dialogue between students that leads to a stronger awareness and understanding of themselves, their experiences, and their peers.

The mindfulness values of nonjudgment, openness, acceptance, and understanding are established in the first class session and reiterated and modeled by facilitators throughout the course to foster honest dialogue and insight-driven experiences around issues of power, privilege, and difference. Dialogue is cultivated through honoring silence during each session and allowing students to process, observe, and experience their emotions and thoughts rather than be reactive to each other. Deep listening exercises are used to give each person an opportunity to share without interruption. In one exercise, for example, students are asked to take at least thirty seconds before responding to what has been communicated. We encourage students to bring all of their awareness to what is being shared instead of partially listening and simultaneously formulating an argument in their mind. This practice of deep listening in IGD is the practice of mindfulness, enabling students to develop an understanding of and compassion for their peers and themselves. By providing the structure for mindful listening and compassionate speaking, students are able to process and reflect on their emotions and thoughts without judgment. Through mindful listening, students are then able to ask mindful questions to help them grow in their understanding of their peers' experiences and views.

Facilitators often model mindful listening to students by providing language for asking questions that demonstrate curiosity, openness, and nonjudgment—for example:

- Can you help me understand this situation better?
- What point of view has not been expressed in the classroom so far?
- Who or what else do we need to consider as part of this dialogue?
- How can that be said in a way that someone else can hear and understand how that affects you?

Reflecting on questions helps students broaden their notions of truth and lessen the emotional and psychosocial harm that can be inflicted by the careless use of words.

After deeply sharing and listening to personal experiences around power, privilege, and difference, many students express how they now see the underlying assumptions, beliefs, and dominant norms behind interactions of people with different social identities. Students see these differentials everywhere on their campus and in their local communities. "The goal of mindfulness is to develop a life-style of participating with awareness" (Linehan, 1993, p. 66), which allows a person to approach each moment of daily living with a continuity of awareness (Kabat-Zinn, 2003).

Through IGD, students develop a fuller awareness of their emotions, prejudices, assumptions, and behaviors from their classroom experiences that provides a new critical lens in which they observe and experience everyday interactions. Many times students experience discomfort or even emotional pain through deepening their understanding of their social identities and the experiences of people who are different from themselves. However, "with the energy of mindfulness, we can overcome our pain and use loving speech" (Nhat Hanh, 2003, p. 22). In telling their stories and being heard, valued, and understood, students experience a powerful connection to themselves, their history, and their communities that is healing and transformative. Such transformation is illustrated in the experience of Murielle, who participated in a gender dialogue course:

> When I began IGR . . . I did not expect . . . to discuss class dialogues with my housemates for hours after each Sunday. I did not expect I would change the way I talk about women and men and others. I also did not realize how much I myself perpetuate sexism. . . . But as I said on the last day, I really do grow the most when I feel ambivalence. . . . I hope to continue to challenge my own and others' ideas about gender and stop perpetuating sexism and begin to perpetuate equality.

Listening deeply to another's suffering requires one to embrace and transform one's own hurt and anger first, particularly in the face of differing viewpoints or beliefs (Nhat Hanh, 2003). Prior to taking this course, Murielle was unaware that her interactions with men and women reflected dominant cultural norms. For example, she commonly used *ladies* when referring to her high school and college friends. To Murielle and many other participants in this gender course, the term seemed innocuous. After classmates and facilitators described how *ladies* made them feel demeaned and acting "lady-like" limited their agency as women, she understood that using the term *lady* was hurtful to some people. With this understanding, Murielle decided that she would no longer use this term and would promote the use of *women* in its place. During the course, she recognized how she unconsciously participated in sexism through her use of language and understood how this language can be hurtful to her own gender. Through dialogue, she wrestled with her thoughts and feelings and arrived at a place where she listened authentically, responded with empathy, and changed her actions.

Through these transformative mindfulness exercises and experiences, students in IGD courses cultivate critical leadership skills. Owen (2011) asserts that critical reflection is essential in designing a leadership learning environment that supports students in the discipline of reflective practice. This sentiment has been captured by Yukl (2006): "Before one can be a successful leader, it is necessary to reconnect with one's feelings, confront the latent fears, and resolve the underlying conflicts" (p. 407). In intergroup dialogue, we seek to awaken students to these ideas and concepts that may be latent within themselves. For example, through the "hopes and fears" exercise that engages students in what they hope to gain and what they fear by being in a space where they discuss their experiences, we bring students to a place of reflection, self-awareness, and honesty they do not often experience in college. At the start of her race dialogue course,

Gillian, a White student, expressed her thoughts about her racial identity and her hopes for the class. She stated,

> I have to be honest. . . . I realize now that the problem is that I don't understand my own racial identity, and it is not really all that important to me. All of my life I have been in the majority and just checked the box "Caucasian" without thinking too much about it. . . . I hope to be better able to define my racial identity [by the end of these classes].

Throughout IGD courses, students are invited to explore in depth who they are and what has shaped their beliefs, values, and perspectives. Such exploration allows them to better understand themselves and people from different social and cultural backgrounds. By the end of the race class, Gillian had a very different perspective on her racial identity:

> I cannot believe what I wrote in my first paper. My thinking has changed so much because of this class and the insights that I've gained from my classmates as well as facilitators. My understanding of my own race has been developed. . . . I did not realize all of the ways being of the majority race has given me advantages in life. . . . It really wasn't until I heard some of the stories of blatant discrimination among my classmates and [facilitators] that I realized how prevalent issues of race still are today . . . and that really made me angry and upset. Until now, I really chose to not believe that there was any real racism nowadays, that it all happened in the past and we are moving forward.

Gillian's insight about her racial identity developed through dialogue, where she was invited to honestly explore her beliefs and values. In IGD courses, we not only promote understanding of self and others, but we also call our students to lead through mindful action to address social injustices. As Thich Nhat Hanh (2003) writes, "Peace is not simply the absence of violence; it is the cultivation of understanding, insight and compassion, combined with action" (p. 5). Mindfulness and leadership are mutually inclusive, requiring students to engage in self-reflection to become effective leaders who have self-understanding and a deep sense of compassion for others. By devoting a significant part of the course to the importance of being an ally in struggles for social justice, IGD invites students to use their new understanding to think critically and realistically about their roles on campus and in society. With a new critical lens, students are able to evaluate, observe, and intervene in situations of injustice through initiating mindful, nonviolent communication and dialogue to help their communities heal and grow into more equitable, just environments. At the end of his race dialogue course, Haden, a White student, discussed his transformation to become more critical and serve as an ally by stepping in when there is injustice:

> In just two short months I went from feeling my racial identity had little meaning in my life to realizing it helped me become almost everything I am today. . . . I've been rather naive towards prejudice my whole life. Because of this it is likely that I have missed many instances of prejudice throughout my life that I could have stepped in on to help. This class has taught me to always stay alert to prejudice and be sure to take action when I witness it no matter how small the injustice seems. . . . Moving forward, the most important thing I have learned is to be an ally, I must be willing to step forward and take action. While this may make me feel uncomfortable, it is a small price to pay to help others understand when they are being oppressive and help minorities know they are not surrounded by people looking to oppress them.

In the past, Haden struggled with speaking out in situations of injustice and even perpetuated racism, yet through dialogue, he looked deeply at race and his role in racism. By engaging in mindful reflection, he increased his attentiveness to race, and he expressed a willingness to take action. By challenging his friendship groups and speaking out in the residence halls, Hayden takes on the roles of ally and leader in transforming the campus environment.

Authentic Leadership

The study of authentic leadership and intergroup dialogue aligns with Fairhurst and Sarr's (1996), Witherspoon's (1997), and Northouse's (2013) communicative definitions of leadership. In the development of his Leadership Competencies Scorecard, Ruben (2006) highlights communication competencies as a critical dimension of effective leadership practice. Authentic leaders have a genuine self-awareness, and this relational and contextual approach to leadership has a profound impact on those they lead (Avolio & Gardner, 2005). The emphasis on being true to oneself and true to others is consistent with the goals of student leadership development initiatives in higher education across the United States. As George (2003) suggests, "Leadership begins and ends with authenticity. It's being yourself; being the person you were created to be" (p. 11).

IGD has immense value for gaining the skills to live and work in an increasingly diverse and global society (Schoem, Hurtado, Sevig, Chesler, & Sumida, 2001; Vasques Scalera, 1999; Zúñiga & Nagda, 1993), yet few studies have addressed IGD within the context of leadership development. Alumni of IGD programs nationally have discussed the value IGD had on their leadership development. One student stated that co-curricular programs such as IGD that encourage students to explore their "multiple and intersecting identities . . . build and strengthen their leadership skills and competencies" (Gurin et al., 2013, p. 364). In addition, this link between dialogue and leadership has been fostered in an international context as Biren (Ratnesh) Nagda has collaborated with the Desmond Tutu Peace

Center to foster leadership development among South African youth (Gurin et al., 2013). This chapter extends Nagda's work that links peacemaking, leadership, and IGD into the US classroom and higher education context.

Within the context of Villanova's IGD program, mindfulness and authentic leadership are intentionally cultivated through the use of specific exercises and deliberate opportunities for dialogue like the "hopes and fears" and "stepping up and stepping back" exercises. In challenging students to step up in addressing difficult topics or conversations in class, IGD develops the leadership skills they will need outside the classroom. We also ask students to step back through participating in an exercise where they listen closely to their classmates and must wait thirty seconds before responding. Knowing when to intervene as ally or when to listen closely to others are critical skills for leaders seeking to understand and meet the needs of their communities.

Colleges and universities have an obligation to attend to the cultivation of their students' humanity (Palmer & Zajonc, 2010). Pope Benedict XVI might refer to this as "intellectual charity." As he noted, "This aspect of charity calls the educator to recognize that the profound responsibility to lead the young to truth is nothing less than an act of love" (2008). This human-centered approach to education comes from a place of love, and the implications for the student experience are significant.

By integrating this authentic approach to leadership with the literature on mindfulness and intergroup dialogue, students are further prepared to deal with the increasing complexities of leadership in a diverse yet disconnected society. IGD empowers students to think more deeply about their authentic self and how they can contribute to the lives of others. By cultivating these skills in our students through curricular and cocurricular dialogue initiatives, student participants begin to hone in on this unique dialogic leadership perspective. As one student noted at the completion of an IGD course, "Now that my eyes are open, I can't stop seeing."

Recognizing the important contributions of IGD to authentic leadership development, it is worth providing a brief snapshot of the various ways IGD participants are using their renewed awareness of dialogue and mindfulness to create change as leaders both on campus and in the community. First, a number of IGD participants are involved with an existing student organization: the Association for Change and Transformation (ACT). ACT educates students on the importance of using dialogue to talk through difference. With the use of performance, ACT hosts weekly dialogue sessions called "Real Talks" run "for students and by students." In these sessions, students use the skills of mindful listening and questioning that are cultivated in IGD to lead their peers in informal dialogues. Many of these same students also volunteer to perform as actors in the annual "Touch of Diversity Skit," which occurs during new student orientation. This performance challenges incoming freshmen to view and reconsider their conceptions of prejudice. Alongside the orientation counselors, student leaders in ACT co-facilitate and debrief the diversity performance. These same ACT students also serve as diversity peer educators and use performance to facilitate conversations about bias incidents with campus community members.

While taking IGD courses, a student named Tommy also assumed leadership positions within student-driven, social justice organizations addressing issues of privilege and oppression on campus. Tommy took multiple IGD courses, honed his skills in dialogue, and engaged with his peers such that they listened more authentically to one another and helped one another develop leadership skills that enabled the organization to flourish. During his last semester, Tommy served as a teaching assistant for a multicultural leadership course. In this role, he used his experiences as an underrepresented student of color on a predominantly White campus to give voice to theoretical perspectives such as standpoint theory being discussed in the class. In this way he served as a resource for the instructors. He also led students by listening to their thoughts on course topics and their ideas for final papers, and he helped them connect their own experiences (and lack of experiences) to the theories and discuss ways they can actively facilitate change on campus.

In other academic contexts, a number of IGD participants used their new knowledge to engage in research for social change (e.g., public health in Latino/Hispanic communities) and pursue Fulbright grants to continue their cultural understanding. Finally, illustrating the collective desire to enact change beyond the walls of Villanova, many IGD participants have gone on to volunteer for a myriad of service organizations (e.g., Teach For America, City Year, Peace Corps) where they employ their knowledge and skills in their work. For example, Lee, a student in IGD, committed to a year of service with City Year after graduation. His experience with dialogue, and specifically his ability to listen and engage with others in thoughtful ways, was a factor in his acceptance and success in the program. In working with diverse populations through City Year, Lee applies his strong cultural competency and leadership skills to teach and mentor inner-city middle school students. Recognizing his privileges as a college graduate, Lee listens carefully to his students' experiences to think critically about the barriers that they face within the education system and how he can best meet their needs. These examples capture the manifestation of authentic leadership on completion of the IGD program.

Conclusion

The value of IGD is not limited to our institution. Many institutions have embraced this program as an opportunity for student development. As the National Clearinghouse for Leadership Programs (2013) posits in its guiding principles, student leadership training and development programs should deepen and expand one's inner knowledge of self and relationships with others and "embrace the values of diversity and inclusion in processes and content, to empower students to be effective change agents in a pluralistic world" (National Clearinghouse for Leadership Programs, 2013, para. 2). Consistent with this analysis on IGD, both students and institutions benefit from this intentional emphasis on mindfulness and dialogue in student leadership initiatives.

As we continue to build IGD at Villanova, we look forward to seeing leadership and mindfulness take root in strong and meaningful ways among our students outside IGD classrooms. We hope to see these students, with "open eyes," take action by creating more inclusive and equitable spaces on campus. We hope that privileged students who have taken IGD courses will now be open not just to being leaders but also to being led by historically underrepresented and disenfranchised individuals and communities. Adopting a new leadership perspective, stepping aside to be led, and opening up opportunities to include others allows students of diverse backgrounds to become members and leaders of the most visible and predominantly White, upper-class, and able-bodied student organizations on campus. We anticipate that students won't "stop seeing" and will instead employ mindful questioning to consider what other opinions need to be considered and what programs would help open the eyes of their peers to inequities. IGD can transform college students into agents of social change. Our world is in need of leaders who are self-aware and oriented toward the welfare of others. By moving students from awareness to action, IGD serves as a useful model for effective leadership development—a model that reflects the unique intersection of authentic leadership, mindfulness, and dialogue.

References

Allport, G. W. (1954). *The nature of prejudice*. Cambridge, MA: Addison-Wesley.

Arnett, R. C., & Arneson, P. (1999). *Dialogic civility in a cynical age*. Albany: State University of New York Press.

Avolio, B. J., & Gardner, W. L. (2005). Authentic leadership development: Getting to the root of positive forms of leadership. *Leadership Quarterly, 16*, 315–338.

Bohm, D. (1996). *On dialogue*. New York: Routledge.

Bohm, D., & Peat, F. D. (1987). *Science, order, and creativity*. New York: Routledge.

Boyatzis, R. E., & McKee, A. (2005). *Resonant leadership*. Boston: Harvard Business School Publishing.

Buber, M. (1947). *Between man and man*. New York: Macmillan.

Fairhurst, G., & Sarr, R. (1996). *The art of framing: Managing the language of leadership*. San Francisco: Jossey-Bass.

Feagin, J. R., & McKinney, K. D. (2003). *The many costs of racism*. New York: Rowman and Littlefield.

George, W. W. (2003). *Authentic leadership: Rediscovering the secrets to creating lasting value*. San Francisco: Jossey-Bass.

Gurin, P., & Nagda, B. A. (2006). Getting to the "what," "how," and "why" of diversity on campus. *Educational Researcher, 35*(1), 20–24.

Gurin, P., Nagda, B. A., & Zúñiga, X. (Eds.). (2013). *Dialogue across difference: Practice, theory, and research on intergroup dialogue*. New York: Russell Sage Foundation.

Kabat-Zinn, J. (2003). Mindfulness based interventions in context: Past, present, and future. *Clinical Psychology: Science and Practice, 10*(2), 144–156.

Kanter, R. M. (1977). Some effects of proportions on group life: Skewed sex ratios and responses to token women. *American Journal of Sociology, 82*(5), 965–990.

Linehan, M. M. (1993). *Skills training manual for treating borderline personality disorder*. New York: Guilford Press.

National Clearinghouse of Leadership Programs. (2013). *Guiding principles*. Retrieved from http://www.nclp.umd.edu/about_nclp/Default.aspx#body_mission

Nhat Hanh, T. (2003). *Creating True Peace: Ending Conflict in Yourself, Your Family, Your Community and the World*. New York, NY: Free Press.

Northouse, P. G. (2013). *Leadership: Theory and practice* (6th ed.). Thousand Oaks, CA: Sage.

Orfield, G. (2001). *Schools more separate: Consequences of a decade of desegregation*. Cambridge, MA: Civil Rights Project at Harvard University.

Orfield, G., & Eaton, S. E. (2003). Back to segregation. *Nation, 276*(8), 5.

Orfield, G., Frankenberg, E. D., & Lee, C. (2003). The resurgence of school segregation. *Educational Leadership, 60*(4), 16–20.

Owen, J. E. (2011). Considerations of student learning in leadership. In S. R. Komives, J. P. Dugan, J. E. Owen, C. Slack, W. Wagner, & Associates, *The handbook for student leadership development*. (pp. 109–133). San Francisco: Jossey-Bass.

Palmer, P. J., & Zajonc, A. (2010). *The heart of higher education*. San Francisco: Jossey-Bass.

Pettigrew, T. F. (1998). Intergroup contact theory. *Annual Review of Psychology, 49*, 65–85.

Pope Benedict XVI. (2008, April 7). Address to Catholic educators. Catholic University of America, Washington, DC.

Rogers, J. L. (2003). Leadership. In S. R. Komives, D. B. Woodard, & Associates (Eds.), *Student services: A handbook for the profession* (pp. 447–465). San Francisco: Jossey-Bass.

Ruben, B. D. (2006). *What leaders need to know and do: A leadership competencies scorecard.* Washington, DC: National Association of College and University Business Officers.

Schoem, D., Hurtado, S., Sevig, T., Chesler, M., & Sumida, S. H. (2001). Intergroup dialogue: Democracy at work in theory and practice. In D. Schoem & S. Hurtado (Eds.), *Intergroup dialogue: Deliberative democracy in school, college, community, and workplace.* Ann Arbor: University of Michigan Press.

Smith, W. A., Allen W. R., & Danley, L. L. (2007). "Assume the position . . . You fit the description": Psychosocial experiences and racial battle fatigue among African American male college students. *American Behavioral Scientist, 51*(4), 551–578.

Solórzano, D., Ceja, M., & Yosso, T. (2000). Critical race theory, racial microaggressions, and campus racial climate: The experiences of African American college students. *Journal of Negro Education, 69*(1/2), 60–73.

Steele, C. M. (1997). A threat in the air: How stereotypes shape intellectual identity and performance. *American Psychologist, 52*(6), 613.

Sue, D. W., & Constantine, M. G. (2008). Racial microaggressions as instigators of difficult dialogues on race: Implications for student affairs educators and students. *College Student Affairs Journal, 26*(2), 136–143.

Sue, D. W., Nadal, K. L., Capodilupo, C. M., Lin, A. I., Torino, G. C., & Rivera, D. P. (2008). Racial microaggressions against black Americans: Implications for counseling. *Journal of Counseling and Development, 86*(3), 330–338.

Vasques Scalera, C. M. (1999). Democracy, diversity, dialogue: Education for critical multicultural citizenship. *Dissertation Abstracts International, 61*(02), 561A. (UMI No. 9959879)

Villanova University. (2013). *Villanova University mission statement.* Retrieved from http://www1.villanova.edu/villanova/mission/heritage/mission.html

Wagner, W. (2011). Considerations of student development in leadership. In S. R. Komives, J. P. Dugan, J. E. Owen, C. Slack, W. Wagner, & Associates, *The handbook for student leadership development,* (pp. 85–108). San Francisco: Jossey-Bass.

Witherspoon, P. D. (1997). *Communicating leadership: An organizational perspective.* Boston: Allyn & Bacon.

Yeung, J. G., Spanierman, L. B., & Landrum-Brown, J. (2013). "Being White in a multicultural society": Critical whiteness pedagogy in a dialogue course. *Journal of Diversity in Higher Education, 6*(1), 17–32.

Yukl, G. A. (2006). *Leadership in organizations* (6th ed.). Upper Saddle River, NJ: Pearson Education.

Zúñiga, X., & Nagda, B. A. (1993). Dialogue groups: An innovative approach to multicultural learning. In D. Schoem, L. Frankel, X. Zuniga, & E. Lewis (Eds.), *Multicultural teaching in the university* (pp. 233–248). Westport, CT: Praeger.

Zúñiga, X., & Nagda, B. A. (2001). Design considerations in intergroup dialogue. In D. L. Schoem & S. Hurado (Eds.), *Intergroup dialogue: Deliberative democracy in school, college, community and workplace* (pp. 306–327). Ann Arbor: University of Michigan Press.

Zúñiga, X., Nagda, B.R.A., Chesler, M., & Cytron-Walker, A. (2007). *Intergroup dialogue in higher education: Meaningful learning about social justice.* San Francisco: Jossey-Bass.

Part Three

Authenticity

Appear Authentic!

The Rhetorical Oxymoron of Authentic Leadership

Lena Lid-Falkman

"Appear authentic! Act spiritual! Remember to be present! Perform mindfully!"

These calls are all paradoxical opposites. They are examples of rhetorical oxymorons, a collocation of two or more words that are logically contradictory, according to the *Encyclopedia of Rhetoric* (Plett, 2001). The word is in itself an oxymoron, coming from the Greek *oxys*, sharp, and *moros*, stupid. An example is when a contradicting epithet is put to a word, such as in a "loud silence." An oxymoron works due to its emotional or comic appeal and through its absurd and paradoxical nature. "Appear authentic" is such an oxymoron. *Authentic* means to be true, real to your own self; when put together with *appear*— as in portraying, performing, seeming to be—it becomes an oxymoron.

Today's leaders are often expected to "appear authentic." In today's social, transparent, and media-trained society, people with power or in the role of a spokesperson are expected to be active online. The online logic for communicating in social media is to be personal, witty, and interactive. It seems that people must seem "real," sharing mistakes and reflections. Small talk taking place in the lunchroom has become public talk due to this evolution of the social world.

We expect people to be online: communicating, reading, writing, and "liking." In the age of smart phones, everyone can do anything everywhere. At the same time, people are expected to be reflective, full people, not only positions. Apparently we expect them to have values, be reflective, and be insightful. The ideal is also to be spiritual and mindful. Yoga and mindfulness in many forms are in fashion.

These two contemporary ideals crash, but they also nourish each other. To be transparent and interactive and act authentic, you need to be constantly online. To be insightful and to become authentic, you need to be offline.

Room for Reflection in the Daily Life of a Leader?

What do people in leading positions actually do? The scholarly study of managerial work suggests some answers. In the classic time study *Executive Behaviour*, Sune Carlson (1951) showed how being in a position of responsibility creates a daily life of fragmented time, variety within tasks, and a reactive rather than proactive unfolding of events through a day. This time study also showed that the majority of a leader's time is spent on communication: talking, writing, reading, and listening, formal and informal. Fifty years after this groundbreaking study, Carlson's study was reproduced. The new research showed that the daily life of people in positions of responsibility was still varied, reactive, and fragmented, but now not only in time but also in place. One of the changes in managers' lives was that they traveled more (Tengblad, 2002). Besides this, the study confirmed that leaders spend most of their time communicating, which has also been shown in research on leaders' different roles (Mintzberg, 1973). It is unlikely that either Sune Carlson in the 1950s or Henry Mintzberg in the 1970s could have imagined the amount of communication we do today and the speed created by the possibility of being constantly online, unheard of in the 1950s and 1970s.

Online and Communicative Leadership in the New Global Social World

A CEO in the banking sector, we can call him Lars, is a modern CEO. The business magazines call him "an Indiana Jones of banking" with his kick-ass attitude. The bank has an expressed strategy of using technological solutions in communicating with customers. As most banks reduce the number of offices, this one has decided to be easier to reach for customers by being where many of those customers are: online. The bank has spicy commercials making fun of old banking, movie posters marketing free webinars where those who are curious can learn about savings, and the bank's representatives are active on social media. I met Lars and his bank in my research projects about how the global world and its technology as social media affect leadership and rhetoric.

Lars the CEO uses Facebook, but not much, since he finds the medium difficult—to whom is he writing and about what? He is also active on a blog. Most of all he is active on Twitter. Writing 140 characters has become a way for him to communicate with the world. He knows that among his followers, he has employees, customers, owners, media, and competitors. When he sits across from me, the coffee cup is comfortable in his hand, but in the other hand, his iPhone looks as if it's glued to his palm. I sense that he is eager to check his iPhone as we speak. "I write as the bank," he says, "not as myself; I would never write about private things." When I read his tweets, I am not as convinced as he is. Lars is thanking and welcoming new followers with interactive replies. He retweets writings from colleagues. He writes about where he travels and the people he meets. He writes about news in the market and news in his bank. But he also writes about his physical training, as when he set a new personal record in a race. He also writes things like, "Friday night, time for some rock & roll" and "Icy Sunday Morning, reading Hemingway."

Who do I think Lars is if I look at social media? Lars seems like a good guy and a passionate leader. He is engaged and positive and enthusiastic about his bank and his mission. He is encouraging and curious. Most of the time, he is on the run, and he is hard working and busy. He is also reflective and catches moments in time. I realize that I have never had such an image of a CEO before. I know, without knowing him, what he likes, where he is, what he does, and what he values even before I meet him. I have a picture of a real person, not only a title and a name. Lars appears online as a professional and hard-working CEO, but also as an authentic good guy.

Training in Authentic Leadership or Image Marketing?

Authentic leadership has been addressed in three ways: the intrapersonal, where the leader's own experiences, visions, and convictions generate the authenticity; the interpersonal, where the process and relationship between leaders and led generate the authenticity; and the training perspective, where authenticity is developed (Northouse, 2013).

The concept of authentic leadership has been identified as a root construction for the area of value-based leadership (Avolio & Gardner, 2005a; May, Hodges, Chan, & Avolio, 2003). These theories deal with leading through values—getting people to follow you because of your vision, what you stand for, and who you are. Authentic leaders lead by creating positive meaning for their followers (Endrissat, Müller, & Kaudela-Baum, 2007). An authentic leader drives from his or her own ideas, not from prior status. Authentic leaders motivate others and create visions based on their own convictions (Michie & Janaki, 2005; Shamir & Eilam, 2005).

In my research on Dag Hammarskjöld and the other seven secretary-generals of the UN, I highlighted the importance of being consistent if one is to come across as authentic, that is, living, leading, and communicating the same message and values

(Lid-Andersson, 2009). Self-knowledge and self-awareness are important for developing into an authentic leader (Shamir & Eilam, 2005). Much leadership education in this perspective uses narrative methods and biographical storytelling to help one get to know oneself and one's values (Shamir & Eilam, 2005; Sparrowe, 2005).

Reading some of the value-based authenticity research on leadership, as presented, for example, in a special issue of *Leadership Quarterly* (Avolio & Gardner, 2005b), I cannot help but wonder whether writing your own story to use as a tool in your leadership, is "to know thyself," or is image management and marketing. Do these stories come across as authentic stories? If you try to be true to yourself, do you always come across as sane and making sense? Or are you simply appearing to be authentic?

Being Authentic

How is it possible to come further beyond appearing into being? Kathryn Goldman Schuyler (2012) has argued that leaders need to go beyond actions toward being in order to a have a larger impact. She also writes in the Introduction to this book that "authenticity refers to moving beyond trying to be present (but really just pretending), to being able to genuinely live values that serve all participants in a given system."

The chapters in part 3 consist of welcome and varied perspectives toward understanding how to be and live authentic leadership. Ubuntu values have emerged in traditional African societies. They place the community first and the individual second; respect for others and interdependence are typical traits. In chapter 7, Sylvia van de Bunt-Kokhuis and Hellicy Ngambi compare Ubuntu with Western servant-leadership, identifying how both value systems focus on the follower, the other human being, which, perhaps paradoxically, increases the authenticity of the leader. They offer insight into the communal and societal aspect of values and authenticity and also place an interesting focus on new digital aspects of being an authentic leader with clear values.

Reflection and contemplative practice are seen as important in the training and developing perspective on authentic leadership, but apparently there is little empirical research on this in the context of leadership. In chapter 8, Deana Raffo explores this literature and offers suggestions and directions for needed future research. She identifies self-reflection as the missing point between self-awareness and authenticity. This is one way of moving beyond learning and doing authentic leadership into being authentic.

Marco Aponte-Moreno discusses in chapter 9 how theater techniques can be used to develop authentic leadership. He focuses on acting training not as a means to come across or appear as authentic, but to develop ways that leaders can express themselves and their truths. He describes how this is done not only externally with body, voice, and language, but also internally with techniques such as the "magic if" and "inner objects." This chapter moves beyond the simple understanding of acting as appearing authentic toward sensing how it is a form of embodiment.

We chose to close the book with a chapter grounded in research to remind readers of the importance of developing or testing theories and models empirically. Susan Skjei, the author of chapter 10, studied leaders who had been identified by others as being authentic. She sees authenticity as moments when leaders face ambiguity, listen to the body, are open to different possibilities, communicate with both vulnerability and honesty, and act with integrity and courage. She contributes to our understanding of how authenticity is actually lived. I find the specification of authentic moments very helpful: it let me overcome the strict opposition between authentic and inauthentic. Her chapter can help leaders and all of us to become and be authentic, one moment a time.

It is my wish and that of the whole editing team to create understanding about how people can become authentic leaders one step and one moment at a time rather than inducing leaders to live up to the absurdity presented by the oxymoron of appearing spiritual, present, mindful, or authentic.

References

Avolio, B. J., & Gardner, W. L. (2005a). Authentic leadership development: Getting to the root of positive forms of leadership. *Leadership Quarterly*, *16*(6), 315–338.

Avolio, B. J., & Gardner, W. L. (Eds.). (2005b). Authentic leadership development: Getting to the root of positive forms of leadership [Special issue]. *Leadership Quarterly*, *16*(3).

Carlson, S. (1951). *Executive Behaviour: A study of the work load and the working methods of managing directors*. Stockholm: Arno Press.

Endrissat N., Müller, W. R., & Kaudela-Baum, S. (2007). En route to an empirically-based understanding of authentic leadership. *European Management Journal*, *25*(3), 207–220.

Goldman Schuyler, K. (2012). *Inner peace—global impact: Tibetan Buddhism, leadership, and work*. Charlotte, NC: Information Age Publishing.

Lid-Andersson, L. A. (2009). *Ledarskapande Retorik*. Stockholm: EFI.

May, D. R., Hodges, T., Chan, A.Y.L., & Avolio, B. J. (2003). Developing the moral component of authentic leadership. *Organizational Dynamics*, *32*(3), 247–260.

Michie, S., & Janaki, G. (2005). Values, emotions, and authenticity: Will the real leader please stand up? *Leadership Quarterly*, *16*(3), 441–457.

Mintzberg, H. (1973). *The nature of managerial work*. New York: Harper.

Northouse, P. (2013). *Leadership: Theory and practice*. Thousand Oaks, CA: Sage.

Plett, H. F. (2001). Oxymoron. In T. O. Sloane (Ed.), *Encyclopedia of rhetoric*. New York: Oxford University Press.

Shamir, B., & Eilam, G. (2005). "What's your story?" A life-story approach to authentic leadership development. *Leadership Quarterly*, *16*(3), 395–417.

Sparrowe, R. T. (2005). Authentic leadership and the narrative self. *Leadership Quarterly*, *16*(3), 419–439.

Tengblad, S. (2002). Time and space in managerial work. *Scandinavian Journal of Management*, *18*(4), 543–565.

Chapter Seven

Leadership Values in Africa and Implications for Online Learning Communities

Sylvia van de Bunt-Kokhuis, Hellicy C. Ngambi

This chapter examines and compares servant-leadership with African leadership as it is grounded in Ubuntu philosophy and RARE (responsible, accountable, relevant, ethical) leadership. We explore how these values support community building and commitment to the growth of others. We discuss the history of servant-leadership in a twenty-first-century digital age perspective, examining how it can be useful in Africa, given the needs for empowerment, motivation, and nurturance that we perceive among African online learners, understanding, finally, that the values of traditional African Ubuntu communities can inspire leaders dedicated to serving online learning communities.

The Role of Leadership Values

Fisher and Lovell (2003) define *values* as "core ideas about how people should live and the ends they should seek." Values are thus core beliefs: the underlying thoughts that stimulate human behavior (Russell, 2001). The role of values in organizations is to elicit behavioral alternatives, and in choosing these alternatives, the leader develops a personal behavior system. The questions we need to ask are what role values play in various

---

This chapter originated from earlier research and publications of both authors.

types of institutions and what role they play in leadership. According to Massey (1979), personal values are influenced by family, friends, religion, education, the media, geographic roots, technology, and current events, among other things. This list reveals that values, unlike principles, are relative and situational. They are also influenced by national cultures, life experiences, and relationships. According to Trompenaars and Woolliams (2003), values are fundamentally within each of us, but they manifest themselves as a series of dilemmas. While the dilemmas themselves exist separate from culture, the way people (e.g., leaders) approach and resolve them are culturally determined. Hence, for example, respect begins from within the individual. It is the individual's own culture inside her head and heart that silently whispers to her. Russell (2001) called this "moral reasoning," where values affect a leader's judgments about ethical and unethical behavior. Research by England and Lee (1974) concluded that there is supporting evidence to suggest a reasonably strong relationship between leaders' levels of success achieved and their personal values; if one's values are debased and toxic, one is unlikely to attain sustainable success.

Dean (2008) defines *value-based leadership* as leading by example, doing the right things for the right reasons, and not compromising one's core values. Inherent in this definition is an appreciation for the idea that principles are universal, whereas values "*evolve*" (Albion, 2006, p. 60) depending on the context. However, values are critical in delivering on the principles. Therefore, Ngambi proposes a leadership principle that is responsible, accountable, relevant, and ethical (RARE) (Ngambi, 2010, 2011).

The RARE-based value system is essential to effective leadership at both personal and organizational levels. Researchers such as Clawson (1999) have argued that certain values, including honesty and integrity, are critical to leadership success. This suggests the importance of appropriate leadership values for online learning communities, especially in Africa, where the number of universities is insufficient to meet the demand for higher education, especially in remote rural areas.

About Servant-Leadership

Traditional African communities are based on the Ubuntu value system, which reinforces behavior among members of the community. For example, in African *subsistence farming*, women would brew traditional beer and soft drinks, called *Munkoyo* in Zambia, and then invite others to come and help cultivate the fields for a day or two without pay. They would work during the day and celebrate together in the evening, drinking and eating together. This practice is based on values such as empathy, caring, informal communication, and self-help entrepreneurship. This kind of shared leadership creates an authentic bond among community members and ensures that all members, even the feeble, are able to have a harvest and feed their families, underscoring their responsibility, accountability, and relevance to one another.

How does the African example of subsistence farming apply to servant-leadership? In servant-leadership, commitment to people's growth and building community are also core values. Major attributes of servant-leadership can be found across cultures and can contain a distinct ethical dimension. These major attributes, which are very similar to those in African communities (Ngambi, 1999), are as follows (see also Nuijten, 2009; Sarayrah, 2004; Spears, 2010; Trompenaars & Voerman, 2009; Vargas & Hanlon, 2007):

1. *Listening*—unbiased listening to the other to get in touch with one's inner voice and the desire to know the other.
2. *Empathy*—understanding others; accepting and recognizing their special and unique behaviors.
3. *Healing of relationships*—care for other people and their welfare; healing is a powerful ethical force for transformation and integration.

4. *Awareness*—achieving mindfulness through reflection. General as well as self-awareness creates a better understanding of power, ethics, and values in groups.

5. *Persuasion*—convincing rather than coercing others, effectively building consensus within groups, and helping others understand and learn.

6. *Conceptualization*—thinking beyond day-to-day realities and helping others see the bigger picture.

7. *Foresight*—understanding the lessons of the past, the realities of the present, and the likely consequences of the future.

8. *Stewardship*—holding the trust of others to serve the needs of all.

9. *Commitment* to the growth of others—being committed to their learning and improvement.

10. *Building community* among those who work within a given organization.

Servant-leadership is multidimensional and enhances the human, ethical, and talent factors in organizations. Traditional leaders tend to focus on tasks, control, and processes in organizations. Servant-leaders focus more on their followers, seeking to strengthen—with spirit—their capacity and whole and inner selves. Servant-leaders are compassionate and connected with people, reconciling dilemmas and empowering them as team members, employees, customers, students, or citizens. The servant-leader is eager to contribute value to others (e.g., pupils, students, trainees) and encourage their talents. Each investment by the servant-leader in the well-being of another is an investment in the common good. The servant-leader's skills can be found in bridging the contrasting dilemmas of leading versus serving, control versus compassion, high-tech versus high-touch, power over versus trust and commitment to others (Trompenaars, 2007).

The African Leadership Approach

This section examines African leadership values and their impact on community building and commitment to the growth of others.

Ubuntu in African Organizations

From a historical perspective, great spiritual and authentic African leaders such as Julius Nyerere, Kenneth Kaunda, Nelson Mandela, and others explicitly taught core values. Mbigi (2004) summarized the most important values in African organizations: respect for the dignity of others; group solidarity, where an insult to an individual is an insult to all; service oriented to others in the spirit of harmony; and interdependence. In other words, "every one of us needs all of us." Nelson Mandela (2006) explained the unifying power of Ubuntu: "Though we differ across cultures and faiths, and though history has divided rich from poor, free from unfree, powerful from powerless, and race from race, we are still all branches on the same tree of humanity."

From a historical point of view, servant-leadership can be compared with Ubuntu in community building. Collectivism is the underlying leadership value of Ubuntu—to serve the other. In Ubuntu philosophy, one is seen to be a person through others, focusing on serving others as a way of life. Ngambi (1999) gives the example of the Fungwe community of Zambia, where the leader acts as an overseer and custodian of the community through dialogue and open informal communication. Trust and integrity are key, like listening to the community and consensus decision making based on "we," not "I."

In languages such as Sotho and Xhosa, *Ubuntu* means "humanness" or "humility" and symbolizes that, to be whole, a person is dependent on other persons. "I am because of others," and "You are who you are because of the others." In this respect, Ubuntu philosophy can be compared with the opposite rational

Western worldview of, "I am because I think I am."[1] The collectivity inherent in the concept of Ubuntu is illustrated in the question *"Ninjani?"* or "How are you?" and the answer, *"Sikhona,"* meaning, "We are here!" (Mangaliso & Mangaliso, 2006; Mbigi, 2006; Bunt-Kokhuis, 2009, 2011). Ubuntu also implies a more inclusive way of thinking—compare the quality, "commitment to the growth of others" in servant-leadership—in terms of learning and education. *Collective wisdom* (Ngambi, 2011) draws on and leverages the benefits of diversity and promotes difference. This is the wisdom that appreciates that the knowledge possessed by the individual is limited compared to that of the collective.

RARE Leadership

The Ubuntu philosophy reflects what Ngambi (2010, 2011), based on her research of chieftaincies and kingdoms in Africa (Ngambi, 1999, 2004), calls the RARE leadership approach: responsible, accountable, relevant, and ethical. RARE leadership can be compared with servant-leadership, where leading with spirit, commitment to the growth and empowerment of others, and building community is evident (Ngambi, 2004). Ngambi (2011) refers to the seven "indisputable D's" that enhance and develop the winning spiritual attitude of a RARE leader in contributing to community development: dreaming (knowing what you want to achieve and focusing on it), desire (not being satisfied with mediocrity), dedication (being committed and loyal to what you want to achieve), devotion (committing to your cause in a RARE way and with enthusiasm), daring (having the courage to take risks without fear of failure), determination (shaking off disappointments and moving on), and discipline (understanding that one cannot succeed in life without mental, moral, and physical control). These attitudes help a leader build positive relationships in community, or what Ngambi (1999) elsewhere calls the African village community.

The African Village

The traditional African leadership model differs from Western and European models, where the leader sets the vision and then works on getting people to support it, resulting in a superficial commitment. In the African traditional model—what Ngambi (1999) calls the African village model—people are committed on a spiritual level to the vision because it mirrors what they care about. As the African saying goes, "You don't have to get people to commit to their children; they are naturally committed." Such spiritual commitment comes out of shared vision and does not require one to surrender uniqueness; rather, everyone expresses it. As such, in an African village, one raises not dependents but interdependents (Ngambi, 2011). Such an environment is possible only if a leader deepens each person's unique sense of vision on a spiritual level. The leader establishes harmony among diverse visions so that people can move forward together (compare the quality of a servant-leader's foresight and conceptualization). The leader is involved, which refers to so-called hands leadership within the RARE leadership approach (see Ngambi, 2011).

Ngambi (2011) exemplifies the essence of RARE African leadership by her research on chieftaincies in South Africa, Ghana, and Zambia in the so-called African village model (Ngambi, 2004). The traditional Fungwe communities of Zambia originated in the sixteenth century, with a population of about twelve thousand people. Observation, conversations, and interviews with Chief Mwenechifungwe, the head of the Chakosamoto village (one of the Fungwe communities), and the people, revealed three broad leadership characteristics, strongly connected with spirituality and authenticity:

1. *Leadership through dialogue and shared vision* (compare the quality of foresight of a servant-leader). Membership in the chieftaincy is voluntary, and the leader has no power to force his opinions on the people. Forums are arranged to discuss issues

concerning the chieftaincy. The chief and his village headmen lead from the front in dangerous situations and from behind if the situation is calm and peaceful.

The Fungwe community is bonded together by shared visions and values. The mental image of a possible and desirable future is developed by the chief and the headmen and elders, who formulate a realistic, credible, and attractive view or vision for the community. The vision is that the Fungwe community "shall be the most secure, healthy, progressive, and prosperous chieftaincy. The Fungwe people will live for each other and ensure that all people are free, healthy, secure, peaceful, and trusting." This vision is articulated through stories, songs, dances, and slogans reflecting a spiritual connection. An annual event, *chambo chalutanga*, is celebrated, wherein the entire population meets to reinforce unity and the spiritual identity of the Fungwe people.

2. *Leadership that fosters discipleship* (compare the quality of community building of a servant-leader). The action-oriented involvement of the chief fosters behaviors that led community members to become disciples of the chieftaincy, with qualities such as discipline and morality, selflessness, service and calm, commitment to hard work, self-confidence and self-empowerment, trust, integrity and reliability, transparency and credibility, and love for the people and the community served.

3. *The leader as overseer and custodian of the community* (compare the quality of stewardship and listening of a servant-leader). The chief acted as overseer of both human and material resources. He presided over all land ownership and was a custodian of traditional values and customs. His goals were to feed the people, maintain peace, promote culture and traditional values, further the chieftaincy, and preserve and defend life. Achieving these goals required the participation of the entire chieftaincy for the good of the whole community. The Chief and his *indunas* (elders) had to monitor and evaluate whatever projects were undertaken.

This kind of leadership sensitizes and mobilizes the people who receive the benefits of such projects. The chief was personally involved. The community had two types of work: community work (mostly voluntary) and paid work in commercial business projects. In community work, the people of a given area or village are asked to do the work without remuneration as a contribution to society. Whether one was selected for commercial work depended on one's skills and the record of one's involvement in community work.

Commercial work was essentially a reward for one's involvement in improving the community. Regardless of whether the Fungwe chief held a different view from those of his followers, he would listen. He generated dialogue and sought to understand his followers' views. That he had genuine feeling for their perspective is apparent in his words: "You don't just tell people that you love them, you show them that you love them." The chief maintained a clear and consistent position as headman of Chakosamoto village (Ngambi, 1999). By listening to the community, the chief and the headman could identify the will of the people. They would reflect on what they had heard and thus grow as leaders and develop character. The headman said, "You have to know and understand yourself to motivate your followers to follow you."

These leaders were aware of themselves and others, which helped them understand issues involving ethics and values. They sought to convince rather than coerce, and they were very effective in building consensus with the community. They looked beyond day-to-day realities (compare foresight quality of the servant-leader) and were able to understand the lessons of the past, the realities of the present, and the likely consequences of a decision for the future. The main objectives of leading with the hands are to get things done, achieve goals and objectives, move the organization or community forward, and achieve the greater good. The Fungwe chieftaincy achieved all this, using various approaches.

Lekgotla Meetings

In line with the case of the Fungwe community, the Lekgotla meetings also illustrate Ubuntu and community building where listening (compare servant-leadership quality of listening) is key. Lekgotla is about the traditional way that some African managers organize and interact (Liefde, 2002). In Lekgotla meetings, the opinions of all participants are reviewed. Nuances of what is said, mutual respect, empathy, and the social context (narrativity) are extremely important, as in the tradition of Ubuntu. During Lekgotla meetings, the primary goal is not to make decisions but to allow all participants to express their opinions by way of reaching consensus (Liefde, 2002).

Listening to others (a key attribute of servant-leaders) to access one's inner voice is one of the defining characteristics of the Lekgotla meeting. Discussions continue until an agreement is reached, signified by concepts such as *omulembe* (peace), *obulala* (togetherness), and *umoja* (oneness) (Nafukho, 2006). In African work and learning processes, these reconciliation concepts are critical. Similar to Arab organizations, seniority and respect for the elders play a major role in Lekgotla meetings (Banutu-Gomez, 2003). A senior person might not possess all the expertise needed for the task, but servant-leadership, with its inherent wisdom, ethics, vision, and focus on harmonious working relations, can motivate others to perform well (Mangaliso & Mangaliso, 2006). This appeals to and encourages other (potential) competences from each participant in a Lekgotla meeting (Bunt-Kokhuis, 2011).

Harambee

In Swahili, the concept of *harambee* means, literally, "all pull together." Harambee stresses community self-reliance and mutual social responsibility rather than individual gain. A collective effort is made for the common good, such as helping a family in need or the construction of a school or church (Koshal & Patterson, 2008). In the harambee context, servant-leaders act with ethical care and compassion, giving moral, emotional, and social support to harambee teams (compare *shosholoza* teamwork in South African communities).

Harambee represents the need for cooperation in a community, pooling resources to help each other, similar to Ubuntu (Chieni, 2010; Bunt-Kokhuis, 2011). Harambee is strongly connected with servant-leadership, including community building and a mutual sense of service and stewardship between leaders and followers. It reflects the strong ancient ethical value of mutual assistance, team effort, and Ubuntu.

In parts of East Africa, harambee events have long been important ways to build and maintain social communities. In harambee community meetings, things are done collectively (Winston & Ryan, 2008). These community events range from informal meetings lasting a few hours, with invitations spread by word of mouth, to formal, multiday events advertised in newspapers.

Servant-Leadership and Online Learning Communities

Servant-leadership has not been prominent in online learning communities. This is remarkable because, especially in virtual learning communities where there is no face-to-face meeting, the meaning of trust, social inclusion, empathy, talent nurturing, commitment, and the seven D's for a winning attitude of a RARE leader (Ngambi, 2011) are very much at stake. The spiritual dimension of both leading and serving becomes even more challenging in the virtual world. Teachers with servant-leadership qualities can make the difference in online learning communities. In the online classroom, more than ever before, the teacher needs to be qualified to listen, care for distance learners, encourage awareness raising, give feedback, and build a robust community. This calls for a compassionate kind of educational leader, one who is able to connect high-tech values (technology-mediated learning, multimedia infrastructure) with "high-touch" values (contact, human interaction, commitment to the growth of others, healing) in the online learning community.

Online learning comprises all forms of computer-enabled learning activities, including Web-based learning, virtual team collaboration, and content exchange over the Internet. The roles of teacher and pupil are changing, and the online learning process can take place through a diverse range of self-paced learning or led by an online instructor, tutor, or coach. Online collaboration goes beyond academic and traditional educational boundaries, and high-quality learning content is available free of charge. For example, massive open online courses (MOOCs) originated from open courseware and the Open Learning Initiative. Stanford University conducted a MOOC on artificial intelligence in 2011, for which 160,000 students in 190 countries enrolled.[2]

Implications for African Online Learning Communities

Most African countries have embraced online learning and are willing to advance and support it to enhance equal learning opportunities for all. However, the pace of online learning development in Africa remains very slow compared to the Western world (van Hoorik & Mweetwa, 2007), and the digital divide remains a serious concern for the near future. For online learning to be fully used in developing countries such as South Africa and Zambia, international authorities, including nongovernmental organizations, governments, and educational leaders, must fully commit themselves and the necessary resources to make it workable. Train-the-trainer programs are necessary for those who will be responsible for coaching African e-learners.

Getting the current and next generation of African talent, especially in rural areas, connected to the global community of online learning (e.g., MOOCs) is a global social responsibility.

Limited experience suggests that online learning can have social and economic benefits in rural Africa. For example, Internet use in rural Zambia has been increasing. Case studies of two villages in Zambia (van Hoorik & Mweetwa, 2007) revealed that people and communities in rural Zambia use the Internet to communicate, search for information, and purchase goods, helping them build a more sustainable future.

Online Community Building in the African Classroom

The servant-leadership attribute and Ubuntu philosophy of community building means that educational leaders help build a learning community. With the rise of the Internet, the impact of leaders on communication and empowerment for community building can be enormous. Today, e-learners may be linked primarily informally to their teachers. Do community-based values and Ubuntu make an easier application of learning on the African e-classroom? In exploring Internet use in rural Zambia, van Hoorik and Mweetwa (2007) found that Zambians were eager to take advantage of the Internet to connect with relatives and friends. This research finding can be extended to African online learning communities.

Online Communication in an African Context

Based on Ngambi's research (1999, 2004, 2011), experience, and observations in more than fifteen African countries, in certain African cultures, the facts and behaviors we have described may alternately hinder and enable effective cross-cultural online communication and community building. For example in some African cultures, direct eye contact is perceived as rude. For some senior professionals, it might be easier to communicate in a "faceless" way, thereby remaining anonymous in terms of their positions. In the African context, communication without these kinds of prejudices can improve the success of online learning communities. Both Hofstede's dimensions of culture[3] and Trompenaars[4] allude to such cultural differences.

Results of a study conducted at the University of South Africa (UNISA; Heydenrych & Viviers, 2002) revealed a successful online learning community in the African context. Some of the benefits identified in the study pertaining to learners include social support, where learners made friends and felt part of the group; learner empowerment, where learners became confident in voicing their opinions in public; critical reflections and self-reflections by learners on their actions and contributions; and engaged learning. The learners reacted positively to being involved, as opposed to the usual isolation and passivity of traditional distance education. Other benefits were that learners wanted to satisfy more of their degree requirements using online learning and discussions enabled them to make their own contributions and gain from others' opinions. Finally, UNISA learners appreciated the facilitator-guided discussion as well as receiving a nearly immediate response to their inquiries.

Heydenrych and Viviers (2002) observed that the underlying African values and Ubuntu philosophies of sharing, consensus, constructive disagreement, interdependent relationships, and caring environments were prevalent in online learning environments. There are still online communication challenges that require additional funding and effort; for example, poor or no Internet connectivity and lack of computers, electricity, and infrastructure, especially in rural areas, perpetuates the urban-rural digital divide (Naidoo, 2012).

Comparing Traditional African and Servant-Leadership Values: A Summary

Pointing out the similarities between traditional African and servant-leadership values helps identify the historical common ground of human nature and leadership. Comparing the meaning of these traditional leadership values contributes to more consistent solutions to the worldwide online leadership dilemmas of the present and future. Considering what we have discussed, we can now identify in table 7.1 points of agreement while comparing (online) African and servant-leadership values:

Table 7.1 Online Servant and African Leadership Values

(Online) Servant-Leadership	Ubuntu Leadership	RARE Leadership	Fungwe Leadership
Listening	Listening to preserve unity and achieve consensus (e.g., Lekgotla meetings)	Listening to one's followers in a responsible, accountable, relevant, and ethical way	Listening when the chief has a different view; dialogue
Empathy	Humanness, humility	Discipline; work and learn purposefully and with integrity on daily basis (e.g., in e-learning)	Trust, integrity
Healing	Promoting care and compassion for the community, striving for harmony in (learning) groups	Devotion; forgive and move on	People live for each others' well-being
Awareness	I am because of others.	Determination; shake off disappointments and move on	Open and informal communication
Persuasion	Belief in collective engagement, collective power	Daring; innovation results from bold steps	Vision is articulated through stories, songs, dances, and slogans Convince followers rather than coerce, building consensus

(*continued*)

Table 7.1 (Continued)

(Online) Servant-Leadership	Ubuntu Leadership	RARE Leadership	Fungwe Leadership
Conceptualization	Make sacrifices in service of others	Leader is involved; hands-on leadership Dreaming; have a clear mental picture of your desired future	Leadership through shared vision and values
Foresight	The sustainability of our future is our unity	Dedication; loyal to your vision; "head leadership"	Look beyond day-to-day realities
Stewardship	Serving others as a way of life	Leader establishes harmony among diverse visions in education	The leader as overseer and custodian of the (learning) community
Commitment to the growth of people	Human commitment to each other	People are committed on a spiritual level to a shared vision; "heart leadership"	Move the (learning) community forward to achieve the greater good
Building Community	Unified individual and community relationships	Building community through a RARE principle-based value system	Leadership that fosters discipleship; love for people and the (learning) community you serve

Avenues for Future Research

There is much to explore and many opportunities for comparing leadership across the globe as the world becomes more connected and more community based. The following questions provide avenues for research on comparing servant- and African (Ubuntu/RARE) leadership in the twenty-first century:

1. What can leaders learn from traditional Ubuntu/RARE values for current online learning communities? Lutz (2009) argues that Ubuntu is essential learning for professionals in the age of globalization. Ubuntu can make any international organization more consistent with humans' basic need for community, belonging, and acceptance. Ubuntu and RARE values could inspire future research on the dilemma of individualism versus collectivism in online learning communities.

2. In the perspective of Ubuntu-related research, what can we learn from the work on the Fungwe community (Ngambi, 1999), an African village where community direction or vision is established through dialogue? Western culture, as pointed out by Peck, Senge, and DePree (1995) suggests a one-way link: the leader directs the followers. However, in a traditional African community, leaders and followers interact and derive a shared vision and values through dialogue and listening. Similarly, in an online learning community, dialogue and listening are vital to fostering a sense of belonging for e-learners. Multimedia applications to optimize sharing opportunities in online learning communities need to be further investigated.

Conclusion and Outlook

In this chapter, we compared the spiritual meaning of African and servant-leadership and its usefulness for building online learning communities. This leadership issue should have a significant place in the agendas of educationalists. Servant-leaders of an online learning community (e.g., teachers, policymakers, peers, parents, elders) can nurture others to discover their inner strengths. Both digital and cultural horizons need to be explored further, inclusively. Servant-leadership will enable younger generations to achieve higher levels of spirituality and community participation in their everyday learning and lives.

In the African context, a comparison of servant-leadership values with Ubuntu and RARE leadership (leading with the head, heart, and hands) illustrates how African and servant-leaders can support and facilitate the growth of others in online learning communities. There is an ethical responsibility for servant-leaders in nurturing and inspiring their online learning communities. This role requires them to have a selfless service attitude and to enforce online learners' competencies, motivation, and inspiration.

Any e-learner, regardless of his or her economic or cultural background in Africa and beyond, should have the right to a quality online learning community and to engage in lifelong learning. Online learning communities can nurture the next generation of servant-leaders. Further comparative studies on African and servant-leadership can be used to enhance more effective online learning, through MOOCs and other online learning communities, and, subsequently, contribute to socioeconomic development in Africa and beyond. This in turn would equip servant-leaders as educators and reinforce their roles as RARE online community teachers and tutors. The confidence and hope gained from the mindful experiences in online African communities and beyond underscore the need for further action.

Notes

1. In his Master lecture, *Cross Cultural Management*, Prof. Trompenaars (Vrije Universiteit Amsterdam, April 2008) noticed that only in the English language is "I" written with a capital letter. This symbolizes the importance of the ego in this part of the world. In The Netherlands, the word "u" was also capitalized in the past, to show respect to the other. In Asian countries, one is addressed by one's last name first to show respect to the family, and one's first name is less relevant.
2. http://edf.stanford.edu/readings/massive-open-online-courses-learning-revolution

3. http://geert-hofstede.com/dimensions.html
4. http://en.wikipedia.org/wiki/Fons_Trompenaars#Dimensions

References

Albion, M. (2006). *True to yourself: Leading a value-based business.* San Francisco: Berrett-Koehler.

Banutu-Gomez, M. B. (2003). Leadership in the government of the Gambia: Traditional African leadership practice, shared vision, accountability and willingness and openness to change. *Journal of American Academy of Business, 2,* 349–359.

Bunt-Kokhuis, S. van de. (2009). Talent diversity: A garden of opportunities. In L. van der Sluis & S. van de Bunt-Kokhuis (Eds.), *Competing for talent* (pp. 90–137). Assen: Royal van Gorcum Publishers.

Bunt-Kokhuis, S. van de. (2011). Servant-leadership in a cross-cultural and ethical perspective. In D. Weir & N. Sultan (Eds.), *From critique to action: The practical ethics of the organizational world* (pp. 273–294). Newcastle-upon-Tyne, UK: Cambridge Scholars Publishing.

Chieni, S. N. (2010). *The Harambee movement in Kenya: The role played by Kenyans and the government in the provision of education and other social services.* Department of Educational Foundations, MOI University, Kenya. Retrieved from http://babelserver.org/bsw?url=boleswa97 .tripod.com%2Fchieni.htm

Clawson, J. G. (1999). *Level three leadership: Getting below the surface.* Upper Saddle River, NJ: Prentice-Hall.

Dean, K. W. (2008). Value-based leadership: How our personal values impact the workplace. *Journal of Value Based Leadership, 1*(1), 59–66.

England, G. W., & Lee, R. (1974). The relationship between managerial values and managerial success in the United States, Japan, India and Australia. *Journal of Applied Psychology, 59*(4), 411–419.

Fisher, C., & Lovell, A. (2003). *Business Ethics and Values: Individual, Corporate and International Perspectives* (2nd ed.). Essex: Pearson Education.

Heydenrych, J. F., & Viviers, A. M. (2002). In search of a learning environment: The online learning community in the African context. *Cluster for Online Learning Environments, 1*(3), 1–14.

Hoorik, P. van, & Mweetwa, F. (2007). *Use of Internet in rural areas of Zambia.* Retrieved from www.link.net.zm

Koshal, J., & Patterson, K. (2008). A Kenyan on servant-leadership: Harambee and service. *International Journal of Servant-Leadership, 4,* 245–280.

Liefde, W.H.J. de. (2002). *African tribal leadership.* Amsterdam: Kluwer.

Lutz, D. (2009). African Ubuntu philosophy and global management. *Journal of Business Ethics, 84,* 313–328.

Mandela, N. (2006). Foreword. In R. J. Khoza (Ed.), *Let Africa lead: African transformational leadership for 21st century business*. Vezubuntu, Johannesburg.

Mangaliso, M. P., & Mangaliso, N. A. (2006). Unleashing the synergistic effects of Ubuntu: Observations from South Africa. In H. van den Heuvel, M. Mangaliso, & L. van de Bunt (Eds.), *Prophecies and protests: Ubuntu in Global management*. Amsterdam: SAVUSA.

Massey, M. (1979). *The people puzzle: Understanding yourself and others*. Reston, VA: Reston Publishing Company.

Mbigi, L. (2004, June). Afrocentric management and Ubuntu. Paper presented at the Afrocentric Management seminar, SAVUSA FEWEB, Vrije Universiteit, Amsterdam.

Mbigi, L. (2006). A vision of African management and African leadership: A southern African perspective. In H. van den Heuvel, M. Mangaliso, & L. van de Bunt (Eds.) *Prophecies and protests: Ubuntu in global management*. Amsterdam: SAVUSA.

Nafukho, F. M. (2006). Ubuntu worldview: A traditional African view of adult learning in the workplace. *Advances in Developing Human Resources, 8*, 408–415.

Naidoo, G. (2012). Improving ICT for ODL in UNISA Department of Public Administration. *Mediterranean Journal of Social Sciences, 3*(12), 127–149.

Ngambi, H. C. (1999). Community leadership: The case of an African village and an American firm. *South African Business Review, 3*(2), 27–34.

Ngambi, H. C. (Ed.). (2004). African leadership: Lessons from the chiefs. In T. N. Meyer & I. Boninelli (Eds.), *Conversations in leadership: South African perspective* (pp. 107–132). Randburg, South Africa: Knowledge Resources.

Ngambi, H. C. (2010, October). *RARE leadership: An alternative leadership approach for Africa*. Thabo Mbeki African Leadership Institute Conference, Johannesburg.

Ngambi, H. C. (2011). *RARE total leadership: Leading with the head, heart and hands*. Claremont, South Africa: Juta Publishers.

Nuijten I. (2009). *Servant-leadership: Paradox or diamond in the rough?* Rotterdam School of Management, Alblasserdam: Haveka Publishers.

Peck, M. S., Senge, P., & DePree, M. (1995). *Reflection on leadership*. New York: Wiley.

Russell, R. F. (2001). The role of values in servant leadership. *Leadership and Organization Development Journal, 22*(2), 76–84.

Sarayrah, Y. K. (2004). Servant leadership in the Bedouin-Arab culture. *Global Virtue Ethics Review, 5*(3), 58–79.

Spears, L. (2010). Character and servant leadership: Ten characteristics of effective, caring leaders. *Journal of Virtues and Leadership, 1*(1), 25–30.

Trompenaars, F. (2007). *A new substantive theory of sustainable creativity and innovation through the integration of cultures.* Inaugural professorial lecture, Amsterdam: Vrije Universiteit Amsterdam.

Trompenaars, F., & Voerman, E. (2009). *Servant-leadership across cultures.* Oxford: Infinite Ideas.

Trompenaars, F., & Woolliams, P. (2003). *Business across cultures.* Chichester: Capstone Publishing.

Vargas, P., & Hanlon, J. (2007). Celebrating a profession: The servant leadership perspective. *Journal of Research Administration, 38,* 45–49.

Winston, B. E., & Ryan, B. (2008). Servant leadership as a human orientation: Using the GLOBE Study Construct of humane orientation to show that servant leadership is more global than western. *International Journal of Leadership Studies, 3*(2), 212–222.

Chapter Eight

Reflection and Authentic Leadership

Deana M. Raffo

It is easy to say that authentic leaders should be self-aware and reflective, but what does this really mean? The literature discusses self-awareness in authentic leadership, concluding that one must be self-aware to be an authentic leader (Avolio & Gardner, 2005; Gardner, Avolio, Luthans, May, & Walumbwa, 2005; Sparrowe, 2005). However, my review of the authentic leadership literature revealed no definition of *reflection* in this context. I believe that people do not fully appreciate the scope of self-reflection, especially as it relates to authentic leadership development and its implications for being a mindful leader. Indeed, reflection is a more complex phenomenon than one might think. I propose that self-reflection is the missing link to self-awareness and mindfulness in authentic leadership theory.

Over the past decade, there has been increasing focus in the leadership literature on a positive approach to leadership, called authentic leadership (Avolio & Gardner, 2005; Cooper, Scandura, & Schriesheim, 2005; George, 2003; Jensen & Luthans, 2006; May, Chan, Hodges, & Avolio, 2003; Sparrowe, 2005; Walumbwa, Avolio, Gardner, Wernsing, & Peterson, 2008). It is a "significant area of inquiry that represents a current pillar in leadership research" (Avolio, Walumbwa, & Weber, 2009, p. 423), representing one of the newest areas of leadership research within both the applied and academic management literature. However, authentic leadership is still considered to be in the formative stages of conceptual development, requiring more clearly defined and conceptualized parameters (Northouse, 2010; Walumbwa et al., 2008).

This chapter integrates a number of works, summarizes their common elements, and extends the work of authentic leadership theory development by explaining the role of self-reflection, following the principles of philosophical conceptualization (Meredith, 1993). After presenting an overview of the conceptual framework that describes the linkages between authentic leadership and self-awareness, self-reflection, and mindfulness, I examine the authentic leadership literature and, more specifically, the role of self-awareness in authentic leadership. Next, I discuss reflective theory and practice and offer Christopher Johns's (2009) typology of reflective practice as the linchpin in connecting self-reflection and mindfulness as a way of being for authentic leaders. I conclude with implications for authentic leadership development. To this end, I hope to develop further and extend the emerging theory of authentic leadership by advancing the understanding of this intrapersonal component of authentic leadership development.

Overview of the Theoretical Model

Avolio and Gardner (2005), in their exhaustive review of the authentic leadership literature, identified a need for research on the relationship between authentic leadership and self-awareness. I propose a model that develops this intrapersonal aspect of authentic leadership. In the authentic leadership literature, self-awareness is presented as a crucial facet of authentic leadership (Avolio & Gardner, 2005; Gardner et al., 2005; Sparrowe, 2005). As such, reflection is commonly referred to in both the general self-awareness literature (e.g., Walumbwa et al., 2008) and, more specifically, the authentic leadership literature (Avolio, Luthans, & Walumbwa, 2004; Gardner et al., 2005), as a practice that can deepen self-awareness.

In this model, I suggest that self-reflection and, on a deeper level, mindfulness are needed in developing authentic leadership. In essence, the leader's ability to be self-reflective and mindful helps encourage greater authenticity. Self-reflection leads to mindful attention to one's identity, values, strengths and weaknesses, purpose, and core beliefs. This mindful attention allows a person to be authentic and develop a deeper clarity that becomes wisdom.

The authentic leadership model I am proposing has three elements: self-awareness, self-reflection, and mindfulness. Self-awareness encompasses knowledge of one's self, beliefs, assumptions, values, talents, and emotions. Self-reflection is the "doing" level of performing mental processing exercises with the intention of making sense, gaining insight, or being aware. Finally, mindfulness is a state of being, with intentional awareness of self, others, and one's surroundings. I delineate the roles of self-reflection and mindfulness as levels of reflection, influenced by Johns's (2009) reflective typology. I also use the term *self-reflection* rather than *reflection* to be more descriptive of the process of gaining insights about oneself specifically rather than oneself or something— although the general term *reflection* is most often used in the authentic leadership literature. Through self-reflection, we can develop mindfulness, a greater capacity for self-awareness, and more authenticity in the way we lead. A more detailed description of each of these foundational elements follows.

Authentic Leadership and Self-Awareness

Authentic leadership is a multidimensional construct that draws on both positive psychological capacities, as found in the positive psychology literature, and highly developed organizational contexts, as articulated in the positive organizational behavior scholarship (Luthans & Avolio, 2003). There are at least four theoretical lenses, or perspectives, scholars have adopted regarding authentic leadership: intrapersonal, developmental, interpersonal, and pragmatic. The intrapersonal lens focuses on processes within the person that are key to functioning as an authentic leader and includes the reflective components of authentic leadership (Chan, 2005). The intrapersonal perspective in authentic leadership builds on the emphasis on this inner work, resulting in both greater self-awareness and self-regulated positive behaviors (Luthans & Avolio, 2003). This means that authentic leaders engage in a continuous search for self-knowledge (Branson, 2007), since self-awareness is key in the pursuit of authenticity (Sparrowe, 2005), and the capacity for reflection and introspection is an assumption in self-awareness (Walumbwa et al., 2008). Surprisingly little research has been done on strategies that can support this authentic leadership development process (Northouse, 2010), and yet the act of self-reflection can certainly guide, reinforce, and sustain self-discovery.

Luthans and Avolio (2003) have defined *authentic leadership* as "a process that draws from both positive psychological capacities and a highly developed organizational context, which results in both greater self-awareness and self-regulated positive behaviors on the part of leaders and associates, fostering positive self-development" (p. 243). Similarly, Walumbwa et al. (2008) defined *authentic leadership* as "a pattern of leader behavior that draws upon and promotes both positive psychological capacities and a positive ethical climate to foster greater self-awareness, an internalized moral perspective, balanced processing of information, and relational transparency on the part of working with followers, fostering positive self-development" (p. 94).

As noted in these definitions, the self-awareness dimension has been included consistently in discussions of authentic leadership and has been considered an essential starting point for authentic leadership development (Avolio & Gardner, 2005). As many researchers have said, authentic leaders are self-aware and cognizant of their purpose, principles, and values (George, 2003); beliefs, assumptions, organizing principles, and feelings (Eriksen, 2009); and emotions, strengths and limitations, and motives (Goleman, Boyatzis, & McKee, 2002)—all qualities that lie at the core of what it means to be self-aware. I have combined these key concepts of self-awareness to include knowledge of one's self, beliefs, assumptions, values, talents, and emotions.

According to Chapman and Kennedy (2010), today's leaders must be self-aware. This ability is key to understanding one's unique talents, shortcomings, perceptions, and biases. Self-awareness allows people to leverage knowledge and experience to make wise decisions (Crossan & Mazutis, 2012) and understand how others affect them (Goldman Schuyler, 2004). Self-awareness is a lifelong process and should not be viewed as a destination, but rather as a continual process (Avolio & Gardner, 2005). Kouzes and Posner (2012) posit that knowing who you are is paramount in leadership, and "being in tune internally" (p. 119) ultimately determines a leader's level of success.

Despite the need for authentic leaders to have a capacity for self-reflection and introspection, there is scant research on the role of self-reflection and how it is necessary in the development of authentic leaders. Research is needed to examine the various construct relationships for each of the four authentic leadership dimensions, including self-awareness (Walumbwa et al., 2008). By the same token, Walumbwa et al. (2008) state that empirical research on authentic leadership has been limited, possibly due to the "inherent difficulty involved in measuring authentic leadership behavior" (p. 118). Notably, Avolio and Gardner (2005) believe that one of the key distinctions between authentic leadership and other forms of leadership—such as transformational leadership, charismatic leadership, servant-leadership, and spiritual leadership—is the attention paid to self-awareness and regulation.

Self-Reflection

Despite the importance of self-awareness, many leaders leave little time for self-exploration (George, Sims, McLean, & Mayer, 2007). According to Gardner et al. (2005), "By reflecting through introspection, authentic leaders gain clarity and concordance with response to their core values, identity, emotions, motives, and goals" (p. 347). However, my extensive review of the authentic leadership literature revealed few connections made with the reflection literature. This leads me to ask what it means to be self-reflective and what models can guide self-reflective practices that support leaders in being authentic.

Moon (1999) outlined a comprehensive history of reflection, mentioning John Dewey, Jürgen Habermas, David Kolb, and Donald Schön as four principal scholars who significantly influenced research on reflection. Dewey's focus was on educational processes—the nature of reflection and how it occurs. Later, Habermas's efforts focused on how reflection generates knowledge, particularly in the realm of the social sciences. In the 1980s, Kolb built on Dewey's work and developed a model of experiential learning in which reflection is considered essential to the learning experience. However, in recent decades it was Schön's seminal book, *The Reflective Practitioner* (1983), that inspired much of the research on reflection in professional practice (Moon, 1999).

Boud, Keogh, and Walker (1985) defined *reflection* as "an important human activity in which people recapture their experience, think about it, mull it over, and evaluate it" (p. 19). It includes cognitive, affective, and motivational components that, ideally, lead to coherence in thoughts, feelings, motivation, and behavior (Rosenberg, 2010). Reflection enables people to make sense of an experience, guides decision making, and corrects distorted beliefs and errors in problem solving. The process of reflection validates meanings, builds schemas, shapes perspectives, interprets information, supports learning, and facilitates higher-order learning processes (Mezirow, 1990).

Although most current research on reflection focuses on it within the education and health professions (Branson, 2007; Loughran, 2002), reflection has emerged continually as a suggested approach to helping practitioners better understand what they do, develop professional knowledge, engage in problem solving, and cultivate wisdom-in-practice (Loughran, 2002). This work can inform an understanding of reflection in various contexts. For example, a greater understanding of the role and use of reflection has important implications in both academic and business communities (Peltier, Hay, & Drago, 2005) as it pertains to leadership and the management sciences (Schön, 1983).

Reflective leaders often have qualities such as higher degrees of consciousness and self-actualization (Bennis & Nanus, 1997), self-efficacy and confidence (van Woerkom, Nijhof, & Nieuwenhuis, 2002), open-mindedness and responsibility (Densten & Gray, 2001), and purpose-centered mindfulness (Rosenberg, 2010)— all intertwined with the core characteristics of authentic leadership, particularly with regard to fostering a heightened level of self-awareness. Nevertheless, while there is wide-ranging research regarding authentic leadership and reflective practice, only three studies were found that touch on the combined subjects, examining personal values and life-story narratives (Branson, 2007; Eriksen, 2009; Shamir & Eilam, 2005).

Reflection is commonly used in three ways: (1) within a process of learning in order to consider something in more detail, (2) for the purpose of study, and (3) to refer to complicated mental processing of issues that seem to have no obvious solution. So while there are slight variations, all uses imply a form of mental processing with a purpose or outcome and an association with learning or thinking (Moon, 1999).

While these works have laid a foundation and shaped reflective theory, I believe that Johns's examination of reflective practice in *Becoming a Reflective Practitioner* (2009) is critical to understanding how self-reflection plays a fundamental role in authentic leadership. Johns expounds on reflective practice, from models, theories, and stages to practices, approaches, and challenges. Although he approaches reflection from a nursing and health care perspective, his examination of reflective practice and its relationship to mindfulness is crucial to understanding how these concepts connect and can ultimately be used to extend authentic leadership theory. Hence, I contend that

Johns's work is the key to bringing reflection theory and mindfulness together in the authentic leadership literature.

In his typology of reflective practice, Johns (2009) explains that reflective practice spans the range from "*doing* reflection, toward reflection as a *way of being*" (p. 9). Drawing on Schön's and Heidegger's works, he outlines five stages in this flow of experience. The first four stages are part of the "doing" stages of reflection:

1. *Reflection-on-experience:* Reflecting on a situation or experience after the event with the intention of gaining insights that may inform future practice in positive ways.

2. *Reflection-in-action:* Pausing within a particular situation or experience in order to make sense of and reframe the situation to proceed toward desired outcomes.

3. *The internal supervisor:* Dialoging with [oneself while talking] with another to make sense [of an experience].

4. *Reflection-within-the-moment:* Being aware of the way I am thinking, feeling, and responding within the unfolding moment [while] holding the intent to realize a vision. It involves dialoging with [oneself] to ensure that one interprets and responds congruently to whatever unfolds and having mental acuity to change ideas rather than being fixed to certain ideas. (p. 10)

From Johns's (2009) and Moon's (1999) definitions, I have combined the key concepts of self-reflection to include performing mental processing exercises with a purpose of making sense, gaining insights, or being aware of oneself. These self-reflective practices may include activities such as journaling, blogging, talking with a trusted confidant, or spending ten minutes reviewing each day (e.g., Daft, 2012; Johns, 2009; Pipe, 2008). They are internal processes with an external product and are action or "doing" oriented.

Mindfulness

The fifth level in Johns's (2009) typology of reflective practice is mindfulness, which represents reflection as a way of being and "involves seeing things for what they really are without distortion, while holding the intention of realizing desirable practice" (p. 10). Johns describes mindfulness as "the quality of mind that notices what is present without judgment, without interferences. It is like a mirror that clearly reflects what comes before it" (p. 11). It is "knowing what I'm doing and why I'm doing it, and what I am doing right now fits with my intention" (p. 11). In their book *Resonant Leadership* (2005), Boyatzis and McKee dedicated a chapter to mindfulness, which they defined as "the capacity to be fully aware of all that one experiences inside the self—body, mind, heart, spirit—and to pay full attention to what is happening *around us*—people, the natural world, our surroundings, and events" (p. 112). From these definitions, I have combined the key concepts of mindfulness to include a state of being with intentional awareness of oneself, others, and one's surroundings.

Notably, while mindfulness can be encouraged through meditation, prayer, meditative walks in nature, deep breathing exercises, somatic practices, and yoga (Boyatzis & McKee, 2005; Goldman Schuyler, 2010; Pipe, 2008; Silverthorne, 2010), mindfulness is not a technique or even a practice, as self-reflection is, but a state of being. Mindfulness is cultivated by paying attention (Kabat-Zinn, 2005), which is supported by self-reflective practices. In particular, self-reflection is frequently mentioned as a technique for achieving self-awareness (Avolio et al., 2004; Gardner et al., 2005; Walumbwa et al., 2008), while mindfulness is rarely mentioned, at least directly, in the authentic leadership literature.

Although mindfulness is an ancient practice, it is enjoying some current popularity as it relates to leadership. In *The Mindful Leader*, Carroll (2007) offered a leadership model based not on ambition, power, and achievement but rather on qualities such as wisdom, gentleness, humility, poise, patience, awareness, and authenticity. This and other books, including *Leading with Soul* (Bolman & Deal, 2011), *Mindful Leadership* (Gonzalez, 2012), *Resonant Leadership* (Boyatzis & McKee, 2005), and *Leadership and Spirit* (Moxley, 2000), offer perspectives and outlooks on leadership concepts that include purpose, significance, fulfillment, compassion, gratitude, community, and spirituality.

Some believe that those who are more reflective and mindful tend to be more effective in leadership roles (Silverthorne, 2010). In an interview, Bill George said that mindfulness is part of the process of self-awareness and should be part of leadership development programs (Silverthorne, 2010). Similarly, Baron and Cayer (2011) included mindfulness as a practice to support leaders in moving toward higher levels of consciousness, which in turn leads to higher levels of effectiveness and productivity in leading change.

In summary, I propose a model (see table 8.1) that provides a conceptual framework of the nature and dynamics of self-reflective practice in authentic leadership development. It connects self-awareness and mindfulness to authentic leadership theory in a way that can develop and expand understanding of authentic leadership. I believe that when people are more self-aware, self-reflective, and mindful, they have the capacity to become more authentic leaders. As such, there are strong implications for including reflection and even mindfulness in leadership development programs.

Table 8.1 A Model of Self-Reflection in Authentic Leadership

Self-awareness	Knowledge of one's self, beliefs, assumptions, values, talents, and emotions
Self-reflection	Doing mental processing exercises with a purpose to make sense, gain insights, or be aware of oneself
Mindfulness	State of being with intentional awareness of self, others, and surroundings

Implications for Authentic Leadership Development

The three factors in my model (self-awareness, self-reflection, and mindfulness) should be valued and nurtured at all levels— individual, interpersonal, team, and organizational. I offer practical suggestions for applying these three elements to authentic leadership development:

1. *Value self-awareness.* A deep knowledge of one's self, beliefs, assumptions, values, talents, and emotions is key to success. Authentic leaders are likely to engage in a continuous search for self-knowledge. This search is a process, or journey, that does not end. Leadership development programs should include activities and opportunities for self-exploration and introspection, while also providing occasions for challenging one's assumptions and examining others' beliefs systems.

2. *Develop and sustain the intention to self-reflect.* Leaders can find the tool or technique that is a good fit for doing mental processing exercises with a purpose of making sense, gaining insights, or being aware of oneself. Universities can incorporate self-reflective activities into graduate and undergraduate programs. Professional training programs should include self-reflective activities in their leadership development activities. While self-reflection may appear to be self-serving or self-absorbing (Boyatzis & McKee, 2005; Pipe, 2008), it is not about being absorbed in one's own problems and issues; rather, it is about cultivating a greater understanding of oneself in order to make a greater contribution to the community. It supports authentic leadership by deepening self-knowledge to glean the information needed to be one's best self, to best lead others. In becoming an authentic leader, one develops a heightened sense of interconnectedness with others and becomes a support for them (Pipe, 2008).

3. *Introduce and nurture mindfulness.* Mindfulness—the state of being with intentional awareness of self, others, and surroundings—may be unfamiliar. For some, the state of being

present and fully aware without judgment may be foreign. Therefore, leadership development programs may consider introducing individuals to what it means to be mindful.

Implications for Research

Walumbwa et al. (2008) argued that research should be conducted to measure authentic leadership and further develop the theory, since the current model probably does not include all relevant or important constructs. Including self-reflection and, subsequently, mindfulness in this dialogue can advance and refine the understanding of authentic leadership at the individual level. Consequently, this model provides a framework to guide future research from which many testable hypotheses and studies can be developed.

From their meta-analysis, Reichard and Avolio (2005) pointed out that there are surprisingly few intervention studies in leadership. Hence, self-reflection as an intervention strategy to cultivate authentic leadership is rich with possibilities. Suggested avenues for research include developing a self-reflection scale for authentic leadership, investigating self-reflection techniques and their long-term impacts on authentic leadership, and comparing self-reflective processes across contexts.

Another area for research is longitudinal studies of authentic leadership development programs that include self-awareness and self-reflection as part of their scaffolding. Such studies could investigate whether self-reflection accelerates authentic leadership development and whether there are lasting impacts. This type of research is needed because self-awareness is emphasized throughout the authentic leadership literature; hence, it would be useful to determine the extent to which self-reflection is core to understanding the intrapersonal perspective of authentic leadership.

Gardner et al. (2005) discussed the importance of triggers or events that stimulate positive growth in authentic leadership development. Such research would illuminate whether self-reflection can be considered a key trigger in the authentic leadership development process. Other questions that merit study include the following: Are there scaffoldings or self-reflective techniques, practices, or conditions that are more conducive to authentic leadership development, and if so, what are they? What are the short- and long-term impacts of those self-reflective practices on authentic leadership and organizational life?

From a personality type perspective, it would be interesting to know whether introverts have an advantage over extraverts in this particular intrapersonal aspect of authentic leadership. Nesbit (2012) pointed out that introverts are "more inclined toward reflection due to introspective nature" (p. 218), and I concur with his call for research to hypothesize and test relationships of personality measures, self-reflection, and their interactions with authentic leadership.

Finally, it would be helpful to have research on how self-reflection on an individual basis translates to authentic leadership on a macrolevel for organizational, institutional, and social change. Can the convergence of the tangible benefits of self-reflection and the spiritual values of mindfulness contribute to authenticity in leadership?

Conclusion

I propose that self-reflective practice is the missing link for understanding and developing authentic leadership, particularly as it relates to the quality of self-awareness. The literature is scant in integrating these topics, which provides an opportunity to contribute to a new and exciting theoretical construct in contemporary leadership. Ultimately the purpose of this chapter is to analyze the underpinnings of self-reflection and mindfulness within the context of authentic leadership development in order to lay the necessary conceptual groundwork for advancing authentic leadership theory.

Kongtrül (2006) wrote that self-reflection allows people to free their minds from ignorance and enables them to see their true nature more clearly. However, the presence of human biases, blind spots, and interpretations of thoughts and emotions means that often we cannot "see" what we do not know, and so an objective quality may be missing. With time and practice, self-reflection and mindfulness lead to clearer self-awareness and a more awakened mind that makes space for neutrality, seeing both positive and negative attributes for what they are. This clarity goes hand-in-hand with authenticity, for being authentic "has to do primarily with being one's true self" (Chan, Hannah, & Gardner, 2005, p. 6).

In *Inner Peace—Global Impact* (2012), Goldman Schuyler wrote about wisdom traditions and contemplative education as foundations for leaders to go beyond "actions" to a "way of being" that can have positive societal impacts. Similarly, I believe that self-reflection is a conduit to mindfulness, which is a contribution to authentic leadership inspired by wisdom. It is my hope that that self-reflection and mindfulness will be seen as critical in deepening self-awareness and will be examined more closely in social science research to help individuals develop their potential to become more authentic leaders.

References

Avolio, B. J., & Gardner, W. L. (2005). Authentic leadership development: Getting to the root of positive forms of leadership. *Leadership Quarterly, 16*(3), 315–338.

Avolio, B. J., Luthans, F., & Walumbwa, F. O. (2004). *Authentic leadership: Theory building for veritable sustained performance.* Lincoln, NE: Gallup Leadership Institute.

Avolio, B. J., Walumbwa, F. O., & Weber, T. J. (2009). Leadership: Current theories, research, and future directions. *Annual Review of Psychology, 60,* 421–449.

Baron, C., & Cayer, M. (2011). Fostering post-conventional consciousness in leaders: Why and how? *Journal of Management Development, 30*(4), 344–365.

Bennis, W., & Nanus, B. (1997). *Leaders: Strategies for taking charge*. New York, NY: HarperBusiness.

Bolman, L. G., & Deal, T. E. (2011). *Leading with soul: An uncommon journey of spirit*. San Francisco: Jossey-Bass.

Boud, D., Keogh, R., & Walker, D. (1985). *Reflection: Turning experience into learning*. London: Kogan Page.

Boyatzis, R. E., & McKee, A. (2005). *Resonant leadership: Renewing yourself and connecting with others through mindfulness, hope, and compassion*. Boston, MA: Harvard Business Press.

Branson, C. (2007). Effects of structured reflection on the development of authentic leadership practices among Queensland primary school principals. *Educational Management Administration and Leadership*, 35(2), 225–246.

Carroll, M. (2007). *The mindful leader: Awakening your natural management skills through mindfulness meditation*. Boston, MA: Trumpeter.

Chan, A. (2005). Authentic leadership measurement and development: Challenges and suggestions. In W. L. Gardner, B. J. Avolio, & F. O. Walumbwa (Eds.), *Authentic leadership theory and practice: Origins, effects and development* (pp. 227–250). Oxford: Elsevier.

Chan, A., Hannah, S. T., & Gardner, W. L. (2005). Veritable authentic leadership: Emergence, functioning, and impacts. In W. L. Gardner, B. J. Avolio, & F. O. Walumbwa (Eds.), *Authentic leadership theory and practice: Origins, effects and development* (pp. 3–41). Oxford: Elsevier.

Chapman, J. A., & Kennedy, J. A. (2010). Psychological perspectives on leadership. In N. Nohria & R. Khurana (Eds.), *Handbook of leadership theory and practice: A Harvard Business School centennial colloquium* (pp. 159–181). Boston, MA: Harvard Business Press.

Cooper, C., Scandura, T. A., & Schriesheim, C. A. (2005). Looking forward but learning from our past: Potential challenges to developing authentic leadership theory and authentic leaders. *Leadership Quarterly*, 16(3), 475–493.

Crossan, M., & Mazutis, D. (2012). Transcendent leadership. In W. E. Rosenbach, R. L. Taylor, & M. A Youndt (Eds.), *Contemporary issues in leadership* (pp. 51–68). Boulder, CO: Westview Press.

Daft, R. L. (2012). First, lead yourself. In W. E. Rosenbach, R. L. Taylor, & M. A. Youndt (Eds.), *Contemporary issues in leadership* (pp. 125–133). Boulder, CO: Westview Press.

Densten, I. L., & Gray, J. (2001). Leadership development and reflection: What is the connection? *International Journal of Educational Management*, 15(3), 119–124.

Eriksen, M. (2009). Authentic leadership: Practical reflexivity, self-awareness, and self-authorship. *Journal of Management Education*, 33(6), 747–771.

Gardner, W. L., Avolio, B. J., Luthans, F., May, D. R., & Walumbwa, F. (2005). Can you see the real me? A self-based model of authentic leader and follower development. *Leadership Quarterly, 16*(3), 343–372.

George, B. (2003). *Authentic leadership: Rediscovering the secrets to creating lasting value.* San Francisco, CA: Jossey-Bass.

George, B., Sims, P., McLean, A., & Mayer, D. (2007). Discovering your authentic leadership. *Harvard Business Review, 85*(2), 129–130, 132–138, 157.

Goldman Schuyler, K. (2004). Practitioner—Heal thyself! Challenges in enabling organizational health. *Organization Management Journal, 1*(1), 28–37.

Goldman Schuyler, K. (2010). Increasing leadership integrity through mind training and embodied learning. *Consulting Psychology Journal: Practice and Research, 62*(1), 21–38.

Goldman Schuyler, K. (2012). *Inner peace—global impact: Tibetan Buddhism, leadership, and work.* Charlotte, NC: Information Age Publishing.

Goleman, D. P., Boyatzis, R. E., & McKee, A. (2002). *Primal leadership: Realizing the power of emotional intelligence.* Boston, MA: Harvard Business School Press.

Gonzalez, M. (2012). *Mindful leadership: The nine ways to self-awareness, transforming yourself, and inspiring others.* San Francisco, CA: Jossey-Bass.

Jensen, S. M., & Luthans, F. (2006). Relationship between entrepreneurs' psychological capital and their authentic leadership. *Journal of Managerial Issues, 18*(2), 254–273.

Johns, C. (2009). *Becoming a reflective practitioner.* Oxford: Wiley-Blackwell.

Kabat-Zinn, J. (2005). *Coming to our senses: Healing ourselves and the world through mindfulness.* New York: Hyperion.

Kongtrül, D. (2006). *It's up to you: The practice of self-reflection on the Buddhist path.* Boston, MA: Shambhala.

Kouzes, J. M., & Posner, B. Z. (2012). Leadership begins with an inner journey. In W. E. Rosenbach, R. L. Taylor, & M. A. Youndt (Eds.), *Contemporary issues in leadership* (pp. 117–123). Boulder, CO: Westview Press.

Loughran, J. J. (2002). Effective reflective practice: In search of meaning in learning about teaching. *Journal of Teacher Education, 53*(1), 33–43.

Luthans, F., & Avolio, B. (2003). Authentic leadership development. In K. S. Cameron, J. E. Dutton, & R. E. Quinn (Eds.), *Positive organizational scholarship: Foundations of a new discipline* (pp. 241–261). San Francisco, CA: Berrett-Koehler.

May, D. R., Chan, A., Hodges, T., & Avolio, B. J. (2003). Developing the moral component of authentic leadership. *Organizational Dynamics, 32*(3), 247–260.

Meredith, J. (1993). Theory building through conceptual models. *International Journal of Operations and Production Management, 13*(5), 3–11.

Mezirow, J. (1990). How critical reflection triggers transformative learning. In J. Mezirow (Ed.), *Fostering critical reflection in adulthood: A guide to transformative and emancipatory learning* (pp. 1–20). San Francisco, CA: Jossey-Bass.

Moon, J. A. (1999). *Reflection in learning and professional development: Theory and practice.* London: Kogan Page.

Moxley, R. S. (2000). *Leadership and spirit: Breathing new vitality and energy into individuals and organizations.* San Francisco, CA: Jossey-Bass.

Nesbit, P. L. (2012). The role of self-reflection, emotional management of feedback, and self-regulation processes in self-directed leadership development. *Human Resource Development Review, 11*(2), 203–226.

Northouse, P. G. (2010). *Leadership: Theory and practice* (5th ed.). Thousand Oaks, CA: Sage.

Peltier, J. W., Hay, A., & Drago, W. (2005). The reflective learning continuum: Reflecting on reflection. *Journal of Marketing Education, 27*(3), 250–263.

Pipe, T. B. (2008). Illuminating the inner leadership journey by engaging intention and mindfulness as guided by caring theory. *Nursing Administration Quarterly, 32*(2), 117–125.

Reichard, R. J., & Avolio, B. J. (2005). Where are we? The status of leadership intervention research: A meta-analytic summary. In W. L. Gardner, B. J. Avolio, & F. O. Walumbwa (Eds.), *Authentic leadership theory and practice: Origins, effects and development* (pp. 203–223). Oxford: Elsevier.

Rosenberg, L. R. (2010). Transforming leadership: Reflective practice and the enhancement of happiness. *Reflective Practice, 11*(1), 9–18.

Schön, D. A. (1983). *The reflective practitioner: How professionals think in action.* New York, NY: Basic Books.

Shamir, B., & Eilam, G. (2005). What's your story? A life-stories approach to authentic leadership development. *Leadership Quarterly, 16*(3), 395–417.

Silverthorne, S. (2010, September 7). *Mindful leadership: When East meets West.* Retrieved from http://hbswk.hbs.edu/item/6482.html

Sparrowe, R. T. (2005). Authentic leadership and the narrative self. *Leadership Quarterly, 16*(3), 419–439.

van Woerkom, M., Nijhof, W. J., & Nieuwenhuis, L.F.M. (2002). Critical reflective working behavior: A survey research. *Journal of European Industrial Training, 26*(8), 375–383.

Walumbwa, F. O., Avolio, B. J., Gardner, W. L., Wernsing, T. S., & Peterson, S. J. (2008). Authentic leadership: Development and validation of a theory-based measure. *Journal of Management, 34*(1), 89–126.

Chapter Nine

Embodying Authentic Leadership

An Actor's Perspective

Marco Aponte-Moreno

Acting can provide valuable insights into achieving greater authenticity by way of becoming a more effective leader. When playing a character, the actor is challenged to strike a balance between the external traits that we tend to associate with a specific character type (e.g., the commanding presence of a president or the seductive allure of a femme fatale) and the truth that defines the character's humanity. Without this truth, the performance lacks substance and authenticity and instead comes across as superficial.

The purpose of this chapter is to provide insights on acting techniques to nonactors who wish to communicate leadership authentically. I argue that the development of strong self-awareness and the application of internal and external theater techniques can contribute to the embodiment of authentic leadership in the same way that they contribute to the development of truthful and authentic performances on stage. I explore these issues as I experienced them while acting in a Greek tragedy and relate them to the process of evincing authentic leadership. It is important to note that my purpose is not intended to provide "acting tricks" to be applied in leadership situations. Rather, I encourage readers to consider how leaders can employ acting techniques to access truth within themselves.

The Great Dionysian Festival

In summer 2012, Theatro Technis produced five tragedies from the Oedipus saga under the direction of George Eugeniou. The event, called The Great Dionysian Festival, took place between July 31 and August 11 at the company's theater in the London borough of Camden.

In the play *Seven against Thebes*, by Aeschylus, Oedipus' son Eteocles leads the citizens of Thebes in a battle against the Argive army, which is led by his brother Polyneices. The two brothers had agreed to take turns ruling Thebes, but when it was Polyneices' turn, Eteocles refused to cede power. As a result, Polyneices decided to raise an army to defeat his brother and take his rightful place as king. The resulting confrontation between the two brothers ended in their killing each other (Aeschylus, 467 BC/2012).

In this chapter, I focus on the role of Eteocles, the leader who must defend Thebes against an attack by his own brother. The complexity of Eteocles' choice lies in the fact that in continuing to rule Thebes, which he considers essential to the well-being of his people, he is compelled to obtain their support in fighting his brother. In the prologue of the play, Eteocles delivers a moving speech, invoking love for the motherland as his main argument in rallying his citizens' support.

For an actor, playing a complex leader such as Eteocles is no easy task. In addition to portraying leadership traits that will influence and inspire others under difficult circumstances, the actor must find the humanity within Eteocles, who feels that his duty is to rule and defend Thebes at all costs, even if it means killing his own brother.

In our production of *Seven against Thebes*, Eteocles was played by a young Italian actor named Ruggiero Dalla Santa. We rehearsed for three hours a day, five days a week, for six weeks. Except for the prologue and one scene with the chorus, all of Eteocles' scenes consisted of interactions with my character, a soldier who served as Eteocles' messenger. Playing this role gave me a unique opportunity to assess Ruggiero's performance as Eteocles; I portrayed not only a follower looking for guidance and inspiration, but also an observer trying to understand Eteocles' motivations in betraying his own brother in the name of defending Thebes. My character needed to be convinced by Eteocles' main argument that his brother's intention to invade Thebes constituted the ultimate disloyalty of a citizen: betrayal of the motherland.

At the beginning of our rehearsals, Ruggerio's delivery appeared forced: his voice was often too loud, and his movements were hesitant. His acting lacked conviction. It was clear that he had yet to find the elements within himself that would allow him to connect with his role and the circumstances of the play. However, as rehearsals progressed, he transformed himself, becoming one with the king's presence and speech. He owned the text, delivering it in the right tone of voice, and adopted postures and movements that were appropriate to the king's exalted position. He was confident, convincing, and truthful. Ruggerio's performance was clearly rooted in something within himself, an internal truth that made his movements and gestures organic. He did not simply seem like Eteocles; rather, he had found the character within himself. His portrayal of Eteocles had become truthful and authentic.

Developing Authentic Leadership Through Theater

The link between performance and leadership is not new. In *The Art of Rhetoric*, Aristotle connects political leadership with the ritual dimensions of rhetoric (Peck, Freeman, 6, & Dickinson, 2009). Most scholars agree that Aristotle's enthymeme involves "an argument built from values, beliefs, or knowledge held in common by a speaker and an audience" (Herrick, 2005, p. 9). Aristotle's conceptualization of followers as audience members suggests the existence of a performance dimension in political leadership.

In the past fifteen years, scholars have examined the connection between stage performance and leadership. Erving Goffman's dramaturgical analysis of individuals in ordinary situations precipitated a new body of work (Jackson & Parry, 2011). In their article "The Charismatic Relationship: A Dramaturgical Perspective," Gardner and Avolio (1998) compared leaders to actors and followers to audience members. They analyzed how leaders (as actors) and followers (as audience members) interact with themselves and the environment to construct a charismatic relationship. Similarly, Dunham and Freeman (2000) examined the leadership styles of theater directors, arguing that business leaders have much to learn from skilled stage directors, given that both have to strike the perfect balance between achieving unity behind an artistic mission and allowing enough creativity for the individuals involved in the play.

In their book *Leadership Presence*, Halpern and Lubar (2003) argue that leaders can develop presence by employing dramatic techniques. They define *leadership presence* as "the ability to connect authentically with the thoughts and feelings of others" (p. 3). They linked presence to both external and internal elements: "presence is a set of skills, both internal and external, that virtually anyone can develop and improve" (p. 3).

The distinction between external and internal acting in nontheatrical settings was addressed by sociologist Arlie Russell Hochschild (1983) in her seminal book, *The Managed Heart*. Drawing on the works of Russian actor and director Constantin Stanislavski, the creator of Method Acting, she distinguished between "surface acting" and "deep acting" in the context of the commercialization of emotions. In surface acting, the person "is only acting as if he had feeling" (p. 37), while in deep acting, feelings come from within.

The embodiment of authentic leadership is the key factor that determines leadership presence. In their article "Enacting the 'True Self': Towards a Theory of Embodied Authentic Leadership,"

Donna Ladkin and Steven Taylor (2010) also draw from Stanislavski's theories "to explore how authentic dramatic performances are created" (p. 64). They argue that "although authentic leadership may be rooted in the notion of a 'true self', it is through the embodiment of that true self that leaders are perceived as authentic or not" (p. 64).

The concept of authentic leadership has been present in academic literature since the 1990s (Ladkin & Taylor, 2010). It has been defined in different ways, depending on the author's focus. In a review of the concept, Northouse (2013) distinguishes three main viewpoints: (1) the intrapersonal perspective, in which the leader's personal experiences are emphasized as the essence of his authenticity; (2) the interpersonal perspective, in which the relationship between leaders and followers is the determining factor of authenticity; and (3) the developmental perspective, which focuses on the idea that authentic leadership can be developed and nurtured. This third perspective, introduced by Avolio and Gardner (2005), is the basis of the developmental approach of authentic leadership through theater techniques, adopted in this chapter.

In their article, "Authentic Leadership: Development and Validation of a Theory-Based Measure," Walumbwa, Avolio, Gardner, Wernsing, and Peterson (2008) define *authentic leadership* as "a pattern of leader behavior that draws upon and promotes both positive psychological capacities and a positive ethical climate, to foster greater self-awareness, an internalized moral perspective, balanced processing of information, and relational transparency on the part of leaders working with followers, fostering positive self-development" (p. 94).

It is important to note that in addition to its focus on self-awareness, this definition stresses the need for authentic leaders to consider the ethical dimensions related to their roles. They need to make sure that their actions and decisions are consistent with their core beliefs (internalized moral perspective), they must be willing to take into consideration other people's views (balanced processing), and they should be honest and able to accept their mistakes (relational transparency).

For our purposes, leadership presence is understood as the leader's ability to express thoughts and feelings authentically, from the inside out, in order to connect with the thoughts and feelings of followers. Authenticity, as conceived by Ladkin and Taylor (2010), is understood here as both the quality of being truthful to oneself and the capacity to embody the true self in such a way that it is perceived as truthful by others. To be convincing in a role, then, an actor must be truthful. As Halpern and Lubar (2003) noted, "It's a paradox of the theater that, in order to pretend, the actor must be real" (p. 7). Similarly, the leader must always strive for the truth, which lies at the heart of authenticity.

The Importance of Self-Awareness in Authentic Leadership

Uta Hagen, the renowned American acting teacher and actress, acknowledged the importance of self-awareness in creating a character. In her book A Challenge for the Actor (1991), she writes, "I must find myself in the role" (p. 53). She also states that "the basic components of the characters we will play are somewhere within ourselves" (p. 55). Hagen points out that individuals change their "sense of self" many times a day, depending on their circumstances, their relationship to others, the nature of events, and even their clothing. She argues that self-discovery is a process that never ends, and she encourages her students to develop the habit of self-observation.

Although I do not know whether Ruggiero engaged in self-reflection while preparing for his portrayal of Eteocles, it was clear from his compelling performance that he had established a deep connection with a deeper truth within himself. I could see clearly in his eyes, face, and body that he was connecting with authentic emotions and thoughts during his performance. It was precisely this authentic inner quality that allowed him to connect with his fellow actors and the audience.

Leaders need to look for values in their own life stories and make them explicit so that they can share them with their followers. Similar to the actor who draws on inner truth to achieve authenticity in a role, the leader who wishes to inspire others must know herself so that she can draw on her own experiences, emotions, and thoughts. According to Halpern and Lubar (2003), leaders' self-knowledge requires "the ability to accept yourself, and to reflect your values in your decisions and actions" (p. 230).

On November 9, 2012, after President Obama was reelected, he gave an emotional speech thanking his campaign staff and volunteers at his Chicago headquarters. In his brief speech, he recalled how much he "grew up" as a community organizer in Chicago. Then, his voice cracking with emotion, he added, "I became a man during that process. And so when I come here and when I look at all of you, what comes to mind is not that you guys actually remind me of myself, it's the fact that you are so much better than I was, in so many ways." As he finished the sentence, he began to shed tears, followed by loud applause from his staff (Memoli, 2012). As was the case in Ruggiero's performance as Eteocles, it was Obama's authentic emotion that made his speech compelling. That authenticity was driven by both Obama's capacity to embody his emotions and, subsequently, being perceived as truthful by his followers.

Acting is sometimes defined as the process of living truthfully under the imaginary circumstances of the play. In my acting experience, in addition to practicing self-observation, I have used two techniques that have allowed me express authentic emotions by connecting my inner self to the imaginary circumstances of a character: Stanislavski's "Magic If" and Hagen's "Inner Objects." I discuss these techniques in the following sections to shed light on the possibility of applying them in leadership development.

Stanislavski's Magic If

Method acting, introduced by Stanislavski in the early twentieth century, refers to actors' drawing from their own life experiences to produce truthful actions and emotions. The method emerged as a reaction to the exaggerated representational acting that was the norm until that point, and it changed the way acting is taught all over the world (Moore, 1960). The method became especially popular with the emergence of the film industry, where the use of close-up shots required a much more contained and truthful acting style.

One of Stanislavski's most popular techniques is the Magic If, the purpose of which is to transform the aims of the character into those of the actor. It takes the actor into the imaginary circumstances of the character as it requires him to imagine what he would do if he were in those circumstances. Stanislavski suggests that actors don't need to believe that they are their characters; it is enough to imagine what they would do if they were the characters. The question actors should ask themselves when preparing for their roles is, "What would I do if I were this character, in these circumstances?" (Stanislavski, 1988).

The truth of the character comes either from real experiences in the actor's life or as a product of her imagination, which serves as a bridge between the actor's inner self and the character's circumstances. Hence, when preparing for the role, the actor imagines what she would do if she were the character instead of what she would do to seem like the character, thereby developing real elements within herself to be truthful within the circumstances of the play. A leader can employ this same process to develop the capacity to express the truth within herself when embodying authentic leadership.

It is important to distinguish Stanislavski's Magic If acting technique from the psychological concept of the "as if" personality, which is associated with "the action of defensive dissociation deriving from very early experiences of internalizing the presence of an absent object, creating the sense of an internal void at the core of the self" (McFarland, 2004, p. 635). Actors use the Magic If technique to examine what they would do if they were in their characters' situations. It is a voluntary technique that allows the actor to imagine himself in his character's situation, as opposed to an involuntary psychological condition. The purpose of the Magic If is to use the actor's own emotions and experiences to create a truthful performance. Obviously this technique has limitations given that what the actor would do is not necessarily what the character would do in any given situation. However, it is an effective technique for bringing truth and realism to a performance.

Similarly, leaders can use the Magic If technique to bring truthfulness to various leadership situations. In a recent production of Aristophanes' political satire, *The Knights*, I played the role of Agoracritus, a commoner who ends up becoming the leader of his country. The character learns how to sway the multitudes with his speeches (Aristophanes, 424 BC/2003).

Despite the comedic aspect of this premise, my performance still had to be authentic to convince the audience that my character's followers believed that Agoracritus was a skilled politician. Although I have no experience as a political leader, I was able to apply the Magic If by imagining what I would have done had I been in Agoracritus's situation. When giving a speech to Agoracritus's followers, for example, I imagined what I would have done by relating his experience to a similar experience in my own life. Specifically, I thought about my behavior when teaching in large university lecture halls. I recalled specific thoughts and emotions that I had experienced while teaching and then incorporated them in Agoracritus's speeches. By drawing on real elements of my own life in this way, I was able to relate to the imaginary circumstances of the play and deliver a truthful performance.

Uta Hagen said that we change our sense of self many times a day depending on the circumstances. Sometimes we are followers, and sometimes we are leaders. A leader can use the Magic If to express leadership elements within herself in any given leadership situation, embodying leadership authentically by exploring what she would do if she were in that situation.

Hagen's Inner Objects

The Inner Objects technique, developed by Uta Hagen, is a visualization technique that allows actors to relate to the imaginary circumstances of the play by invoking images from their own lives to trigger desired emotions and physiological reactions (Hagen, 1991). For this technique to work, actors have to practice over and over until they know that a certain image will produce the desired reaction.

Finding inner objects is not as easy as it might sound. Actors have to explore various objects and see how they feel about them before knowing which ones work. One common technique consists of sitting comfortably in a chair, relaxed and with eyes closed, visualizing moments in one's life that might trigger the desired physiological reaction. For example, if my character reacts with fear, I need to think of something that makes me fearful. I have a fear of snakes and therefore might visualize the time I saw a snake in my mother's house in Venezuela. Recalling that moment, I would try to remember every detail: the time of day, the objects in the room, and the colors, textures, smells, and sounds. I would visualize everything and monitor my reactions.

When I first tried this visualization exercise, I was surprised at how difficult it was. Despite visualizing the moment when I saw the snake, the fear did not come. I kept trying, focusing on my memory of the objects in the room, along with the colors, smells, sounds, and textures. I monitored how I felt, and yet the reaction did not come. I kept trying, but nothing happened. Then, as I continued to visualize my surroundings on that day, I saw a purple velvet pillow lying on the sofa where I was sitting when I saw the snake. As I felt the soft texture of the pillow, the reaction finally came. I felt extreme fear; my heart began to pound, and I began sweating. The inner object that produced fear was not the image of the snake crawling from beneath the table, but rather the sensation of my right hand touching the velvet pillow.

Now when I need to express fear, I know that I can do so by recalling the sensation of my hand touching the velvet pillow. By using this inner object repeatedly in rehearsals, the desired reaction will eventually become a reflex in that particular part of the play. This is what is commonly referred to in the acting literature as sense memory.

Was Obama's emotional reaction in front of his staff truly provoked by the presence of young followers and volunteers who reminded him of his years as a community organizer in Chicago, or was it triggered by an inner object from his own life? It is clear that his reaction came from a truthful place within himself, which his audience perceived as authentic. By practicing identifying and recalling inner objects, leaders, like actors, can become more adept at expressing their feelings and emotions. This openness is essential when expressing authentic leadership as its embodiment requires both being truthful to oneself and being perceived as truthful by others.

External Elements: Language, Voice, and Body

Stanislavski's work is compiled in three books: *An Actor Prepares* (1988), *Building a Character* (2003), and *Creating a Role* (2003). *An Actor Prepares* explores the inner work an actor must undergo when preparing for a role. The internal elements of the Magic If and Inner Objects originated with this book. In *Building a Character*, Stanislavski discusses external acting techniques, highlighting the importance of language, voice, and body. *Creating a Role*, which is less relevant to leadership development, describes the preparation that precedes actual performance.

According to Uta Hagen (1991), along with high responsiveness to their senses, actors need to have fine standard speech, a trained voice, a sound body, an unshakable desire to be an actor, a need to express emotions, and an insatiable curiosity about the human condition.

Unlike leaders, actors are provided with scripts. Interpreting the playwright's words is an essential part of the actor's job. For example, in the prologue of Seven against Thebes, metaphors such as "this land is your mother," which links defense of the land to the followers' bond with their mothers, are used to achieve the king's objective of rallying the citizenry against an imminent attack. Although actual leaders do not necessarily speak from scripts, they can use metaphors and other rhetorical devices to communicate in a moving and inspirational way. Reading plays, along with novels and poetry, can help leaders master language and become more effective communicators.

Regarding the voice, giving each of the character's words the right intonation requires the actor to understand the writer's intent. For example, when using a metaphor to influence others, the actor needs to adopt a tone that corresponds to a specific intention. There is no right or wrong tone, but some tones will fit a specific intention more effectively than others. When using the "this land is your mother" metaphor, an actor playing Eteocles might employ a soft tone to help his followers recall pleasant memories about their mothers. Another choice might be adopting a more assertive tone to make followers react more strongly. Both choices are valid. Laughter or joy would fail in this situation because these would be unlikely to help achieve the objective of rallying the followers.

Mastering the voice is an essential element in leadership development; hence, the leader can benefit from regular voice training through breathing and singing exercises. The leader needs to modulate the tones of the voice like notes in a symphony: long and short notes, high and low notes, soft and hard notes. The notes must be congruent with the words so that the speech becomes a "concert" aimed at moving followers through both sound and content. Otherwise the actor is simply uttering a string of meaningless words.

Actors often spend years training to use their bodies as instruments of expression. They need flexibility to play a variety of roles. In some acting exercises, actors use physical expression to play out entire scenes without saying a word. Sometimes they use masks so that the focus of the audience is on their physical expression.

In the case of Eteocles, we expect the postures, movements, and gestures of a leader. He is strong. He moves with assurance. He owns the space and acts with self-assurance. He is the king. When Ruggiero began work on the character, his movements were clumsy and his steps hesitant. He did not have a royal bearing. After trying various improvisational exercises suggested by the director, Ruggiero decided to base his character on a lion. Studying animals as sources of characterization is known in Method Acting as animal exercises (Easty, 1981). He began observing how lions move and how they relax. For days he practiced these movements during rehearsals, and he then began incorporating the bearing of a lion into his portrayal of Eteocles.

A subtle display of vulnerability can sometimes help boost the leader's image among followers. As Goffee and Jones (2000) asserted, one of the essential qualities of inspirational leadership is the display of weakness. Showing genuine vulnerability allows leaders to "reveal their approachability and humanity" (p. 51). A case in point is Hillary Clinton, who ended up winning the 2008 New Hampshire primary after having cried in public in the late stages of her campaign. She won despite Obama's clear lead in the state's polls (Ladkin & Taylor, 2010).

Although Eteocles generally behaves as one might expect of a strong leader, he must also at times show a vulnerable side in order to achieve his objectives. In such cases, using the body correctly can help. Instead of trying to portray a fake emotion, the actor can convey a much more authentic one by connecting with real vulnerability within himself and then using his body to counteract that emotion. The struggle of a character working to hide vulnerability has a stronger impact on the audience than simply pretending to be vulnerable. This is also true in expressing physical conditions such as drunkenness. Struggling to maintain control over the physiological effects of drunkenness is much more effective than simply aping the clumsy movements of a drunken man.

Leaders, like actors, can use physical actions to express intentions and moods beyond words. The body allows the leader to communicate the subtext of a speech and express intentions without words. For this reason, having control over the body allows leaders to match their physical expression with their inner selves.

Conclusion

Authenticity is both the quality of being truthful to oneself and the capacity to embody the true self in such a way that it is perceived as truthful by others. Actors work with their inner selves, voices, and bodies; hence, it is appropriate to incorporate acting training as a valuable component of leadership development. Also, as actors often portray leaders on stage, the dramatic techniques they employ are useful for developing leadership skills. Self-awareness, which is at the center of acting training, is acquiring more and more importance in leadership development (Boyatzis & McKee, 2005; Cook-Greuter, 2004; Goldman Schuyler, 2012, 2013; Scharmer, 2009; Senge, 1994).

Internal acting techniques require that actors work from the inside to produce authentic emotions. Techniques drawn from Method Acting such as the Magic If and Inner Objects are useful when leaders include them in their repertoire of leadership skills. Although these techniques are designed for actors, they shed light on how to develop leadership from within.

External acting training involves the development of language, voice, and body. This training is important when actors prepare for their roles. Some leaders are very skilled at capitalizing on language, modulating their voices, and using their bodies to communicate leadership, but many are not. Using embodiment in leadership development is an important element (Melina, 2013). Physical techniques such as animal exercises may also prove useful in communicating leadership qualities.

When acting does not come from within, the performance is much less likely to be believable. This creates a discontinuity in the illusion and prevents the audience from being moved and inspired by the play. The same can be said about leadership. Unless leaders succeed in accessing truth within themselves and expressing it, others will not be moved and inspired. Incorporating a combination of internal and external acting techniques into leadership development can help leaders express their inner selves more authentically.

References

Aeschylus. (2012). *Seven against Thebes* (T. A. Buckley, Trans.). Auckland: Floating Press. (Original work published in 467 BC)

Aristophanes. (2003). *The Birds and Other Plays: The Knights* (D. Berrett & A. Summerstein, Trans). London: Penguin. (Original work published in 424 BC)

Avolio, B. J., & Gardner, W. L. (2005). Authentic leadership development: Getting to the root of positive forms of leadership. *Leadership Quarterly, 16,* 315–338.

Boyatzis, R. E., & McKee, A. (2005). *Resonant leadership.* Boston: Harvard Business School Press.

Cook-Greuter, S. (2004). Making the case for a developmental perspective. *Industrial and Commercial Training, 36,* 1–10.

Dunham, L., & Freeman E. (2000). There is business like show business: Leadership lessons from the theatre. *Organizational Dynamics, 29*(2), 108–122.

Easty, E. D. (1981). *On method acting.* New York: Ivy Books.

Gardner, W., & Avolio, B. (1998). The charismatic relationship: A dramaturgical perspective. *Academy of Management Review, 23*(1), 32–58.

Goffee, R., & Jones, G. (2000). Why should anyone be led by you. In *Harvard Business Review Ten More Reads: On Leadership* (pp. 51–59). Boston: HBR Press.

Goffman, E. (1959). *The presentation of self in everyday life*. London: Penguin Books.

Goldman Schuyler, K. (2012). *Inner peace—global impact: Tibetan Buddhism, leadership, and work*. Charlotte, NC: Information Age.

Goldman Schuyler, K. (2013). From the ground up: Revisioning sources and methods of leadership development. In L. Melina (Ed.), *The embodiment of leadership*. San Francisco: Jossey-Bass.

Hagen, U. (1991). *A Challenge for the Actor*. New York: Scribner.

Halpern, B., & Lubar, B. (2003). *Leadership presence*. New York: Penguin.

Herrick, J. (2005). *The history of theory and rhetoric* (3rd ed.). Boston: Pearson Education.

Hochschild, A. R. (2003). *The managed heart*. Berkeley: University of California Press.

Jackson, B., & Parry, K. (2011). *A very short, fairly interesting and reasonably cheap book about studying leadership* (2nd ed.). London: Sage.

Ladkin, D., & Taylor, S. S. (2010). Enacting the "true self": Towards a theory of embodied authentic leadership. *Leadership Quarterly, 21*(1), 64–74.

McFarland, S. H. (2004). Self creation and the limitless void of the dissociation: The "as if" personality. *Journal of Analytical Psychology, 49*, 635–656.

Melina, L. (Ed.). (2013). *The embodiment of leadership*. San Francisco: Jossey Bass/Wiley.

Memoli, M. (2012, November 8). Obama's emotional, teary thank-you to staff [Video and article]. *Los Angeles Times*. Retrieved from http://articles.latimes.com/2012/nov/08/news/la-pn-obama-emotional-video-20121108

Moore, S. (1960). *The Stanislavski system*. New York: Penguin.

Northouse, P. (2013). *Leadership*. London: Sage.

Peck, E., Freeman, T., 6, P., & Dickinson, H. (2009). Performing leadership: Towards a new research agenda in leadership studies? *Leadership, 5*(1), 25–40.

Scharmer, C. O. (2009). *Theory U*. San Francisco: Berrett-Koehler.

Senge, P. (1994). *The fifth discipline: The art and practice of the learning organization*. New York: Doubleday.

Stanislavski, C. (1988). *An actor prepares*. London: Methuen.

Stanislavski, C. (2003). *Building a Character*. New York: Routledge.

Walumbwa, F. O., Avolio, B. J., Gardner, W. L., Wernsing, T. S., & Peterson S. J. (2008). *Authentic leadership: Development and validation of a theory-based measure*. *Journal of Management, 34*(1), 89–126.

Chapter Ten

Leaders' Lived Experience of Authentic Moments

Susan Skjei

What is a leader's lived experience of authentic moments? What conditions or practices foster the experience of authentic moments both individually and collectively? If, in order to be authentic, leaders must be both true to themselves and willing to engage fully in relationships, how can they be genuine yet willing to enact some emotions and not others? These and other questions drew me to engage in a phenomenological study of authentic leadership.

Researchers currently define authentic leaders as those who know who they are and what they believe in; display transparency and consistency among their values, ethical reasoning, and actions; focus on developing positive psychological states such as confidence, optimism, hope, and resilience within themselves and their associates; and are widely known and respected for their integrity (Avolio, Gardner, Walumbwa, Luthans, & May, 2004; Gardner, Avolio, & Walumbwa, 2005). My background and training in Buddhism enriched this definition of authenticity. According to Buddhism, human beings are basically good and inherently authentic. However, this authenticity is covered over when they are afraid. This generates grasping, pushing away, or ignoring in an attempt to control what is happening and leads to defensive patterns, which adds further confusion and inauthenticity to interactions. In this tradition, the way out of such confusion is to return to the authentic experience of what is occurring in the present moment and let go of defensive patterns (Mipham, 2005, p. 77).

According to research (Avolio et al., 2004), authentic leaders are said to be unique in that they are highly self-aware and build credibility with followers by earning their respect and trust and supporting them in achieving their goals. They create a sense of personal and social identification and belonging and use positive role modeling and ethical action to inspire loyalty. They model vulnerability and self-reflection while staying focused on growth and goal achievement. All of these qualities lead to higher levels of commitment, engagement, and job satisfaction, in addition to increased employee effort and organizational productivity (Avolio et al., 2004). These descriptions of the qualities and behaviors of authentic leadership have been used to measure and assess (Avolio & Gardner, 2005; Walumbwa, Avolio, Gardner, Wernsing, & Peterson, 2008), but they do not help one to understand the lived experience of authenticity itself. What is the internal experience of such leaders? What choices do they make, and how do they actually practice authenticity in the moments that really matter?

To explore these questions, I focused on leaders' lived experience of authentic leadership moments in the complex, unfolding reality of the workplace. In these moments leaders are confronted with a challenge or an opportunity that at first may seem disorienting or beyond their current capacity, and yet they are able to engage with the people or events with an increased level of authenticity and courage rather than defensiveness. I asked participants specifically about these moments, rather than about their understanding of authentic leadership in general, because these specific examples yield richer descriptions and put a sharper focus on the essence of the authentic leadership experience. The intended benefit of this research is to help leaders become more aware of the potential of these moments in their own lives and recognize when they are taking place so that they can engage more genuinely, skillfully, and effectively in a variety of complex, emergent situations.

The Method

In order to pursue my quest for deep understanding of this lived experience, I chose to use mindful inquiry as described by Valerie Malhotra Bentz and Jeremy Shapiro (1998). Mindful inquiry combines "the Buddhist concept of mindfulness with phenomenology, critical theory, and hermeneutics in a process that puts the inquirer in the center" (p. 171). I then used transformative phenomenology (Rehorick & Bentz, 2008), which draws on elements of Husserlian eidetic phenomenology (Husserl, 1999), Heideggerian ontology (Heidegger, 1962), and Gadamerian self-reflective, hermeneutic analysis (Gadamer, 1975).

I wanted to do a research project on authentic leadership that went beyond conventional approaches to data collection and analysis. Phenomenology allowed me to get past my preconceptions of the experience of authenticity in the workplace and look more deeply for the underlying essence or meaning. According to Max van Manen (2002), the core purpose and function of the phenomenological method is to provoke a profound shift in understanding for both the researcher and for those reading phenomenological accounts: "For a phenomenological text to 'lead' the way to human understanding, it must lead the reader to wonder" (p. 5).

Hermeneutic reflection helped me to grasp the essential meaning, which is usually multidimensional, many layered, and communicated through the texture and organization of the prose. Using Gadamer's (1975) three levels of hermeneutics, I reflected on the data to discover (1) the universal characteristics, generalities, or abstractions from the data, (2) an understanding of the persons themselves (which may contradict my interpretations of them), and (3) an openness to my own transformation as a researcher, in the process of engaging with the data.

Sample and Data Collection

I sought participant nominations from faculty members who were well versed in authentic leadership theory and practice from Naropa University's Authentic Leadership certificate program, and the Authentic Leadership in Action Institute. To qualify for the study, nominees had to be seen as authentic leaders who were self-aware and reflective and were able to articulate their lived experience of authentic moments. From this pool of nominees, I selected ten leaders who represented diverse backgrounds and organizations. I conducted seventy-five-minute semistructured interviews with each leader about his or her lived experience of authentic moments in the workplace. Each interview was audiorecorded and transcribed, after which I reviewed the recording and corrected transcription errors.

The study participants were four white men, ages forty-five to sixty-two; four white women, ages forty-eight to fifty-eight; one black woman, thirty-nine years old; and one Hispanic woman, thirty-eight years old. The organizations represented four nonprofit organizations, three businesses, two educational institutions, and one government agency. The organizations were based in the United States with the exception of two located in Canada and one located in Zimbabwe. Although not a requirement for the study, most of the interviewees had a personal practice of meditation or another form of contemplative practice such as prayer. Three participants identified as Buddhist practitioners.

Analysis

I began the analysis by exploring my own life as the context for the study and wrote four protocols, or short descriptions of my own lived experience of authentic leadership moments. As a Buddhist practitioner for over thirty years, I wrote these protocols to be aware of my own taken-for-granted way of seeing the world, and therefore to be better able to bracket out or set aside that perspective to analyze the data with fresh eyes (Dahlberg, 2006). I identified the invariant horizons (meaning units) of the experience and clustered these into themes. Next, I wrote a preliminary textural description of an authentic leadership moment based on my own experiences.

I then reviewed each of the ten interview transcripts while listening again to the recording of the interview and selected specific stories from each participant, crafting them into first-person vignettes to reveal the existential uniqueness of each participant's situated lifeworld. I read through each interview again, identified each participant's definition of *authenticity*, and crafted a thick description of their experience of the authentic moment based on quotes of their actual lived experience. I explored imaginative variations and reflected on my own preconceptions and assumptions in response to each interview in order to bracket my own biases, surface my own interpretations, and open up new possibilities of meaning.

I next developed a composite structural description and identified five invariant horizons or themes that were contained in each participant interview: (1) dwelling in ambiguity, (2) listening to the body, (3) opening to possibilities, (4) communicating with honesty and vulnerability, and (5) acting with integrity and courage. These themes overlap and are not discrete. Each theme contains elements of the other themes and points to the complexity inherent in lived experience. While not discussed in every interview, the role of mindfulness and contemplative practice was mentioned in many of the interviews, and I discuss it further in the discussion and conclusion section.

Essential Structure of an Authentic Leadership Moment

The challenges of uncertainty and change are a constant reality for leaders; however, when they are experiencing an

authentic leadership moment, they respond in ways that foster genuineness and openness in themselves and others. The
leader acknowledges the experience of ambiguity and anxiety
and abides in it rather than trying to avoid it. She listens to
her embodied experience as it unfolds in the moment. Her
openness to possibilities allows her to relax defensiveness and
explore fresh learning and new options. She expresses care
and vulnerability in her relationships but is also honest and
willing to challenge the status quo in her interactions with
others. She acts with integrity and courage, based on her connection with the situation, and she makes conscious choices,
knowing that each choice has risks and consequences. Her
words and actions tend to remove obstacles and clear the air,
allowing innovation and creativity to occur. The leader's confidence increases, as does the group's well-being and productivity, and there is an expanded sense of purpose in the group or
organization.

Essential Themes

In this section, I describe the five composite themes, with specific examples, along with my interpretation and selected references to transformative learning, phenomenology, and Buddhist
principles and practices.

Abiding in Ambiguity

Participants in the study experienced the threshold of an
authentic leadership moment as an encounter with ambiguity
and uncertainly. During times of change and transition, things
are not definite, and situations are not necessarily as they seem.
However, when the leader is able to abide in ambiguity and not
defend against the accompanying feelings of fear and anxiety,
new opportunities for learning and creativity open up. A clearing is created in which "things as they are" can be revealed.

This experience can be uncomfortable as well as exhilarating, as the following examples illustrate.

Juanita, a thirty-five-year-old staff leader for a political campaign, expresses the power and transformative potential of dwelling in ambiguity:

> They knew I was there. And yet there wasn't any indication that I would be speaking up. And so when I did, the shock that it sent into the crowd was really what I think an authentic moment feels like for me. It's like there's a nut that gets cracked in that moment. It's right before anything . . . things get quieter and more intense and the moments get longer—every second feels longer and I can feel my fear. And then the nut cracks and people respond. And it's in that response that the sense of security that everybody had in what they thought was going to be, is different.

Her metaphor of the "nut that gets cracked" is reminiscent of Jack Mezirow's (Mezirow & Associates, 2000) description of the first stage of transformational learning in which learners experience a "disorienting dilemma" and then are able to examine the feelings that arise in the moment (p. 22). In this case Juanita's disorienting dilemma was her strong desire to speak up about the negative campaigning of the other candidate, combined with her desire to be invisible. Her experience that "things get quieter and more intense and the moments get longer—every second feels longer and I can feel my fear" captures the essence of abiding in ambiguity: time slows down, and things become more distinct. She also mentions "that the sense of security that everybody had in what they thought was going to be is different," indicating that the moment itself affects not only the leader but those around her, inviting them into their own experience of ambiguity. Juanita, who has practiced meditation for about five years, described the importance of focusing on the breath, which helped her to abide in ambiguity and anxiety rather than reacting: "One of the most fundamental practices for me is any time I recognize my anxiety, I focus on my breath. That is a tool I know I have. And it changes the situation a lot. Within seconds it changes the sensation of panic that's beginning to arise. And that happens a lot in this work. I tend to get a lot of panic at the onset of anything. So it's been helpful."

Frank, a fifty-five-year-old executive director of a small nonprofit organization, describes his experience of becoming defensive and then relaxing into it as an entry point into an authentic leadership moment during a board meeting:

> I wanted to keep my anxiety at bay. I wanted to keep it at a distance. I was thinking that I was protecting myself and that I was defending myself against an impending crisis, and what was fascinating was, in that moment when I relaxed, I came in direct contact with what was really going on and faced it, out in the open with everyone, and a huge burst of energy arose.

His ability to abide in ambiguity and stay with his own feelings of anxiety allowed him and the group to connect more directly with reality and access new levels of energy and creativity. Frank had been a practitioner of meditation for over twenty-five years and had this to say about the role of contemplative practice in his ability to not react: "It's the idea that you take a thousand breaths in meditation so in any moment if you can remember to take one breath, you can open up the space for something other than just reacting." Leadership, from this point of view, is a process of harnessing energy rather than directing or managing oneself or others. When leaders abide in ambiguity, they demonstrate trust in the situation and invite resourcefulness from themselves and others.

Listening to the Body

Listening to the body provided an opportunity to deeply inform one's understanding of the situation. Participants described the "felt sense" of the body and the wisdom and clarity revealed in the present moment. For some, this experience was initially uncomfortable, but when they were able to listen, the body provided important signals about what was needed for positive change to occur. The comments of many leaders were consistent with the perspective of phenomenologist Maurice Merleau-Ponty (1962), who asserted that the body is not merely an object but actually our means of communicating with our world.

Casey, a forty-five-year-old sales manager for a technology company, described how the "feeling in the pit of his stomach" was a clue that there was an issue he needed to address. By listening to his body, he was able to direct his attention to something that needed to be looked at more closely: "When I'm able to be present, the trigger for me is the feeling that something could be done differently or just flat out shouldn't be done at all . . . and I literally feel it in my gut. Sometimes it's just this empty feeling in the pit of my stomach that something is not quite right and perhaps should be looked at a little more closely."

To prepare for a difficult conversation, Casey analyzed the situation and developed scenarios that would rationally explain his concerns, but he also prepared by training himself "to pause and observe the moment a little bit more carefully instead of responding directly or reacting directly." Casey does not have a regular meditation practice, although his intention to bring awareness into his work as a leader has shaped his ability to attend to his internal state, allowing him to be more conscious and effective in his responses to others.

Joan, a fifty-six-year-old high school principal, described a time when she was having a conflict with her staff and was able to listen to her embodied emotions as a source of deep knowing and as opportunity for becoming more aware of how she wished to be in the world:

My reaction was hugely physical, and that was a good wake-up call. I mean I was almost quaking with anger. Some of it was

> targeted at this one person who I felt betrayed by, because he could have mediated the situation but he chose to take an adversarial role, and it was scary. It was scary to have my staff rebelling and pissed at me and, you know, angry. . . . It took me back to old places of being afraid . . . but I was able to be with these feelings and didn't act them out.

Although the feelings she was experiencing were frightening, by continuing to listen to her body rather than "acting out," she was able to respond and act skillfully with her team instead of reacting to a threatening situation. Joan had been practicing mindfulness and seeing a therapist for several years, and she attributes this "inner work" to her ability to continue to listen. As she explained, "I couldn't do it without mindfulness and therapy—all of the things that have trained me to recognize when I'm going into a defensive mode."

Listening to the body can provide a sense of confidence and certainty that goes beyond conceptuality, as in this example from Greg, a sixty-year-old business owner who was facing a difficult decision. As he listened to his body, he experienced a realization and a sense of "knowing" that was beyond "rational argument":

> In this particular case it was unusual in that I wasn't sitting with an uneasy gnawing sense in my body that I was trying to understand. Instead, the realization just hit me "boom" like a ton of bricks. There was a clear sense of knowing that I experienced in my body. And it was so clear that any kind of rational argument I could have was minuscule in comparison to the clarity of that sense of knowing.

According to Buddhist philosophy, the experience of synchronizing the body and mind can offer new insights and perspectives that extend far beyond the conceptual mind. Leaders who listen to the wisdom of the body have access to this resource as they make decisions (Trungpa, 2013).

Opening to Possibilities

The process of opening to possibilities involves extending one's awareness beyond the current situation and exploring a vision of what might be possible. Dana, a thirty-nine-year-old leader of a sustainable village and ten-year meditation practitioner, provides a clear example:

> I think a big part of what I did as well was to give other people faith in what we could do and be and that we could live our way through . . . to continue to move toward the sense of possibility rather than staying with the sense of victimhood and despair which we had been in for a long time.

The ability to open to a vision of the future while acknowledging the challenges of the present moment is an important leadership skill, especially during times of change and transition. Joan's commitment to a larger vision of how she wanted the relationships in her staff to be motivated her to let go of defenses and remain open to the moment: "So what allows me to do it differently, I think, is the commitment to the larger vision of how I want relationships to be and the experience of knowing that if I stay defended or angry in my situational position of power, nothing good can come from that."

Tom, a sixty-two-year-old director of a large medical association, describes a conversation with a coworker in which he shared a vision of what was possible while listening to her concerns. Although the coworker was caught up in the despair of the current situation, she was able to open up to new possibilities for herself and for the clinic by listening to a different perspective:

> On that particular day when she said she didn't know what to do, I said to her, "The experience of the clinic is just nothing but volunteers and physicians and others coming together. And we

create an environment there where we actually love those people. For some of them, it may be one of very few moments where they actually feel being loved." And she broke down and said, "I know I can love people," . . . and she got it! It seems to have relieved her of carrying a burden that was impossible. We both sat at the table with tears in our eyes about what we understood that clinic to be.

For all of the participants, stepping beyond self-concerns and the concerns of the moment enabled a feeling of openness and "a breath of fresh air" and was an important element in their experience. They accessed a sense of resourcefulness and connectedness to the future that was inspiring to themselves and others.

Communicating with Honesty and Vulnerability

For the leaders in this study, the experience of an authentic leadership moment meant communicating with others in ways that were emotionally transparent and honest, taking responsibility for their own perspectives and sharing them appropriately with others.

Frank describes the conversation he had with his board during which his willingness to be vulnerable and tell the truth transformed the situation. The founder of the organization had recently been diagnosed with late-stage breast cancer and they had not been able to accomplish their fundraising goals. He and the founder met just before the board meeting and decided not to put on a "happy face" and to just be honest:

So we got to the check-in, and it came around to me, and I hadn't really thought about what I was going to say. We didn't have a strategy other than the conversation we had earlier, which was that we were going to tell the truth—which sort of set the tone. And I just said, "I feel terrible. I'm trying to put ten pounds of stuff into a five-pound bag, and I feel like I'm not doing a good job of it. I am miserable, and Jean's diagnosis is devastating and I'm embarrassed to even be saying all of this, considering what she is facing." What happened next really surprised me. Suddenly board members were really engaged, offering help and strategic ideas, and I thought, "Wow, is this what vulnerability is all about?" I realized that by trying to be so competent ourselves, we hadn't allowed them to really help us or feel like they were making a difference.

For Frank, vulnerability and honesty opened the door for others to understand what was actually happening and to step in with their own competence and resourcefulness. By letting go of his identity as the "competent leader," he allowed others to contribute in new ways that provided more meaning and engagement.

Much can be learned about the experience of authentic leadership moments by setting them in relief against inauthentic leadership moments. In inauthentic moments, the leader reacts with defensiveness, disengagement, or even aggression instead of with openness. Sometimes the best a leader can do under these circumstances is to simply be aware of his or her inability to act differently in the moment. Nancy, a fifty-two-year-old university department chair and faculty member, describes a moment in which she was unable to engage with honesty and vulnerability during a confrontation with a student in her leadership class whom she had accused of plagiarism:

Later he sent me an e-mail saying, "You don't practice what you teach." It just hit me right between the eyes. I knew he was right, but I didn't know what to do. Instead I stayed behind the wall of, "Look, this is just plagiarism, period." There was no conversation. I don't think I would have changed my decision, but I didn't honor him enough and respect him enough to understand what was going on for him and to see what his side of it was. I've thought a lot about it since then, and now I use this in my classes as a teaching story about a challenging situation that I faced and didn't handle very well.

Nancy described two practices she uses that support her to be authentic in this way: "One is a daily meditation practice, which makes a big difference. And the second is to try to consciously hold the perspective of the 'observer' and be present at the same time and that practice also helps in work situations."

Acting with Integrity and Courage

The process of acting with integrity and courage means that the leader acted in accordance with his or her core values and overcame some fear or hesitation in order to act. For many of the participants, these actions reinforced their personal feelings of well-being and self-confidence. As Juanita explained:

> I do remember feeling a lot taller. And I could feel the air in my nose. I could feel this deep breath going through my body, and then I remember just watching them responding and the shock of them doing it. And my face turning red and just wanting to run away because I'd caused this crack, you know? It all happened within seconds. And then I was really calm and felt that sense of integrity that I had actually asked the question.

For Juanita, her courage to act also reinforced her authenticity. Her embodied experience of "feeling taller" and being "really calm" were the way she expressed her integrity. This example shows how the themes from the study are intertwined.

Acting with integrity and courage looks different for each leader. Tom expressed it as "talking from a place that was an essential part of me," which was meaningful for him in the context of people he had known most of his life:

> And I felt like I was talking from a place that was an essential part of me. I was with people I had known most of my adult life—other community leaders—and I was coming from a place that they had never seen me come from before. I had this

experience of courage—there was no way I couldn't say what I had to say. There was a feeling of it almost not being me.

In many traditions, both spiritual and philosophical, authenticity is considered innate. It is "who we actually are" beyond our concepts of "who we think we are" (Trungpa, 1969). To paraphrase Dogen Zenji, the founder of Soto Zen, "To know yourself is to forget yourself, and if you forget yourself you become enlightened by all things" (Chödrön, 1997). In Tom's case, by acting courageously and accessing his authenticity, his idea of himself was too small to accommodate his actual experience and he had the feeling of it "not being me."

In some cases, the courageous actions had to do with speaking the truth to people in positions of authority and accepting the consequences. In others, such as this example from Dana, courageous actions were linked to her experience of being connected to others and responding to what is really needed: "Authentic leadership to me is about having the courage to step in and to lead, but in a way that really is both listening to yourself and that sense of yourself as a connected being. It's a broader, bigger self almost—tuning into the group and coming to your sense of expression or response to whatever the need is."

All actions take place within the context of the leader's lifeworld. How much a leader expresses emotional transparency and honesty must be balanced with what is appropriate and skillful for the followers and the situation. Joan describes the inner conflict that all of the leaders in this study confronted, which was how to courageously balance transparency with authenticity:

If you're an authentic teacher, you are choosing what you say and how you say it, because you're teaching, and when you're leading, and you're not just being authentic and telling everyone about your inner child but you're having to think, "I'm having this reaction, how do I use this? How do I present this? How do I share it courageously in a way that enriches my relationships with others?"

This passage shows the interconnectedness of the five themes. Joan's question about how to enrich her relationships with others implies that she is carrying an intention based on her vision of possibility for the future. She is also willing to abide in ambiguity rather than allow her personal reactions to jeopardize her vision. In Buddhism the aspiration to be of benefit to others is called the Bodhisattva vow, and it represents an intention that guides one's choices in the present moment (Chödrön, 2003).

Implications and Conclusion

This study explored the first-person experience of authentic leadership moments. The themes that emerged from the data reinforce the prevailing literature on authentic leadership, which states that authentic leaders demonstrate self-awareness, relational transparency, ethical action, and unbiased processing (Gardner et al., 2005). The examples and descriptions from the first-person perspective add a depth and richness previously lacking in the literature to the picture of the internal experience of authentic leaders. In addition, the critical theme of abiding in ambiguity is a new element, not previously included in models of authentic leadership.

There seem to be important implications for leading with spirit, presence, and authenticity:

1. *Spirit:* The participants saw their recognition and practice of authentic leadership moments as an ongoing journey of self-development, ideally suited for leading in times of uncertainty and change. More than half of the participants in the study regularly practiced meditation, prayer, yoga, or martial arts, and these practices helped them stay present and engaged in the face of ambiguity. Ongoing practice in mindfulness and awareness seems to develop tolerance for ambiguity and allows one to experience authentic leadership moments more frequently and to learn from inauthentic moments as well.

2. *Presence:* There are constant opportunities for experiencing authentic leadership moments, although it can be difficult to recognize them. Experiencing them begins with self-awareness and willingness on the part of the leader to recognize and embrace ambiguity rather than defend against it. Although critical moments or crucible moments have been mentioned in the literature (Bennis, 1994), research about these moments tends to focus on historical events that shaped the identities of the participants as authentic leaders (George & Sims, 2007) rather than on their day-to-day experience. This study expands the concept of moments to include immediate opportunities to practice authenticity in the moment and also reveals the importance of reflective or contemplative practice for leaders.

3. *Authenticity:* Authentic leadership moments are not just about "being yourself" or even "knowing yourself" but instead are moments in which the leader is deeply connected with embodied experience and with the situation as it is unfolding. These revelatory moments in a person's life are aptly described by William James as those times in which "he felt himself most deeply and intensively active and alive. At such moments, there is a voice inside which speaks and says, 'This is the real me'" (James & Hardwick, 1993). To sustain these glimpses and manifest authentic leadership in an ongoing way requires that one engage the situation with openness and curiosity, remaining present, even when one realizes she is being inauthentic. Rather than viewing inauthenticity as a problem or something to be overcome, participants in this study recognized inauthentic moments as a stepping-stone or wake-up call for them to become more present and engaged.

This exploratory study provided a unique window into authentic leadership moments. For most participants, describing these moments and reflecting on them in the framework of the interviews provided an opportunity for further insight and self-awareness. For me as a researcher, it was inspiring and humbling to hear these stories and realize just how difficult it is for me and other leaders to be authentic in the moments that really matter. Leaders in this study who had a contemplative or meditative practice seemed to be more prone to experiencing authentic leadership moments. If this is true, it has tremendous potential for informing how we develop our next generation of leaders. Further research will be needed to explore these implications in more depth.

References

Avolio, B. J., & Gardner, W. L. (2005). Authentic leadership development: Getting to the root of positive forms of leadership. *Leadership Quarterly, 16*(3), 315–338.

Avolio, B. J., Gardner, W. L., Walumbwa, F. O., Luthans, F., & May, D. R. (2004). Unlocking the mask: A look at the process by which authentic leaders impact follower attitudes and behaviors. *Leadership Quarterly, 15*(6), 801–823.

Bennis, W. G. (1994). *On becoming a leader*. Reading, MA: Perseus Books.

Bentz, V. M., & Shapiro, J. J. (1998). *Mindful inquiry in social research*. Thousand Oaks, CA: Sage.

Chödrön, P. (1997). *When things fall apart: Heart advice for difficult times*. Boston: Shambhala.

Chödrön, P. (2003). *Start where you are: A guide to compassionate living*. Boston: Shambhala.

Dahlberg, K. (2006). The essence of essences: The search for meaning structures in phenomenological analysis of lifeworld phenomena. *International Journal of Qualitative Studies on Health and Well-Being, 1*, 11–19.

Gadamer, H.-G. (1975). *Truth and method* (2nd ed.). New York: Continuum Books.

Gardner, W. L., Avolio, B. J., & Walumbwa, F. O. (Eds.). (2005). *Authentic leadership theory and practice: Origins, effects and development* (Vol. 3). Oxford: Elsevier.

George, B., & Sims, P. (2007). *True north: Discover your authentic leadership*. San Francisco: Jossey-Bass.

Heidegger, M. (1962). *Being and time* (J. Macquarrie & E. Robinson, Trans.). New York: Harper Perennial.

Husserl, E. (Ed.). (1999). *The essential Husserl: Basic writing in transcendental phenomenology*. Bloomington: Indiana University Press.

James, W., & Hardwick, E. (1993). *The selected letters of William James*. New York: Anchor Books.

Manen, M. van. (1997). *Researching lived experience: Human Science for an action sensitive pedagogy* (2nd ed.). London, Ontario: Althouse Press.

Manen, M. van. (2002). *Writing in the dark: Phenomenological studies in interpretive inquiry*. London, Ontario: The Althouse Press.

Merleau-Ponty, M. (1962). *Phenomenology of perception* (C. Smith & P. Kegan, Trans.). London: Routledge.

Mezirow, J., & Associates. (2000). *Learning as transformation: Critical perspectives on a theory in progress*. San Francisco: Jossey-Bass.

Mipham, S. (2005). *Ruling your world: Ancient strategies for modern life*. New York, NY: Morgan Road Books.

Rehorick, D. A., & Bentz, V. M. (2008). *Transformative phenomenology: Changing ourselves, lifeworlds, and professional practice*. Lanham, MD: Lexington Books.

Trungpa, C. (1969). *Meditation in action*. London: Stuart & Watkins.

Trungpa, C. (2013). *The path of individual liberation*. Boston: Shambhala.

Walumbwa, F., Avolio, B., Gardner, W., Wernsing, T., & Peterson, S. (2008). Authentic leadership: Development and validation of a theory-based measure. *Journal of Management, 34*(1), 89–126.

Name Index

Subject Index

If you enjoyed this book, you may also like these:

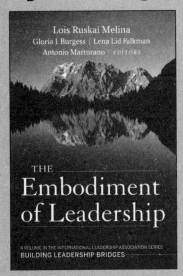
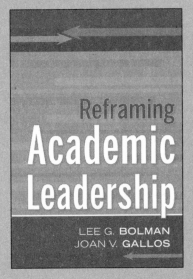